Mandarin
Chinese

phrase book

WITHDRAWN

FRANKLIN PARK LIBRARY
FRANKLIN PARK, IL

Berlitz Publishing Company, Inc.

Princeton   Mexico City   London   Eschborn   Singapore

ISBN 2-8315-6265-1
Seventh printing - April 2001
Printed in Spain

Developed and produced for Berlitz Publishing Company by:
G&W Publishing Services, Oxfordshire, U.K.
Mandarin Chinese edition: Dr. Cheng Ma, Emma Ardern, and Chen Ji.

Contents

Pronunciation 6

Basic Expressions 10

Greetings/Apologies	10	How much/many?	15
Communication difficulties	11	Who?/Which?/Whose?	16
		How?	17
Questions	12	Is it ...?/Are there ...?	17
Where?	12	Can/May?	18
When?	13	What do you want?	18
What sort of ...?	14	Other useful words	19
Why?	14	Exclamations	19

Accommodations 20

Reservations	21	Renting	28
Reception	22	Youth hostel	29
Price/Decision	24	Camping	30
Requirements	26	Checking out	32

Eating Out 33

Restaurants	33	Soups	44
Chinese cuisine	34	Fish and seafood	45
Finding a place to eat	35	Meat	46
Reserving a table	36	Vegetables	47
Ordering	37	Rice	48
Fast food/Café	40	Noodles/Dofu	48
Complaints	41	Dessert/Fruit	49
Paying	42	Drinks	50
Course by course	43	Beer/Wine/Spirits	50
Breakfast	43	Non-alcoholic drinks	51
Appetizers/Starters	43	Menu Reader	52

Travel 65

Safety	65
Arrival	66
Plane	68
Train	72
Long-distance bus [Coach]	78
Subway [Metro]	80
Ferry	81
Bicycle/Motorbike	83
Hitchhiking	83
Taxi [Cab]	84
Transportation	85
Car rental	86
Gas [Petrol] Station	87
Breakdown	88
Accidents	92
Legal matters	93
Asking directions	94
Road signs	96

Sightseeing 97

Tourist information	97
Excursions	98
Sights	99
Admission	100
Impressions	101
Tourist glossary	102
Who/What/When?	104
In the countryside	106

Leisure 108

Tickets	109
Movies [Cinema]	110
Theater	110
Opera/Ballet/Dance	111
Music/Concerts	111
Nightlife	112
Children	113
Sports	114
At the beach	116
Skiing	117

Making Friends 118

Introductions	118
Where are you from?	119
Who are you with?	120
What do you do?	121
Enjoying your trip?	123
Invitations	124
Encounters	126
Telephoning	127

Stores & Services   129

Opening hours	132	Jeweler	149
Service	133	Newsstand [News-	
Paying	136	agent]/Tobacconist	150
Complaints	137	Photography	151
Repairs/Cleaning	137	Police	152
Bank/Changing money	138	Lost property/Theft	153
Pharmacy	140	Post office	154
Clothing	143	Souvenirs/Gifts	156
Health and beauty	147	Antiques	157
Household articles	148	Supermarket/Minimart	158

Health   161

Doctor/General	161	Gynecologist	167
Accident and injury	162	Hospital	167
Symptoms	163	Optician	167
Doctor's inquiries	164	Dentist	168
Parts of the body	166	Payment and insurance	168

English–Chinese dictionary & index   169
Chinese–English glossary   208

Reference   216

Numbers	216	Time	221
Days	218	Map	223
Months/Dates/Seasons	219	Quick reference	224
Public holidays	220	Emergency	224

Pronunciation

This section is designed to familiarize you with the sounds of Chinese using our simplified phonetic transcription. You'll find the pronunciation of the Chinese sounds explained below, together with their "imitated" equivalents. This system is used throughout the phrase book. When you see a word spelled phonetically, simply read the pronunciation as though it were English, noting any special rules.

The Chinese language

Mandarin Chinese is spoken by the majority of people and is the official language of the People's Republic of China (P.R.C.). It is properly known as **poo-tong-hwaa** (literally, common speech). The population of China is between 1.2 and 1.3 billion. This means that more people speak Mandarin Chinese than any other language, including English.

Besides **poo-tong-hwaa**, there are nine other groups of dialects, including Cantonese (spoken in Hong Kong, Guangdong; and Guangxi) and, in addition, a number of different ethnic languages, for example Mongolian, Manchurian, and Miao.

Written Chinese

Poo-tong-hwaa is not written using an alphabet, but with characters or ideograms. The system evolved in basic pictograms used by primitive hunter gatherers to record men, animals, and objects. Over thousands of years, however, this representational language has changed beyond recognition and, with the exception of a few characters, it is impossible to see how any particular character came to represent its current meaning. Today, about 50,000 ideograms exist, of which 5,000 or so are in common use. It is generally thought that a well-educated Chinese person today would know between 6,000 and 8,000 characters. To read a Chinese newspaper you will need to know 2,000 to 3,000 characters, but 1,200 to 1,500 would be enough to get the gist.

While the building block of the Chinese language is the single character, words are usually a combination of two or more characters ➤ 8.

Traditionally, **poo-tong-hwaa** was written in columns and read from top to bottom, and from right to left. Nowadays, however, the policy is to write horizontally from left to right.

Chinese sounds

Poo-tong-hwaa (Mandarin Chinese) is composed less of vowels and consonants than of syllables, consisting of a consonant and a vowel. It is also a language with a large number of homonyms (words of different meaning but with identical spelling). In reality every syllable is pronounced with one of four tones (high, rising, falling~rising, and falling). It is very difficult for non-natives to even hear these tones, let alone reproduce them – hence the phonetic transliteration system used in the phrase book has been much simplified, and excludes tonal markers.

The phrase book also contains the Chinese script. If, despite your efforts, your listener does not seem to understand you, show him or her the book and indicate what you want to say.

Consonants

Letter	Approximate pronunciation	Symbol	Example	Pronunciation
b, d, f, g, j, l, m, n, p, s, t, w, y	approximately as in English			
c	like *ts* in pi*ts*	ts	草	*tsao*
h	like *ch* in Scottish lo*ch*	h	花	*hwaa*
q	like *ch* in *ch*ip	ch	情	*ching*
r	like the English **r**, but with tip of tongue turned up and back, something like the sound of the *s* in pleasure	r	人	*ren*
x	like the *sh* in *sh*ip	sh	心	*shin*
z	like *ds* in ki*ds*	ds	在	*dsai*
zh	like *j* in *j*oke	j	中	*jong*

Vowels

Letter	Approximate pronunciation	Symbol	Example	Pronunciation
a	like *a* in c*a*r, but with no **r** sound	*a*	八	*ba*
e	like *e* in h*e*r, but with no **r** sound	*e*	根	*gen*
i	1. like *ee* in b*ee* 2. not pronounced after ts, r, s, ds, ch, sh, j	*ee*	米	*mee*
o	like *o* in *o*	*o*	口	*ko*
u	like *oo* in sp*oo*n	*oo*	路	*loo*
ü	like *ee* in b*ee*, but with lips closely rounded	*ü*	去	*chü*
üe	like *ee* in b*ee*, but with lips closely rounded + *e*	*üe*	学	*shüe*

Basic Chinese characters

The chart gives some basic Chinese characters which still demonstrate the characters' origin in pictograms, e.g., the character for *mountain* looks very much like a mountain or hill. In addition, you will see how two characters can be combined to form another word that still has an obvious meaning when its two constituent parts are known, e.g., *fire* and *mountain* together give you the word *volcano*. You will also notice that some combinations have both a straightforward "concrete" meaning and an additional "abstract" or poetic meaning. However, this is at the simplest level only. There are many more cases of character combinations in which the meaning is not obvious even if the individual characters are known. In this case a student of the language would have to refer to the dictionary. Beyond two character combinations there are also three and multiple combinations. To add to the growing complexity, there are also single characters made up of parts of other characters. As you can see, written Chinese it is not as simple as it might first appear!

Some basic Chinese characters

山	mountain/hill	*shan*
火	fire	*huo*
火山	volcano	*huo-shan*
水	water	*shwee*
山水	landscape, natural scenery	*shan-shwee*
日	the sun, day	*r*
月	the moon, month	*yüe*
日月	time (*poetic*)	*r-yüe*
上	upper, up, upward, previous	*sharng*
下	under, down, downward, forthcoming	*shia*
风	wind	*fung*
雨	rain	*yü*
风雨	the elements, trials and hardships	*fung-yü*
大	big	*da*
小	small	*shiao*
大小	size	*da-shiao*
人	human being, person	*ren*
大人	grown-up	*da-ren*
小人	vile person, villain	*shiao-ren*

Basic Expressions

Greetings/ Apologies	10	How much/many?	15
Communication difficulties	11	Who?/Which?	16
		Whose?	16
Questions	12	How?	17
Where?	12	Is it...?/Are there ...?	17
When?	13	Can/May?	18
What sort of ...?	14	What do you want?	18
Why?	14	Other useful words	19
		Exclamations	19

ESSENTIAL

Yes.	对。	*dwee*
No.	不对。	*boo dwee*
Okay.	行。	*shing*
Please.	请。	*ching*
Thank you.	谢谢。	*shie-shie*
Thank you very much.	非常感谢。	*fay-charng gan-shie*

Greetings/Apologies 打招呼与道歉

Hello./Hi!	你好。	*nee-hao*
Good morning/afternoon.	早上好 / 你好。	*dsao-sharng hao/nee-hao*
Good evening.	晚上好 / 你好。	*wan-sharng hao/nee-hao*
Good night.	晚安。	*wan-an*
Good-bye.	再见。	*dsai-jian*
Excuse me! (getting attention)	请问。	*ching-wen*
Excuse me. (May I get past?)	劳驾。	*lao-jia*
Excuse me!/Sorry!	对不起!	*dwee-boo-chee*
Don't mention it.	没关系。	*may-gwan-shee*
Never mind.	不要紧。	*boo-yao-jin*

INTRODUCTIONS ➤ 118

Communication difficulties

语言交流困难

Do you speak English?
你会说英语吗?
nee hway shuo ying-yü ma

Does anyone here speak English?
这儿有人会说英语吗?
jer-r yo-ren hway shuo ying-yü ma

I don't speak (much) Chinese.
我不会说汉语/汉语说得不好。
wo boo-hway shuo han-yü/han-yü shuo de boo-hao

Could you speak more slowly?
您能不能说慢点?
nin nung-boo-nung shuo man dian

Could you repeat that?
您能不能再说一遍?
nin nung-boo-nung dsai shuo yee-bian

Excuse me? [Pardon?]
对不起? *dwee-boo-chee*

Please write it down.
请您写下来。 *ching nin shie shia-lai*

Can you translate this for me?
你能为我翻译一下吗?
nee nung way wo fan-yee yee-shia ma

What does this/that mean?
这/那是什么意思?
jer/na sh shen-me yee-s

Please point to the phrase in the book.
请在书上为我指一指这句话
ching dsai shoo-sharng way wo j-yee-j jer jü hwaa

I understand.
我懂了。
wo dong le

I don't understand.
我不懂。
wo boo dong

Do you understand?
你懂了吗?

– *yee-bai-san-sh-woo kwai.*
– *wo boo dong.*
– *yee-bai-san-sh-woo kwai.*
– *ching nin shie shia lai ba …*
ah "one hundred and thirty-five yuan"
… *ming-bai le.*

Questions 问题

Chinese nouns have no articles (a, an, the) and, with the exception of very few nouns, no plural forms. Whether the noun is singular or plural is judged from the context, or by a number modifying the noun.

Wo yao mai yee-jarng chü Sharng-hai de piao.
I'd like a ticket to Shanghai.

Wo yao mai san-jarng chü Sharng-hai de piao.
I'd like three tickets to Shanghai.

Where? 在哪儿?

Where is it?	它在哪儿? *ta dsai na-r*
Where are you going?	你去哪儿? *nee chü na-r*
at the meeting place [point]	在约会地点 *dsai yüe-hway dee-dian*
downstairs	楼下 *lo-shia*
from the U.S.	从美国来 *tsong may-guo lai*
here (to here)	这儿(来这儿) *jer-r (lai jer-r)*
in the car	在车里 *dsai cher lee*
in China	在中国 *dsai jong-guo*
inside	在里面 *dsai lee-mian*
near the bank	靠近银行 *kao-jin yin-harng*
next to the post office	在邮局旁边 *dsai yo-jü parng-bian*
opposite the market	在集市对面 *dsai jee-sh dwee-mian*
on the left/right	在左边/右边 *dsai dsuo-bian/yo-bian*
there (to there)	那儿(去那儿) *na-r (chü na-r)*
to the hotel	去旅馆 *chü lü-gwan*
towards Xi'an	往西安方向 *warng shee-an farng-shiarng*
outside the café	在咖啡馆门外 *dsai ka-fay-gwan men-wai*
up to the traffic lights	直到交通灯那儿 *j-dao jiao-tong-dung na-r*
upstairs	楼上 *lo-sharng*

When? 什么时间?

When does the museum open? 博物馆什么时间开门?
bo-woo-gwan shen-me sh-jian kai-men

When does the train arrive? 火车什么时间到达?
huo-chee shen-me sh-jian dao-da

10 minutes ago 十分钟前 *sh fen-jong chian*

after lunch 中饭后 *jong-fan ho*

always 总是 *dsong-sh*

around midnight 半夜前后 *ban-ye chian-ho*

at 7 o'clock 七点钟 *chee dian jong*

before Friday 星期五前 *shing-chee-woo chian*

by tomorrow 不迟于明天
boo-ch-yü ming-tian

early 早 *dsao*

every week 每星期 *may shing-chee*

for 2 hours (连续) 两小时 *(lian-shü) liarng shiao-sh*

from 9 a.m. to 6 p.m. 从上午九点到下午六点 *tsong sharng-woo jio dian dao shia-woo lio dian*

immediately 立刻 *lee-ker*

in 20 minutes 二十分钟后 *er-sh fen-jong ho*

never 从来没有/决不会
tsong-lai may-yo/jüe-boo-hway

not yet 还没有 *hai-may-yo*

now 现在 *shian-dsai*

often 经常 *jing-charng*

on March 8 三月八号 *san-yüe ba-hao*

on weekdays 星期一到星期五 *shing-chee-yee dao shing-chee-woo*

sometimes 有时 *yo-sh*

soon 不久 *boo-jio*

then 那时 *na-sh*

within 2 days 两天之内 *liarng-tian j-nay*

What sort of ...? 什么样的 ... ?

	I'd like	我想要--点 ...
	something ...	*wo shiarng yao yee-dian* ...
	It's ...	这个 ... *jer ge* ...
	beautiful / ugly	漂亮 / 丑陋 *piao-liarng / cho-lo*
better / worse		更好 / 更糟 *gung-hao / gung-dsao*
big / small		大 / 小 *da / shiao*
cheap / expensive		便宜 / 贵 *pian-yee / gway*
clean / dirty		干净 / 不干净 *gan-jing / boo-gan-jing*
dark / light (color)		深 / 浅 *shen / chian*
delicious / revolting		好吃 / 难吃 *hao-ch / nan-ch*
easy / difficult		容易 / 难 *rong-yee / nan*
empty / full		空 / 满 *kong / man*
good / bad		好 / 坏 *hao / hwai*
heavy / light		重 / 轻 *jong / ching*
hot / warm / cold		热 / 暖 / 冷 *re, nwan / lung*
modern / old-fashioned		时髦 / 过时 *sh-mao / guo-sh*
narrow / wide		窄 / 宽 *jai / kwan*
old / new		旧 / 新 *jio / shin*
open / shut		开 / 关 *kai / gwan*
pleasant, nice / unpleasant		好 / 不好 *hao / boo-hao*
quick / slow		快 / 慢 *kwai / man*
quiet / noisy		安静 / 吵闹 *an-jing / chao-nao*
right / wrong		对 / 错 *dwee / tsuo*
tall / small		高大 / 矮小 *gao-da / ai-shiao*
vacant / occupied		没人 / 有人 *may-ren / yo-ren*
young / old		年轻 / 年老 *nian-ching / nian-lao*

Why? 为什么?

Why is that?	为什么会这样 *way-shen-me hway jer-yarng*
because of the weather	因为天气的缘故 *yin-way tian-chee de yüan-goo*
because I'm in a hurry	因为我有急事 *yin-way wo yo jee-shee*
I don't know why	我不知道原因 *wo boo-j-dao yüan-yin*

14

Word order in Chinese is usually: *subject – verb – object*, which is also the usual order in English sentences.

Adjectives and other modifying phrases are usually placed in front of nouns.

Yes/No questions (i.e., questions which can be answered by either *yes* or *no*) are formed by adding the question word **ma** at the end of a statement.

Jer-r sh sho-piao-choo ma?

(here is ticket office + **ma**) Is this the ticket office?

Other questions are formed by inserting the specific question words (e.g., where, when, who, how many, etc.) in the place in the statement where the information asked for would come. For example, the statement "I am <u>20 years old</u>", would produce the question: You are <u>how many years old</u>? (i.e., How old are you?). Hence:

Sho-piao-choo dsai <u>na-r</u>?   Where is the ticket office?

(ticket office is <u>here</u> ⇨ ticket office is <u>where</u>?)

How much / many? 多少?

How much is that?	这个多少钱? *jer-ge duo-shao chian*
How many are there?	一共有多少? *yee-gong yo duo-shao*
1/2/3	一/二/三 *yee/er/san*
4/5	四/五 *s/woo*
none	一个没有 *yee-ge may-yo*
about 100 yuan	大约一百元 *da-yüe yee-bai yüan*
a little	一点点 *yee dian-dian*
a lot of milk	很多牛奶 *hen duo nio-nai*
enough	够了 *go-le*
a few of them	少来几个 *shao lai jee ge*
more than that	比这多 *bee jer duo*
less than that	比这少 *bee jer shao*
much more	多得多 *duo de duo*
nothing else	就这些 *jio jer-shie*
too much	太多了 *tai duo le*

Who?/Which? 谁?/哪个?

Who's there?	是谁呀?	*sh shwee ya*
It's me!	是我!	*sh wo*
It's us!	是我们!	*sh wo-men*
someone	有人	*yo-ren*
no one	没有人	*may-yo ren*
Which one do you want?	您要哪个?	*nin yao na-ge*
this one/that one	这个/那个	*jer-ge/na-ge*
one like that	象那个一样的 *shiarng na-ge yee-yarng de*	
not that one	不是那个	*boo-sh na-ge*
something	某个东西	*mo ge dong-shee*
nothing	没什么	*may shen-me*
none	一个没有	*yee-ge may-yo*

Whose? 谁的

Whose is that?	那是谁的?	*na sh shwee-de*
It's ...	那是 ...	*na sh ...*
mine/ours/yours	我的 / 我们的 / 你(们)的 *wo de/wo-men de/nee (men) de*	
his/hers/theirs	他的 / 她的 / 他们的 *ta de/ta de/ta-men de*	
It's ... turn.	轮到 ... 了	*lwun-dao ... le*
my/our/your	我 / 我们 / 你(们) *wo/wo-men/nee-(men)*	
his/her/their	他 / 她 / 他们	*ta/ta/ta-men*

Negatives: **boo** (no/not) is added in front of the verb to indicate negation.

Wo yao dan-ren farng-jian.	I want a single room.
Wo boo yao dan-ren farng-jian.	I don't want a single room.

Yes/No: There is no specific word in Chinese for *yes* or *no*. You can affirm or negate something by using **dwee** (right) and **boo-dwee** (not right), or simply repeat the verb which was used in the question.

Nin <u>yao</u> cha ma?	Would you like some tea?
<u>Yao</u>.	Yes, I would.
Boo <u>yao</u>, shie-shie.	No, thank you.

How? 怎么?

How would you like to pay?	您想怎么付钱? *nin shiarng dsen-me foo-chian*
by credit card	用信用卡付钱 *yong shin-yong-ka foo-chian*
cash	现金 *shian-jin*
How are you getting here?	你们怎么去那儿? *nee-men dsen-me chü na-r*
by car/by bus/by train	开车去/坐公共汽车去/坐火车去 *kai-cher chü/dsuo gong-gong-chee-cher chü/ dsuo huo-cher chü*
on foot	步行 *boo shing*
quickly	快点 *kwai dian*
slowly	慢点 *man dian*
too fast	太快 *tai kwai*
very	非常 *fay-charng*
with a friend	和朋友一起 *her pung-yo yee-chee*
without a passport	不用护照 *boo-yong hoo-jao*

Is it ...?/Are there ...? 是不是 ... ? /有没有... ?

Is it ...?	是不是? *sh-boo-sh*
Is it free of charge?	是不是免费的? *sh-boo-sh mian-fay de*
It isn't ready.	还没准备好。 *hai may jwun-bay hao*
Is/Are there ...?	有没有 ... ? *yo-may-yo ...*
Is there a shower in the room?	房间里有没有淋浴? *farng-jian lee yo-may-yo lin-yü*
Are there buses into town?	去城里有没有公共汽车? *chü chung-lee yo-may-yo gong-gong-chee-cher*
There is a good restaurant near here.	附近有家好餐馆。 *foo-jin yo jia hao tsan-gwan*
There aren't any towels in my room.	我的房间里没有毛巾。 *wo-de farng-jian lee may-yo mao-jin*
Here it is/they are.	在这儿。 *dsai jer-r*
There it is/they are.	在那儿。 *dsai na-r*

Can/May? 能不能/可不可以?

Can I have ...?	我能要 ... 吗?
	wo nung yao ... ma
Can we have ...?	我们能要 ... 吗?
	wo-men nung yao ... ma
May I speak to ...?	我能不能跟 ... 说句话?
	wo nung-boo-nung gen ... shuo jü hwaa
Can you tell me ...?	你能不能告诉我 ... ?
	nee nung-boo-nung gao-soo wo ...
Can you help me?	能帮个忙吗?
	nung barng ge marng ma
Can you direct me to ...?	请问去 ... 怎么走? *ching-wen chü ...*
	dsen-me dso
I can't.	我不能。 *wo boo-nung*

What do you want? 你想要什么?

I'd like ...	我想要 ... *wo shiarng yao ...*
Could I have ...?	我能要 ... 吗 ?
	wo nung yao ... ma
We'd like ...	我们想要 ... *wo-men shiarng yao ...*
Give me ...	给我 ... *gay wo ...*
I'm looking for ...	我找 ... *wo jao ...*
I need to ...	我需要 ... *wo shü-yao ...*
go ...	去 ... *chü ...*
find ...	找 ... *jao ...*
see ...	看 ... *kan ...*
speak to ...	跟 ... 说话 *gen ... shuo-hwaa*

– dwee-boo-chi.
– yo shen-me sh?
– wo nung-boo-nung gen warng shian-shung shuo jü hwaa?
– ching shao dung.

18

Other useful words
其它有用的词语

fortunately	幸好 *shing-hao*
of course	当然 *darng-ran*
perhaps/possibly	也许 *ye-shü*
probably	很可能 *hen-ker-nung*

Exclamations 感叹词

At last!	终于 …！ *jong-yü*
Go on.	接着来 *jie-je lai*
I don't mind.	我不在乎 *wo boo-dsai-hoo*
No way!	我才不干呢！ *wo tsai boo-gan ne*
Really?	真的? *jen-de*
Nonsense.	胡说。 *hoo-shuo*
That's enough.	别再说了。 *bie dsai shuo le*
That's true.	是真的。 *sh jen-de*
How are things?	你怎么样? *nee dsen-me-yarng*
Fine, thank you.	很好，谢谢你。 *hen-hao, shie-shie nee*
It's …	这个 … *jer ge …*
great/terrific	太棒了 *tai-barng-le*
very good	太好了 *tai-hao-le*
fine	行 *shing*
not bad	不错 *boo tsuo*
okay	可以 *ker-yee*
not good	不好 *boo-hao*
terrible	很糟糕 *hen dsao-gao*

GRAMMAR

Chinese verb forms are even more invariable than English ones, with no differences between the singular and plural forms.

Personal pronouns (I/me, you, he/him, she/her, etc.) have the same form whether they are the subject or the object.

Wo gay ta piao le. I gave him the ticket.

Ta gay wo piao le. He gave me the ticket.

19

Accommodations

Reservations	21	Requirements	26
Reception	22	Renting	28
Price	24	Youth hostel	29
Decision	24	Camping	30
Problems	25	Checking out	32

Whether you are going to China on your own or as part of a group, your hotel accommodation will probably be reserved in advance by the China International Travel Service (**CITS**).

Hotels 旅馆 (**lü-gwan**) in China range from first class to grimly spartan. The newest hotels, often built with foreign co-operation, offer facilities and standards similar to their counterparts in Europe and the United States. Some cities still have their famous hotels dating from earlier, grander times, for example *The Peace Hotel* in Shanghai. These may have seen better days and may not have all the modern conveniences of the new hotels, but they make up for this in their architectural splendor and grandeur.

In general, hotels in small or remote towns offer few comforts. Air conditioning is a relatively new feature in China; however, radios and telephones are usually provided, and an increasing number of hotels are equipped with small refrigerators and television sets.

In almost every room you'll find cups and a large thermos of hot water for making tea, (which is usually provided as well). The separate carafe of "drinking water" may not always be trusted. Similarly, do not drink water straight from the tap.

In the larger hotels there is a service desk on each floor, manned by staff who often speak some English. They keep room keys, handle laundry, deal with telephone problems, and sell cigarettes, snacks, drinks and postcards. Postal, telegraph, and telephone desks, as well as a foreign-exchange facility and gift shops are usually located on the ground floor.

A suggestion: When you wander out on your own take a hotel card with you (available from reception) with the hotel's name written in Mandarin and English. This is useful if you need to ask the way or direct a taxi.

Reservations 预订房间

In advance 事先

Can you recommend a
hotel in …?

您能推荐一家在 … 的旅
馆吗? *nin nung twee-jian
yee-jia dsai … de lü-gwan ma*

Is it near the center of town?

这家旅馆离市中心近吗?
jer jia lü gwan lee sh-jong-shin jin ma

How much is it per night?

每晚多少钱? *may wan duo-shao-chian*

Is there anything cheaper?

有没有便宜一点的?
yo-may-yo pian-yee yee-dian de

Could you reserve [book]
a room for me there, please?

请您给我在那儿订一个房间, 好吗?
*ching nin gay wo dsai na-r ding yee-ge
farng-jian, hao-ma*

How do I get there?

去那儿怎么走? *chü na-r dsen-me dso*

At the hotel 到达旅馆后

Do you have any vacancies?

您这儿有空房间吗?
nin jer-r yo kong-farng-jian ma

Is there another hotel nearby?

附近还有其它旅馆吗?
foo-jin hai-yo chee-ta lü-gwan ma

I'd like a single/double room.

我想要一个单人／双人房间。
*wo shiarng yao yee-ge dan-ren/
shwarng-ren farng-jian*

Can I see the room, please?

我可以看一看房间吗? *wo ker-yee
kan-yee-kan farng-jian ma*

I'd like a room with …

我想要一个有 … 的房间。 *wo shiarng yao
yee-ge yo … de farng-jian*

twin beds

两张单人床 *liarng-jarng dan-ren-chwarng*

a double bed

一张双人床 *yee-jarng shwarng-ren-chwarng*

a bath/shower

浴缸／淋浴 *yü-garng/lin-yü*

– *nin jer-r yo kong-farng-jian ma? Wo shiarng yao yee-ge
shwarng-ren farng-jian.*
– *dwee-boo-chee, wo-men jer-r ker-man le.*
– *ah, foo-jin hai yo-may-yo chee-ta lü-gwan?*
– *yo, hong-shing lü-gwan jio-dsai foo-jin.*

Reception 接待处

I have a reservation.	我已经预订了房间。 *wo yee-jing yü-ding le farng-jian*
My name is ...	我的名字是 ... *wo-de ming-ds sh ...*
We've reserved a double and a single room.	我们预订了一间双人房和一间单人房 *wo-men yü-ding le yee-jian shwarng-ren-farng her yee-jian dan-ren-farng*
I confirmed my reservation by mail.	我写信来确认过。 *wo shie-shin lai chüe-ren guo*
Could we have adjoining rooms?	您能不能安排我们的房间靠在一起? *nin nung-boo-nung an-pai wo-men de farng-jian kao-dsai-yee-chee*

Amenities and facilities 旅馆设施

Is there (a/an) ... in the room?	房间里有 ... 吗? *farng-jian lee yo ... ma*
air conditioning	空调 *kong-tiao*
TV/telephone	电视 / 电话 *dian-sh/dian-hwaa*
Does the hotel have a(n)...?	旅馆里有没有 ... ? *lü-gwan lee yo-may-yo ...*
cable TV	有线电视 *yo-shian dian-sh*
laundry service	洗衣服务 *shee-yee-foo-woo*
solarium	日光浴 *r-gwarng-yü*
swimming pool	游泳池 *yo-yong-ch*
Could you put ... in the room?	您可不可以给房间里 ... ? *nin ker-boo-ker-yee gay farng-jian lee ...*
an extra bed	加一张床? *jia yee-jarng chwarng*
a crib [child's cot]	加一张幼儿床? *jia yee-jarng yo-er-chwarng*
Do you have facilities for children/the disabled?	您这儿有没有儿童 / 残疾人专用设施? *nin jer-r yo-may-yo er-tong/tsan-jee-ren jwan-yong sher-sh*

Public toilets in towns, villages, and tourist sites are basic: often just holes in the ground with low partitions (without doors). Toilet paper is never provided, so carry tissues with you. However, a program is underway to upgrade facilities for foreign tourists.

How long? 多久？

We'll be staying …	我们在这儿要住 … *wo-men dsai jer-r yao joo …*
one night only	一晚 *yee wan*
a few days	几天 *jee tian*
a week (at least)	(至少) 一星期 *(j-shao) yee shing-chee*
I don't know yet.	还没定呢。*hai may-ding ne*
I'd like to stay an extra night.	我想再住一晚 *wo shiarng dsai joo yee wan*
What does this mean?	这是什么意思? *jer sh shen-me yee-s*

– nee-hao, wo jiao John Newton.
– *nin-hao, Newton shian-shung.*
– wo shiarng joo liarng-wan.
– *shing, ching nin tian yee-shia jer-jarng (dung-jee) biao, hao-ma?*

我看看您的护照，好吗?	May I see your passport, please?
请填写这张表。	Please fill out this form.
您的汽车牌照号码是什么?	What is your car registration number?

不包早餐房价 … 元	room only … yuan
包早餐	breakfast included
有饭菜供应	meals available
姓／名	last name/first name
家庭住址/街道/门牌号码	home address/street/number
国籍/职业	nationality/profession
出生日期/出生地点	date/place of birth
护照号码	passport number
汽车牌照号码	car registration number
地点/日期	place/date
签名	signature

23

Price 价格

How much is it ...?	... 多少钱?	... duo-shao-chian
per night/week	每晚/每星期	may-wan/may shing-chee
for bed and breakfast	包早餐	bao dsao-tsan
excluding meals	不包括吃饭	boo bao-kuo ch-fan
for full board (American Plan [A.P.])	吃住全包	ch-joo chüan bao
for half board (Modified American Plan [M.A.P.])	吃住半包	ch-joo ban bao
Does the price include ...?	房价中包括 ... 吗? farng-jia jong bao-kuo ... ma	
breakfast	早餐	dsao-tsan
sales tax [VAT]	增值税	dsung-j-shwee
Do I have to pay a deposit?	我需要预付押金吗? wo shü-yao yü-foo ya-jin ma	
Is there a reduction for children?	儿童住打折扣吗? er-tong joo da jer-ko ma	

Decision 作决定

May I see the room?	我能不能看看房间? wo nung-boo-nung kan-kan farng-jian	
That's fine. I'll take it.	可以，我要了。 ker-yee, wo yao le	
It's too ...	就是太 ...	jio-sh tai ...
dark/small	暗/小	an/shiao
noisy	吵	chao
Do you have anything ...?	还有没有 ... ?	hai yo-may-yo ...
bigger/cheaper	大点的/便宜点的 da dian de/pian-yee dian de	
quieter/lighter	安静点的/光线好点的 an-jing dian de/gwarng-shian hao dian de	
No, I won't take it.	算了，我不要了。 swan-le, wo boo yao le	

24

Problems
碰到问题

The ... doesn't work.   ... 坏了。 *... hwai le*

air conditioning   空调 *kong-tiao*

fan   电风扇 *dian-fung-shan*

heating   暖气 *nwan-chee*

light   电灯 *dian-dung*

I can't turn the heat [heating] on/off.   暖气打不开／关不掉。 *nwan-chee da-boo-kai/gwan-boo-diao*

There is no hot water/ toilet paper.   房间里没有热水／卫生纸 *farng-jian lee may-yo rer-shwee/way-shung-j*

The faucet [tap] is dripping.   水龙头总是滴水。 *shwee-long-tou dsong-sh dee-shwee*

The sink/toilet is blocked.   水池／厕所塞住了。 *shwee-ch/tser-suo sai-joo le*

The window/door is jammed.   窗户／门卡住了。 *chwarng-hoo/men chia-joo le*

My room has not been made up.   我的房间还没打扫。 *wo de farng-jian hai may da sao*

The ... is broken.   ... 坏了。 *... hwai le*

blinds/lamp   窗帘／灯 *chwarng-lian/dung*

lock/switch   锁／开关 *suo/kai-gwan*

There are insects in our room.   我们房间里有虫子。 *wo-men farng-jian lee yo chong-ds*

Action 行动

Could you have that seen to?   这件事您能不能过问一下? *jer-jian sh nin nung-boo-nung guo-wen yee-shia*

I'd like to move to another room.   我想换个房间。 *wo shiarng hwan ge farng-jian*

I'd like to speak to the manager.   我要向你们的经理提意见。 *wo yao shiarng nee-men de jing-lee tee yee-jian*

Requirements 一般要求

In theory the voltage everywhere in China is 220 volts, 50 cycles. In practice the voltage fluctuates from time to time. Also socket types and sizes vary. Some hotels have adapters that you can borrow.

About the hotel 与旅馆有关的话题

Where's the ...?	... 在哪儿? ... *dsai-na-r*
bar	酒吧 *jio-ba*
bathroom	洗澡间 *shee-dsao-jian*
parking lot [car park]	停车场 *ting-cher-charng*
dining room	餐厅 *tsan-ting*
elevator [lift]	电梯 *dian-tee*
sauna	桑拿浴 *sarng-na-yü*
shower	淋浴间 *lin-yü jian*
swimming pool	游泳池 *yo-yong-ch*
tour operator's bulletin board	旅行社布告牌 *lü-shing-sher boo-gao-pai*
Where is the bathroom [toilet]?	厕所在哪儿? *tser-suo dsai na-r*
What time is the front door locked?	前门几点上锁? *chian-men jee-dian sharng-suo*
What time is breakfast served?	早餐几点供应? *dsao-tsan jee-dian gong-ying*
Is there room service?	有没有客房用餐服务? *yo-may-yo ker-farng yong-tsan foo-woo*

电须刀插座	razors [shavers] only
紧急出口	emergency exit
安全门	fire door
请勿打扰	do not disturb
外线请拨 ... 号	dial ... for an outside line

Personal needs 个人需求

The key to room ..., please.	请给我 ... 号房门钥匙。 *ching gay wo ... hao farng-men yao-sh*
I've lost my key.	我的钥匙丢了。 *wo de yao-sh dio le*
I've locked myself out of my room.	我把钥匙锁在房间里了。*wo ba yao-sh suo dsai farng-jian lee le*
Could you wake me at ...?	您能不能 ... 点钟叫醒我? *nin nung-boo-nung ... dian-jong jiao-shing wo*
I'd like breakfast in my room.	我想在房间里用早餐。*wo shiarng dsai farng-jian lee yong dsao-tsan*
Can I leave this in the safe?	我能不能把这个寄存在保险柜里? *wo nung-boo-nung ba jer-ge jee-tswun dsai bao-shian-gway lee*
Could I have my things from the safe?	请您把我的东西从保险柜里拿出来好吗? *ching nin ba wo de dong-shee tsong bao-shian-gway lee na choo-lai hao-ma*
Where is our tour guide?	我们的旅行团导游在哪儿? *wo-men de lü-shing-twan dao-yo dsai na-r*
May I have (an) extra ...?	我能不能再要 ... ? *wo nung-boo-nung dsai yao ...*
bath towel/blanket	一条浴巾 / 毯子 *yee-tiao yü-jin/tan-ds*
hangers/pillow	一些衣架 / 一个枕头 *yee-shie yee-jia/yee-ge jen-tou*
soap	一块肥皂 *yee-kwai fay-dsao*
Is there any mail for me?	有没有我的信件? *yo-may-yo wo de shin-jian*
Are there any messages for me?	有没有人给我留言? *yo-may-yo ren gay wo lio-yan*

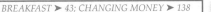

BREAKFAST ➤ 43; CHANGING MONEY ➤ 138

Renting 自炊式住宿

We've reserved an apartment/cottage in the name of …
我们预订了一套公寓房 / 一幢乡间别墅，预订人姓名是 … *wo-men yü-ding le yee-tao gong-yü farng/yee-jwarng shiarng-jian bie-shoo, yü-ding ren shing-ming sh …*

Where do we pick up the keys?
到哪里取钥匙? *dao na-lee chü yao-sh*

Where is the…?
… 在哪儿? *… dsai na-r*

electricity meter
电表 *dian-biao*

fuse box
保险丝盒 *bao-shian-s her*

valve [stopcock]
总阀门 *dsong-fa-men*

water heater
热水器 *rer-shwee-chee*

Are there any spare …?
有没有备用的 … ? *yo-may-yo bay-yong de…*

fuses
保险丝 *bao-shian-s*

gas bottles
煤气罐 *may-chee-gwan*

sheets
床单 *chwarng-dan*

Which day does the maid come?
清洁工哪天来? *ching-jie-gong na-tian lai*

Where/When do I put out the trash [rubbish]?
垃圾拿出去放哪儿 /什么时候拿出去? *la-jee na choo-chü farng na-r/shen-me sh-hou na choo-chü*

Problems 出毛病了

Where can I contact you?
我怎么跟你联系? *wo dsen-me gen nee lian-shee*

How does the stove [cooker]/water heater work?
炉子 /热水器怎么用? *loo-ds/rer-shwee-chee dsen-me yong*

The … is/are dirty.
… 不干净。 *… boo-gan-jing*

The … has broken down.
… 坏了。 *… hwai le*

We have accidentally broken/lost …
我们不小心打破了 /丢了 … *wo-men boo-shiao-shin da-po le/dio le …*

That was already damaged when we arrived.
我们住进来时，那已经坏了。 *wo-men joo jin-lai sh, na yee-jing hwai le*

HOUSEHOLD ARTICLES ➤ 148

Useful terms 有用的词语

boiler	锅炉 *guo-loo*
crockery	碗碟 *wan-die*
cutlery	(西餐) 餐具 *(shee-tsan) tsan-jü*
frying pan	炒锅 *chao-guo*
kettle	水壶 *shwee-hoo*
lamp	灯 *dung*
refrigerator/freezer	冰箱/冷冻柜 *bing-shiarng/ lung-dong-gway*
saucepan	炖锅 *dwun-guo*
stove [cooker]	炉子 *loo-ds*
toilet paper	卫生纸 *way-shung-j*
washing machine	洗衣机 *shee-yee-jee*

Rooms 房间

balcony	阳台 *yarng-tai*
bathroom	盥洗室 *gwan-shee-sh*
bedroom	卧室 *wo-sh*
dining room	餐厅 *tsan-ting*
kitchen	厨房 *choo-farng*
living room	客厅 *ker-ting*
toilet	卫生间 *way-shung-jian*

Youth hostel 青年招待所 (简易旅馆)

Do you have any places left for tonight?	你们今晚有空床位吗? *nee-men jin-wan yo kong chwarng-way ma*
Do you rent out bedding?	你们这儿出租床褥吗? *nee-men jer-r choo-dsoo chwarng-roo ma*
What time are the doors locked?	你们夜里什么时间锁大门? *nee-men ye-lee shen-me sh-jian suo da-men*
I have an International Student Card.	我有国际通用学生证。 *wo yo guo-jee tong-yong shüe -shung-jung*

REQUIREMENTS ➤ 26; CAMPING ➤ 30

Camping 露营

Camping is not known as a leisure activity in China – and is not easy to do. Camping within sight of a town or village would probably result in a visit from the police (Public Security Bureau). Wilderness camping is appealing, but such areas require special permits and are difficult to reach.

Reservations 登记

Is there a campsite near here?	这附近有没有露营地? *jer foo-jin yo-may-yo loo-ying-dee*
Do you have space for a tent/trailer [caravan]?	你们有没有支帐篷/停放活动住房的空位? *nee-men yo-may-yo j jarng-pung/ting-farng huo-dong-joo-farng de kong-way*
What is the charge ...?	... 收费是多少? *...sho-fay sh duo-shao*
per day/week	每天/每星期 *may-tian/may-shing-chee*
for a tent/a car	支一顶帐篷/停放一部车 *j yee-ding jarng-pung/ting-farng yee-boo-cher*
for a trailer [caravan]	停放一个活动住房 *ting-farng yee-ge huo-dong-joo-farng*

Facilities 设施

Are there cooking facilities on site?	露营地有没有炊具? *loo-ying-dee yo-may-yo chwee-jü*
Are there any electric outlets [power points]?	有没有电源插座? *yo-may-yo dian-yüan cha-dsuo*
Where is/are the ...?	... 在哪儿? ... *dsai-na-r*
drinking water	饮用水 *yin-yong-shwee*
trashcans [dustbins]	垃圾箱 *la-jee-shiarng*
laundry facilities	洗衣设备 *shee-yee sher-bay*
showers	淋浴间 *lin-yü-jian*
Where can I get some butane gas?	哪里能买到烧饭用的天然气? *na-lee nung mai-dao shao-fan yong de tian-ran chee*

禁止露营	no camping
饮用水	drinking water
禁止生火 / 禁止烧烤	no fires/barbecues

Complaints 抱怨

It's too sunny/shady/crowded here.	这里太晒了 / 太荫凉了 / 太拥挤了。 *jer-lee tai shai le/tai yin-liarng le/tai yong-jee le*
The ground's too hard/uneven.	这里地面太硬/不平。 *jer-lee dee-mian tai ying/boo-ping*
Do you have a more level spot?	你们有没有平坦点的地方？ *nee-men yo-may-yo ping-tan dian de dee-farng*
You can't camp here.	这里怎么能露营! *jer-lee dsen-me nung loo-ying*

Camping equipment 露营用具

butane gas	天然气 *tian-ran chee*
campbed	折叠床 *jer-die-chwarng*
charcoal	木炭 *moo-tan*
flashlight [torch]	手电筒 *sho-dian-tong*
groundcloth [groundsheet]	铺地防水布 *poo-dee farng-shwee-boo*
guy rope	拉绳 *la shung*
hammer	小锤子 *shiao chwee-ds*
kerosene [primus] stove	便携式煤油炉 *bian-shie-sh may-yo-loo*
knapsack	背包 *bay-bao*
mallet	大锤子 *da chwee-ds*
matches	火柴 *huo-chai*
(air) mattress	(充气)床垫 *(chong-chee) chwarng-dian*
paraffin	煤油 *may-yo*
penknife	小刀 *shiao dao*
sleeping bag	睡袋 *shwee-dai*
tent	帐篷 *jarng-pung*
tent pegs	帐篷桩 *jarng-pung jwarng*
tent pole	帐篷支柱 *jarng-pung j-joo*

Checking out 退房结帐

What time do we have to check out by?	我们应该什么时候退房？ *wo-men ying-gai shen-me sh-hou tway-farng*
Could we leave our baggage here until … p.m.?	我们能不能把行李留在这儿，下午…来取？ *wo-men nung-boo-nung ba shing-lee lio dsai jer-r, shia-woo … lai chü*
I'm leaving now.	我这就走。 *wo jer jio dsou*
Could you order me a taxi, please?	请您给我叫一部出租车好吗？ *ching nin gay wo jiao yee-boo choo-dsoo-cher hao ma*
We've had a very enjoyable stay.	这次住得非常愉快。 *jer-ts joo de fay-charng yü kwai*

Paying 付钱

Tipping is officially discouraged, although it is becoming more acceptable, particularly in the coastal cities. However, a small gift – such as a souvenir from home is appropriate (and much appreciated) when someone has been really helpful to you. If the gift is refused, don't insist.

May I have my bill, please?	我要付帐。 *wo yao foo-jarng*
I think there's a mistake in this bill.	我觉得帐单上有错。 *wo jüe-de jarng-dan sharng yo-tsuo*
I've made … telephone calls.	我打过 … 次电话。 *wo da-guo … ts dian-hwaa*
I've taken … from the mini-bar.	我从小酒吧里拿了 … 。 *wo tsong shiao-jio-ba lee na-le …*
Can I have an itemized bill?	能不能给我一张分项帐单？ *nung-boo-nung gay wo yee-jarng fen-shiarng jarng-dan*
Could I have a receipt, please?	请给我一张收据。 *ching gay wo yee-jarng sho-jü*

Eating Out

Restaurants	33	Egg dishes	45	
Chinese cuisine	34	Meat	46	
Finding a place to eat	35	Vegetables		47
Reserving a table	36	Rice		48
Ordering	37	Noodles/Dofu		48
Fast food/Café	40	Dessert		49
Complaints	41	Fruit		49
Paying	42	Drinks		50
Course by course	43	Beer		50
Breakfast	43	Wine		50
Appetizers/Starters	43	Spirits and liqueurs		50
Soups	44	Other drinks		51
Fish and seafood	45	Menu Reader		52

Restaurants

Almost every country in the world now has Chinese restaurants. However, the authenticity of the food suffers greatly when essential ingredients are hard to come by and the chef makes compromises for local tastes. Real Chinese cuisine will hopefully be one of the hightlights of your trip.

There are many regional variations in Chinese cooking due to the size of the country, the difference in ingredients available, and local tastes.

Most Chinese restaurants outside of China feature Cantonese food because it was the people from Guangdong Province who emigrated far and wide.

Cantonese cuisine 粤菜 yüe-tsai

Steaming and stir-frying are the signatures of Cantonese cooking and preserve the food's natural flavor, as well as colors and vitamins. Look for steamed dumplings filled with meat or shrimp [prawns], deep-fried spring rolls, and of course, sweet and sour pork or shrimp [prawns]. Steamed rice is the usual accompaniment, or fried rice if you prefer.

Beijing cuisine 北京菜 bay-jing-tsai

Wheat, not rice, is the staple in northern China, so Beijing cuisine is composed mainly of noodles, steamed bread and dumplings. Beijing is the place to try Peking (or Beijing) duck: freshly roasted crispy-skinned duck wrapped in wafer-thin pancakes with spring onions and sweet bean sauce.

Shanghai cuisine 沪菜 hoo-tsai

Shanghai cuisine requires time and care. The flavors are full of interesting surprises: sweet and salty with hints of garlic and vinegar. Meats are often marinated and braised in soy sauce, wine, and sugar. Shanghai is famous for its seafood: steamed freshwater crab, honey-fried eel, yellowfish, and sautéed shrimp.

Szechwan cuisine 川菜 chwan-tsai

Sichuan Province is well-known for its hot, peppery dishes. However, the food is not simply hot but rather combines a number of tastes: bitter, sweet, tart, and sour. Even beancurd, often thought bland, becomes something more in Chengdu or Chongqing. If you do not care for hot food, there are other dishes to choose, such as sautéed shredded pork with spring onions and soybeans.

Hunan cuisine 湖南菜 hoo-nan-tsai

Here the chili pepper is also a great favorite. However, dishes are generally less spicy and oily than their neighboring Sichuan counterparts. While in Hunan Province try the chili-smoked pork or chicken.

Banquets 酒席 jio-shee

Tourists are often given banquets or formal dinners in which protocol problems compound any uncertainty over the food. Do not worry, the Chinese are most understanding about foreigners' etiquette mistakes, but the following tips may help. Don't be late. Don't touch any of the food or drink until your host gives the signal. Drink the firewater, usually **mao tai jio** ➤ 50, in your smallest glass only when toasting or replying to a toast. Taste a bit of every dish offered, but as there may be as many as 13 courses start sparingly. Do not take the last morsel from a serving dish as this might imply there is not enough food. And do not ask for rice as it is not served at banquets.

Chinese cuisine 中国菜

Chinese cuisine links a progression of tastes, textures, and colors. The Chinese love culinary contrasts: bitter and sweet, crunchy and tender, and bright, appetizing colors. The progression of courses may seem strange to the Western palate with a sweet course in the middle and soup towards the end.

All dishes are shared; thus, the more people in your party the more chance to sample flavors. In restaurants tables often have revolving platters to facilitate the distribution of food, and using chopsticks lengthens the reach, so dishes don't have to be passed around.

A table for …, please.	要一张 … 座位的桌子
	yao yee jarng … dsuo-way de juo-ds
1/2/3/4	一/二/三/四 *yee/er/san/s*
Thank you.	谢谢。 *shie-shie*
I'd like to pay.	我要结帐。 *wo yao jie-jarng*

Finding a place to eat 找地方吃饭

Can you recommend a good restaurant?	你能不能给推荐个好餐馆? *nee nung-boo-nung gay twee-jian ge hao tsan-gwan*
Is there a … near here?	这附近有没有 …? *jer foo-jin yo-may-yo …*
traditional local restaurant	地方传统风味的餐馆 *dee-farng chwan-tong-fung-way de tsan-gwan*
Chinese restaurant	中餐馆 *jong-tsan-gwan*
fish restaurant	鱼/海鲜餐馆 *yü/hai-shian tsan-gwan*
Italian restaurant	意大利餐馆 *yee-da-lee tsan-gwan*
inexpensive restaurant	价格不贵的餐馆 *jia-ger boo-gway de tsan-gwan*
Korean restaurant	韩式餐馆 *han-sh tsan-gwan*
Japanese restaurant	日式餐馆 *r-sh tsan-gwan*
vegetarian restaurant	素菜馆 *soo-tsai-gwan*
Where can I find a(n) …?	哪里有 … ? *na-lee yo …*
fast food stand	快餐小卖部 *kwai-tsan shiao-mai-boo*
café/restaurant	咖啡馆 / 餐馆 *ka-fay-gwan / tsan-gwan*
with a beer garden	有园林雅座的 *yo yüan-lin ya-dsuo de*
fast food restaurant	快餐馆 *kwai-tsan-gwan*
ice-cream parlor	冷饮店 *lung-yin dian*

DIRECTIONS ➤ 94

Reserving a table 预订餐桌

I'd like to reserve a table for two.	我想预订一张两人餐桌。 *wo shiarng yü-ding yee-jarng liarng-ren tsan-juo*
For this evening / tomorrow at …	今晚 / 明天 … 点钟 *jin-wan / ming-tian … dian-jong*
We'll come at 8:00.	我们八点钟到。 *wo-men ba dian-jong dao*
A table for two, please.	请安排一张两人桌。 *ching an-pai yee-jarng liarng-ren juo*
We have a reservation.	我们订了桌子。 *wo-men ding le juo-ds*

请问贵姓?	What's the name, please?
对不起, 我们很忙 / 满座了。	I'm sorry. We're very busy / full up.
… 分钟后, 我们会有空桌子。	We'll have a free table in … minutes.
请 … 分钟后再来。	Please come back in … minutes.

Where to sit 坐在哪儿

Could we sit …?	我们能不能坐在 … ? *wo-men nung-boo-nung dsuo dsai …*
over there	那儿 *na-r*
outside	外面 *wai-mian*
in a non-smoking area	不吸烟区 *boo shee-yan chü*
by the window	靠窗子的地方 *kao chwarng-ds de dee-farng*
Smoking or non-smoking?	吸不吸烟? *shee boo shee-yan*

> – wo shiarng ding yee-jarng juo-ds jin-wan lai ch-fan.
> – jee-way?
> – s way.
> – nee-men jee dian-jong lai?
> – ba dian.
> – ching-wen nin gway-shing?
> – sh-mee-s.
> – hao-le, dao sh-ho jian.

TIME ➤ 221; NUMBERS ➤ 217

Ordering 点菜

Waiter! / Waitress!	服务员! *foo-woo-yüan*
May I see the wine list, please?	能让我看看酒单吗? *nung rarng wo kan-kan jio-dan ma*
Do you have a set menu?	你们有没有套餐菜单? *nee-men yo-may-yo tao-tsan tsai-dan*
Can you recommend some typical local dishes?	您能不能推荐一些典型的地方风味菜? *nin nung-boo-nung twee-jian yee-shie dian-shing de dee-farng-fung-way tsai*
Could you tell me what … is?	请问这 … 是什么? *ching-wen jer … sh shen-me*
What's in it?	里面是什么? *lee-mian sh shen-me*
What kind of … do you have?	你们有哪种 … ? *nee-men yo na-jong …*
I'd like …	我要 … *wo yao …*
I'll have …	我要 … *wo yao …*
a bottle / glass / carafe of …	一瓶 / 一杯 / 一瓶 … *yee-ping / yee-bay / yee-ping …*

您要点菜吗?	Are you ready to order?
您想吃什么?	What would you like?
您要不要先来点饮料?	Would you like to order drinks first?
我建议 …	I recommend …
我们没有 …	We don't have …
需要等 … 分钟。	That will take … minutes.
请慢用。	Enjoy your meal.

– *nin yao dian-tsai ma?*
– *nung-boo-nung gay twee-jian yee-ge dian-shing de dee-farng fung-way tsai?*
– *ker-yee, wo jian-yee nin charng-charng …*
– *hao, ching gay wo lai yee-fen jer-ge, jia liarng-ban-tsai.*
– *hao-lay, yin-liao her shen-me?*
– *lai yee-ping hong poo-tao-jio ba.*
– *hao de.*

DRINKS ➤ 50; *MENU READER* ➤ 52

Side dishes/Accompaniments

配菜

Could I have ... without the ...?	我的 … 里能不能不加 … ? *wo de … lee nung-boo-nung boo jia …*
With a side order of ...	要一点 … 作配菜 *yao yee-dian … dsuo pay-tsai*
Could I have salad instead of vegetables, please?	能不能把蔬菜换成凉拌菜? *nung-boo-nung ba shoo-tsai hwan-chung liarng-ban-tsai*
Does the meal come with rice or noodles/steamed buns?	主食是米饭还是面条/馒头? *joo-sh sh mee-fan hai-sh mian-tiao/man-tou*
Do you have any ...?	有没有…? *yo-may-yo …*
vegetables/salad	蔬菜 / 凉拌菜 *shoo-tsai/liarng-ban-tsai*
potatoes/fries	土豆 / 炸土豆条 *too-dou/ja too-dou-tiao*
sauces	调味汁 *tiao-way-j*
ice	冰块 *bing kwai*
May I have some ...?	请给我一点 … 好吗? *ching gay wo yee-dian … hao-ma*
bread	面包 *mian-bao*
butter	黄油 *hwarng-yo*
lemon	柠檬 *ning-mung*
mustard	芥末 *jie-muo*
pepper	胡椒 *hoo-jiao*
salt	盐 *yan*
seasoning	调料 *tiao-liao*
sugar	糖 *tarng*
artificial sweetener	人造糖 (糖精) *ren-dsao tarng (tarng-jing)*
vinaigrette [French dressing]	香醋沙司 *shiarng-tsoo sha-s*

General questions 一般要求

Could I/we have a(n) (clean) …, please?
请给我一个 (干净的) …
ching gay wo yee-ge (gan-jing de) …

ashtray
烟灰缸 *yan-hway-garng*

cup/glass
杯子 *bay-ds*

fork/knife/spoon
叉子 / 刀 / 调羹 *cha-ds/dao/tiao-gung*

serviette [napkin]
餐巾 *tsan-jin*

plate
盘子 *pan-ds*

I'd like some more …, please.
请给我再来点 … 。
ching gay wo dsai lai dian …

Nothing more, thanks.
不要了，谢谢。 *boo-yao le, shie-shie*

Where are the bathrooms [toilets]?
厕所在哪儿？
tser-suo dsai na-r

Special requirements 特殊要求

I mustn't eat food containing …
我不能吃含有 … 的食物。
wo boo-nung ch han-yo … de sh-woo

flour/fat
面 / 脂肪 *mian/j-farng*

salt/sugar
盐 / 糖 *yan/tarng*

Do you have meals/drinks? for diabetics
你们供应不供应适合糖尿病人的饮食？
nee-men gong-ying boo gong-ying sh-her tarng-niao-bing-ren de yin-sh

Do you have vegetarian meals?
你们有没有素食饭菜？
nee-men yo-may-yo soo-sh fan-tsai

For the children 儿童餐

Do you have children's portions?
你们做不做儿童餐？
nee-men dsuo-boo-dsuo er-tong tsan

Could we have a child's seat, please?
请问，你们有没有儿童座椅？
ching-wen, nee-men yo-may-yo er-tong dsuo-yee

Where can I feed/change the baby?
哪儿能给婴儿喂饭 / 换尿片？
na-r nung gay ying-er way-fan/hwan niao-pian

CHILDREN ➤ 113

Fast food/Café 快餐店

Something to drink 饮料

I'd like a cup of …	我要一杯 … *wo yao yee-bay* …
tea/coffee	茶 / 咖啡 *cha/ka-fay*
black/with milk	不加牛奶/加牛奶 *boo-jia nio-nai/jia nio-nai*
I'd like a … of red/white wine.	我要一 …红葡萄酒/白葡萄酒。 *wo yao yee … hong poo-tao-jio/bai poo-tao-jio*
glass/carafe/bottle	杯/瓶 *bay/ping*
Do you have beer?	你们有啤酒吗? *nee-men yo pee-jio ma*
bottled/draft [draught]	瓶装啤酒/散装啤酒 *ping-jwarng pee-jio/san-jwarng pee-jio*

And to eat … 食物

A piece of …, please.	请来一块 … *ching lai yee-kwai*
I'd like two of those.	这我要两个。 *jer wo yao liarng-ge*
burger	汉堡包 *han-bao-bao*
cheeseburger	奶酪汉堡包 *nai-lao han-bao-bao*
fries	炸土豆条 *ja-too-dou-tiao*
A … portion, please.	请给一 … 份 *ching gay yee … fen*
small/large	小 / 大 *shiao/da*
regular [medium]	中等 *jong-dung*
omelet	煎鸡蛋饼 *jian-jee-dan-bing*
sandwich	三明治 *san-ming-jee*
cake	蛋糕 *dan-gao*
ice cream	冰淇淋 *bing-chee-lin*
vanilla/chocolate/strawberry	香草/巧克力/草莓 *shiarng-tsao/chiao-ker-lee/tsao-may*
It's to go [take away].	不在店里吃。 *boo dsai dian-lee ch*
That's all, thanks.	就这些，谢谢。 *jio jer-shie, shie-shie*

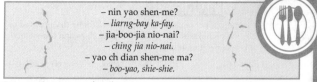

Complaints 提意见

I have no …	我没有 … 。 wo may-yo
knife/fork/spoon	刀/叉子/调羹 dao/cha-ds/tiao-gung
chopsticks	筷子 kwai-ds
There must be some mistake.	一定是出了错。 yee-ding sh choo le tsuo
That's not what I ordered.	我点的不是这个菜。 wo dian de boo-sh jer-ge tsai
I asked for …	我要了 … wo yao le …
I can't eat this.	这我怎么吃。 jer wo dsen-me ch
The meat is …	这肉 … jer ro …
overdone	煮得太老 joo de tai lao
underdone	不熟 boo sho
too tough	嚼不动 jiao-boo-dong
This is too …	这太 … jer tai …
bitter/sour	苦/酸 koo/swan
The food is cold.	这菜不热。 jer tsai boo rer
This isn't fresh/clean.	这不新鲜/不干净。 jer boo shin-shian/boo gan-jing
How much longer will our food be?	我们点的菜还要等多久？ wo-men dian de tsai hai yao dung duo-jio
We can't wait any longer. We're leaving.	我们不能再等了。我们走啦。 wo-men boo-nung dsai dung le. wo-men dso la
I'd like to speak to the head waiter/manager.	我要找你们的领班/经理提意见。 wo yao jao nee-men de ling-ban/jing-lee tee yee-jian

Paying 付帐

Tipping is not usual in China and is officially disapproved of by the authorities. However, in coastal cities and tourist areas it is becoming more acceptable.

I'd like to pay.	请结帐吧。 *ching jie-jarng ba*
The bill, please.	请给我帐单 *ching gay wo jarng-dan*
We'd like to pay separately.	我们想分开结帐。 *wo-men shiarng fen-kai jie-jarng*
It's all together.	请把我们的帐算在一起。 *ching ba wo-men de jarng swan dsai yee-chee*
I think there's a mistake in this bill.	我觉得帐单算错了。 *wo Jue-de jarng-dan swan tsuo le*
What is this amount for?	这笔数哪儿来的? *jer bee shoo na-r lai de*
I didn't have that. I had …	我没有吃那个。我吃的是 … *wo may-yo ch na-ge. wo ch de sh …*
Is service included?	包不括服务费? *bao boo bao-kuo foo-woo-fay*
Can I pay with this credit card?	你们收不收信用卡? *nee-men sho-boo-sho shin-yong-ka*
I've forgotten my wallet.	我忘了带钱包。 *wo warng-le dai chian-bao*
I haven't got enough money.	我身上钱不够。 *wo shen-sharng chian boo-go*
Could I have a receipt, please?	请给我一张发票。 *ching gay wo yee-jarng fa-piao*
That was a very good meal.	这顿饭吃得真美。 *jer-dwun-fan ch de jen may*

– foo-woo-yüan! ching jie-jarng.
– hao-lay, gay.
– jer bao boo bao-kuo foo-woo-fay?
– bao- kuo foo-woo-fay
– yong shin-yong-ka foo-jarng ker-yee ma?
– darng-ran ker-yee …
– shie-shie, jer dwun fan ch-de jen may.

Course by course 一日三餐
Breakfast 早餐

In almost every hotel in China, Western tourists are automatically served a European/American-style breakfast. This will consist of eggs, toast, butter, jam, and tea or coffee. But be warned: the coffee is often an interpretation of the real thing! If you want a Chinese breakfast you must make this clear.

Hotels serve American, British or continental breakfast from about 7 a.m. to 10 a.m. A traditional Chinese breakfast consists of a rice gruel or porridge (**jo/shee-fan**), to which almost anything may be added, from fried batter to salted fish. You'll also see early risers digging into noodle soup with hunks of pork and/or vegetables.

I'd like …	我想吃 … *wo shiarng ch …*
bread/butter	面包/黄油 *mian-bao/hwarng-yo*
a boiled egg	一个煮鸡蛋 *yee-ge joo-jee-dan*
fried/scrambled eggs	煎荷包蛋/炒鸡蛋 *jian her-bao-dan/chao-jee-dan*
fruit juice	果汁 *guo-j*
orange/grapefruit	橙子/柚子 *chung-ds/yo-ds*
honey/jam	蜂蜜/果酱 *fung-mee/guo-jiarng*
milk	牛奶 *nio-nai*
rolls	小面包 *mian-bao*
toast	烤面包 *kao-mian-bao*

Appetizers/Starters 头道菜

spring/pancake roll	春卷 *chwun-jüan*
steamed meat bun	肉包子 *ro-bao-ds*
assorted hors d'oeuvres	拼盘 *pin-pan*
assorted vegetarian food	素什锦 *soo sh-jin*
fried breaksticks	油条 *yo-tiao*
shrimp toast [prawn crackers]	虾片 *shia-pian*
steamed dumplings	蒸饺 *jung-jiao*

43

Soups 汤

馄饨	*hwun-twun*	wonton soup
清汤	*ching-tarng*	clear soup
汤面	*tarng-mian*	noodle soup
玉米蛋汤	*yü-mee dan-tarng*	thick corn and egg soup
豆腐汤	*dou-foo-tarng*	bean curd and vegetable soup
三鲜汤	*san-shian-tarng*	mixed meat and vegetable soup
蛋花菜汤	*dan-hwaa tsai-tarng*	egg and vegetable soup
鲜鱼汤	*shian-yü-tarng*	fresh fish soup
鱿鱼汤	*yo-yü-tarng*	squid soup

肉丝青菜汤 *ro-s ching-tsai tarng*
meat and vegetable broth

鸡汤 *jee-tarng*
chicken broth

西红柿蛋汤 *shee-hong-sh dan-tarng*
tomato and egg soup

酸辣汤 *swan-la-tarng*
hot and sour soup

海鲜汤 *hai-shian-tarng*
seafood soup

鱼翅汤 *yü-ch-tarng*
shark fin soup

青菜汤 *ching-tsai-tarng*
Chinese green cabbage soup

榨菜汤 *ja-tsai-tarng*
pickled mustard green soup

Fish and seafood 鱼和海鲜

Cantonese cuisine in particular is renowned for its imaginative use of fish and seafood.

大马哈鱼	*da-ma-ha-yü*	salmon
黄鱼	*hwarng-yü*	yellow croaker
银鱼	*yin-yü*	whitebait
蚝	*hao*	oysters
小鱿鱼	*shiao yo-yü*	baby squid
对虾	*dwee-shia*	prawns
龙虾	*long shia*	lobster
螃蟹	*parng-shie*	crab
章鱼	*jarng-yü*	octopus
鲤鱼	*lee-yü*	carp

清蒸鱼 *ching-jung-yü*

Steamed whole fish seasoned with soy sauce, vinegar, cooking wine, and sugar, and garnished with shreds of ginger and spring onions.

虾仁炒饭 *shia-ren chao-fan*

Fried rice with shrimp [prawns].

鱿鱼锅巴 *yo-yü guo-ba*

Squid with crispy rice.

红烧鱼 *hong-shao-yü*

Fish braised in soy sauce.

Egg dishes 蛋类

松花蛋 *song-hwaa-dan*

Preserved duck egg (cured in lime for 60 days which creates a cheese-like taste), served with soy sauce, vinegar and sugar as a cold dish).

芙蓉蛋 *foo-rong-dan*

Egg yolks and whites mixed with salt, monosodium glutamate, and crumbled crab meat. This preparation is then fried and served sprinkled with coriander or chopped spring onions.

韭菜炒鸡蛋 *jio-tsai chao jee-dan*

Stir-fried eggs with Chinese chives.

虾仁炒鸡蛋 *shia-ren chao jee-dan*

Stir-fried eggs with peeled freshwater shrimp.

Meat　肉类

牛肉	*nio-ro*	beef
猪肉	*joo-ro*	pork
羊肉	*yarng-ro*	lamb
小牛肉	*shiao-nio-ro*	veal
兔子肉	*too-ds-ro*	rabbit
野鸡	*ye-jee*	pheasant
牛排	*nio-pai*	steak
猪肝	*joo-gan*	pig's liver
火腿	*huo-tway*	ham
鸭肉	*ya-ro*	duck
火鸡肉	*huo-jee-ro*	turkey
鸡肉	*jee-ro*	chicken
腰子	*yao-ds*	kidneys
香肠	*shiarng-charng*	sausages
咸肉	*shian-ro*	bacon

Meat cuts　肉类

里脊牛排	*lee-jee nio-pai*	fillet steak
普通牛排	*poo-tong nio-pai*	sirloin steak
腿肉	*tway-ro*	leg joint
排骨	*pai-gu*	spare ribs

古老肉　*goo-lao-ro*

Sweet and sour pork. Chunks of pork are dipped into egg yolk and then deep fried. The pork is then mixed with pineapple, sweet pepper, carrots, and spring onions, and dressed with a spicy sauce.

猪肉炖豆腐　*joo-ro dwun dou-fu*

Braised pork with bean curd. Stir-fried minced pork with yellow bean sauce, soy sauce, rice wine, chili bean sauce, spring onions, and bean curd.

姜葱牛肉　*jiarng-tsong-nio-ro*

Stir-fried beef with ginger and spring onions.

涮羊肉　*shwan-yarng-ro*

Mongolian hot pot. Each diner gets a plate of thinly sliced lamb, fresh spinach, and Chinese cabbage leaves, small pieces of which are dipped into a communal stock pot with garlic, ginger, spring onions, and coriander. The cooked morsels are then dipped in a sauce.

Vegetables 蔬菜

大白菜	da-bai-tsai	cabbage
洋葱	yarng-tsong	onions
豌豆	wan-dou	peas
荷兰豆	her-lan-dou	snow peas [mangetout]
豆角	dou-jiao	green beans
茄子	chie-ds	eggplant [aubergine]
生菜	shung-tsai	lettuce
菠菜	buo-tsai	spinach
芹菜	chin-tsai	celery
花菜	hwaa-tsai	cauliflower
芥蓝	jie-lan	Chinese broccoli
西红柿	shee-hong-sh	tomatoes
土豆	too-dou	potatoes
青椒	ching-jiao	green peppers
小白菜	shiao-bai-tsai	Chinese green cabbage
蘑菇	muo-goo	mushrooms
胡萝卜	hoo-luo-buo	carrots
黄瓜	hwarng-gwaa	cucumber
山药	shan-yao	Chinese yams
蒜苗	swan-miao	garlic stems
莲藕	lian-o	lotus root
豆腐	dou-foo	bean curd
豆芽	dou-ya	bean sprouts

炒什锦菜 *chao sh-jin tsai*

Mixed vegetables. A selection of vegetables stir-fried and then braised in soy sauce, salt, and sugar.

烧茄子 *shao chie-ds*

Braised eggplant. Deep-fried with spring onions and mushrooms in a sauce of ginger, garlic, soy, rice wine, and chili, with Sichuan pepper.

炒芥蓝 *chao-jie-lan*

Chinese broccoli stir-fried with shredded ginger in sesame oil.

Rice 米饭

In a Chinese meal rice is usually served separately in an individual bowl. It is short grained and slightly sticky. Although generally plain, rice is perhaps the most important part of the meal. When eating out, it is not polite to pour any sauce or gravy onto your rice.

米饭	*mee-fan*	rice
蛋炒饭	*dan-chao-fan*	egg-fried rice
锅巴	*guo-ba*	crunchy rice

Noodles 面条

Noodle dishes are very popular. They make delicious and filling simple meals. You will find that noodle dishes break down into two basic types: those served in a broth or soup with different meat, fish/seafood, and vegetables; and those fried with meat, fish/seafood, and vegetables.

面条	*mian-tiao*	noodles
米粉	*mee-fen*	rice noodles*
炒面	*chao-mian*	crispy fried noodles
汤面	*tarng-mian*	noodles in broth

*rice noodles are thin and almost transparent

Dofu 豆腐

Dofu (or tofu) is a pale soybean curd with a delicate, creamy flavor. There are two main varieties of **dofu**: the coarser type more suitable for frying, and the silken type, which is better suited for inclusion in soups.

老豆腐	*lao dou-foo*	coarse dofu
嫩豆腐	*nen dou-foo*	silken dofu
砂锅豆腐	*sha-guo dou-foo*	dofu casserole
麻辣豆腐	*ma-la dou-foo*	spicy hot dofu
凉拌豆腐	*liarng-ban dou-foo*	cold dofu with soy and crushed garlic

Dessert 甜点

The Chinese seldom finish their meals with sweets or cakes but often have fruit. Some upmarket restaurants have added ice cream (**bing-chee-lin**) to their menu. However, in general sweet things are eaten as snacks and are seldom available in restaurants, with the exception of those in Western-style hotels.

Fruit 水果

Canned and bottled fruit is readily available everywhere. You will find good quality fruit commonly sold on street corners, but the supply drops off in winter. Melons are abundant in the more severe climate of the northwest, and along the southeast coast pineapples and lychees are common in the summer.

Sugarcane is the traditional poor man's candy, and is probably the most commonly available snack. You will find it at train and bus stations.

櫻桃	*ying-tao*	cherries
李子	*lee-ds*	plums
草莓	*tsao-may*	strawberries
石榴	*sh-lio*	pomegranates
苹果	*ping-guo*	apples
桃子	*tao-ds*	peaches
橙子	*chung-ds*	oranges
橘子	*jü-ds*	satsumas
香蕉	*shiarng-jiao*	bananas
柚子	*yo-ds*	pomelo
葡萄	*poo-tao*	grapes
梨	*lee*	pears
杏子	*shing-ds*	apricots
枣子	*dsao-ds*	Chinese dates
荔枝	*lee-j*	lychees
菠萝	*buo-luo*	pineapple

Drinks 饮料

Beer 啤酒

By far the best known Chinese beer is **tsingtao**, brewed from the spring water of the Laoshan mountain. There are also numerous local brands.

| bottled | 瓶装 *ping-jwarng* |
| draft [draught] | 散装 *san-jwarng* |

Wine 果酒

The Chinese have been making wine for thousands of years. Each region has its own wine or liqueur, often rather sweet, made from local fruits, flowers, or herbs.

The red wines of Shanghai and the dry white wines of Yantai have drawn praise from connoisseurs. There are also many rice wines. Some are very potent like the colorless **xifeng** wine in Xi'an.

red wine	红葡萄酒 *hong poo-tao-jio*
white wine	白葡萄酒 *bai poo-tao-jio*
blush [rosé] wine	玫瑰酒 *may-gway jio*
dry/sweet/sparkling	干/甜/有汽 *gan/tian/yo-chee*

Spirits and liqueurs 白酒与烈性酒

Chinese brandies also display regional variations, incorporating flavorings such as bamboo leaves, chrysanthemums, and cloves. The best known, a staple for banquet toasts, is **mao-tai-jio**, which is fragrant and mellow but potent!

Chinese brandy (clear)	茅台酒 *mao-tai jio*
Five-grain spirit (clear)	五粮液 *woo-liarng-ye*
Fen-river spirit (clear)	汾酒 *fen-jio*
Jianlanchun spirit (clear)	剑兰春 *jian-lan-chwun*
whisky/gin/vodka	威士忌/杜松子酒/伏特加 *jian-lan-chwun/doo-song-ds-jio/foo-ter-jia*
with water/soda	搀水/苏打水 *tsan-shwee/soo-da-shwee*
straight [neat]/on the rocks	不搀水/加冰块 *boo-tsan-shwee/jia-bing-kwai*
single/double	单份/双份 *dan-fen/shwarng-fen*
a glass/a bottle	一杯/一瓶 *yee-bay/yee-ping*

Tea and coffee 茶和咖啡

Tea is the most commonly served beverage in China. It is usually offered to guests before a banquet, in an anteroom. In modern China teahouses have become something of a rarity, but where they exist you will find that tea is taken without milk or sugar. Among the varieties available are black (fermented) tea, fragrant green tea, tea scented with jasmine or magnolia, and slightly fermented **oolong** tea.

Indian tea is not generally available outside of international supermarkets.

Ground or whole-bean coffee is hard to find. However, instant coffee (brands like Nescafé and Maxwell House) is widely available.

green tea	绿茶	*lü-cha*
oolong tea	乌龙茶	*woo-long-cha*
jasmine tea	茉莉花茶	*muo-lee hwaa-cha*
milk tea	奶茶	*nai-cha*
lemon tea	柠檬茶	*ning-mung-cha*
iced tea	冰茶	*bing-cha*

Other drinks 其它饮料

Chinese soft drinks are cheap and sold everywhere. However, some are so sweet that you can feel your teeth complaining as you imbibe! Both genuine and copycat versions are available.

Fresh milk is rare as an off-the-shelf item, but you can buy imported UHT milk from international supermarkets. You will also find a rather pleasant fresh sweet yogurt drink available in many parts of China. It is sold in small milk bottles and is drunk rather than eaten with a spoon. This makes a good breakfast drink for those in a hurry.

cola	可乐	*ker-ler*
lemonade	柠檬汽水	*ning-mung-chee-shwee*
fresh milk	鲜奶	*shian-nai*
UHT milk	消毒牛奶	*shiao-doo-nio-nai*
yogurt drink	活性乳	*huo-shing-roo*
water	水	*shwee*

Menu Reader 菜单对照表

This Menu Reader gives listings under main food headings. You will see that the Chinese characters are shown in large type. This is to help you to identify, from a menu that has no English, at least the basic ingredients making up a dish.

Meat, fish, and poultry

肉	*ro*	meat (general)
牛肉	*nio-ro*	beef
(猪) 肉	*(joo) ro*	pork
狗肉	*go-ro*	dog
羊肉	*yarng-ro*	lamb/mutton
鸡 (肉)	*jee (ro)*	chicken
鸭 (肉)	*ya (ro)*	duck
鱼	*yü*	fish (general)
海鲜	*hai-shian*	seafood (general)
虾	*shia*	shrimp [prawns]
龙虾	*long-shia*	lobster
鱿鱼	*yo-yü*	squid
蛋	*dan*	eggs (general)
蛇	*sher*	snake

Vegetables

蔬菜	*shoo-tsai*	vegetable(s) (general)
豆	*dou*	beans
菠菜	*buo-tsai*	spinach
荷兰豆	*her-lan-dou*	snow peas [mangetout]
西红柿	*shee-hong-sh*	tomatoes
生菜	*shung-tsai*	lettuce
黄瓜	*hwarng-gwaa*	cucumber
大白菜	*da-bai-tsai*	Chinese leaves
海带 or 海草	*hai-dai* or *hai-tsao*	seaweed
竹笋	*joo-swun*	bamboo shoots
豆芽	*dou-ya*	bean sprouts
荸荠 or 马蹄	*bee-chee* or *ma-tee*	water chestnuts
蘑菇	*muo-goo*	mushrooms
草菇	*tsao-goo*	straw mushrooms
冬菇	*dong-goo*	shitake mushrooms

Fruit

水果	*shwee-guo*	fruit (general)
苹果	*ping-guo*	apples
梨	*lee*	pears
橙子	*chung ds*	oranges
香蕉	*shiarng-jiao*	bananas
香瓜	*shiarng-gwaa*	melon
西瓜	*shee-gwaa*	watermelon
桃子	*tao-ds*	peaches
李子	*lee-ds*	plums
草莓	*tsao-may*	strawberries
獼猴桃	*mee-ho-tao*	kiwi fruit
荔枝	*lee-j*	lychees
菠萝	*buo-luo*	pineapple
葡萄	*poo-tao*	grapes

Staples: bread, rice, pasta, etc.

米饭	mee-fan	rice
面条	mian-tiao	noodles
粥	jo	rice porridge
馒头	man-tou	steamed buns
米粉	mee-fen	rice noodles
汤圆	tarng-yüan	dumplings *stuffed dumplings made from glutinous rice flour served in broth*
饺子	jiao-ds	dumplings *dumplings stuffed with meat and vegetables*
馄饨	hwun-twun	wontons
蛋面	dan-mian	egg noodles

Basics

盐	yan	salt
胡椒	hoo-jiao	pepper
酱油	jiarng-yo	soy (sauce)
醋	tsoo	vinegar
豆豉酱	dou-ch-jiarng	black bean sauce

烤	*kao*	roasted (for meat)
烘	*hong*	baked or grilled
炒	*chao*	sautéed/stir-fried
蒸	*jung*	steamed
煮	*joo*	boiled
煨	*way*	stewed
红烧	*hong-shao*	braised
烧烤	*shao-kao*	barbecued
熏	*shūn*	smoked
油炸	*yo-ja*	deep-fried
干制	*gan-j*	dried
风干	*fung-gan*	air-dried
腌制	*yan-j*	salted/pickled

Classic dishes

点心，小吃	*dian-shin, shiao-ch*	dim sum *selection of light steamed buns with various fillings*
烧排骨	*shao-pai-goo*	braised pork spareribs
红烧鲤鱼	*hong-shao-lee-yü*	braised carp
干烧明虾	*gan-shao-ming-shia*	Sichuan (Szechwan) shrimp [prawns]
豉椒鱿鱼	*ch-jiao-yo-yü*	squid with black bean sauce
北京烤鸭	*bei-jing-kao-ya*	Beijing duck
腰果炒鸡丁	*yao-guo-chao-jee-ding*	chicken with cashew nuts
青椒鸡丁	*ching-jiao-jee-ding*	chicken with peppers and yellow bean sauce
什菜炒牛肉片	*sh-tsai-chao-nio-ro-pian*	sliced beef with mixed vegetables
蚝油牛肉	*hao-yo-nio-ro*	stir-fried beef with oyster sauce
葱爆羊肉	*tsong-bao-yarng-ro*	stir-fried lamb with scallions (northern China)
回锅肉	*hway-guo-ro*	spicy "twice cooked" sliced pork, a Sichuan (Szechwan) dish

白开水	bai-kai-shwee	water
		hot water for making tea
牛奶	nio-nai	milk
茶	cha	tea
绿茶 / 红茶	lü-cha/hong-cha	green/black tea
		"black" tea is actually called "red" tea in China
花茶	hwaa-cha	jasmine tea
荔枝茶	lee-j-cha	lychee tea
咖啡	ka-fay	coffee
米酒	mee-jio	rice wine
红葡萄酒	hong pu-tao-jio	red (grape) wine
白葡萄酒	bai pu-tao jio	white (grape) wine
威士忌	way-sh-jee	whisky
啤酒	pee-jio	beer
散装啤酒	san-jwarng pee-jio	draft [draught] beer
茅台	mao tai	Chinese brandy

Drinks (continued)

果汁	*guo-j*	(fruit) juice
橘子汁	*jü ds-j*	orange juice
柠檬汽水	*ning-mung-chee-shwee*	lemonade
可口可乐	*ker-ko-ker-ler*	Coca-Cola
芬达	*fen-da*	Fanta
雪碧	*shüe-bee*	Sprite
七喜	*chee-shee*	Seven-Up
汽水	*chee-shwee*	soda water
奶昔	*nai-shee*	milkshake
矿泉水	*kwarng-chüan-shwee*	mineral water

锅贴	*guo-tie*	pan-fried dumplings
饺子	*jiao-ds*	boiled dumplings *dumplings stuffed with meat and vegetables*
春卷	*chwun-jüan*	spring roll *a pancake roll filled with minced pork and vegetables*
馒头	*man-tou*	steamed buns
包子	*bao-ds*	steamed meat buns *filled with pork and vegetables (sometimes filled with sweet bean paste)*
油条	*yo-tiao*	fried breadsticks *eaten with soy milk or rice porridge for breakfast*
虾片	*shia-pian*	prawn cracker
饼干	*bing-gan*	cookies [biscuits]
香酥花生	*shiarng-soo hwaa-shung*	roasted peanuts
瓜子	*gwaa-ds*	roasted seeds *of watermelon, pumpkin or sunflower*

Soups/soup-based dishes

汤	*tarng*	soup
酸辣汤	*swan-la-tarng*	hot and sour soup *a substantial dish* *from northern* *China*
馄饨汤	*hwun-twun-tarng*	wonton soup *clear soup with small* *pork-and-ginger-filled* *dumplings*
鸡丁玉米汤	*jee-ding yü-mee tarng*	chicken and sweetcorn soup
什锦豆腐汤	*sh-jin-dou-foo-tarng*	bean curd soup
菠菜蛋花汤	*po-tsai-dan-hwaa-tarng*	spinach soup with beaten egg
鸭肉三丝汤	*ya-ro-san-s-tarng*	duck soup *made from shredded* *Beijing duck and* *vegetables*
肉丸洋菜汤	*ro-wan-yarng-tsai-tarng*	pork balls and watercress in a stock with cellophane noodles

米饭	*mee-fan*	plain steamed rice
炒面	*chao-mian*	fried noodles with shredded meat and/or vegetables
汤面	*tarng-mian*	boiled noodles in a soy sauce or chicken broth, sprinkled with chopped scallions or served with vegetables and/or meat
蛋炒饭	*dan-chao-fan*	egg fried rice
什锦炒饭	*sh-jin-chao-fan*	special fried rice *rice mixed with a number of other ingredients; the exact mix will vary from restaurant to restaurant*
扬州炒饭	*yarng-jo-chao-fan*	Yangchow fried rice: rice mixed with ham, peas, and diced vegetables

Dairy products and soy products

牛奶	*nio-nai*	milk
酸奶	*swan-nai*	yogurt
活性乳	*huo-shing-roo*	drinking yogurt
黄油	*hwarng-yo*	butter
奶油	*nai-yo*	cream
奶酪	*nai-lao*	cheese
豆腐	*dou-foo*	dofu [tofu]
豆浆	*dou-jiarng*	soy milk
豆腐花	*dou-foo-hwaa*	jelly dofu *spicy or* *sweetened*
豆腐干	*dou-foo-gan*	hard dofu
卤汁豆腐干	*loo-j dou-foo-gan*	savory snack dofu
百页	*bai-ye*	dofu sheets *used for braising,* *or shredded and* *added to salads*

糕点	gao-dian	cake
冰淇淋	bing-chee-lin	ice cream
拔丝苹果	ba-s-ping-guo	glazed toffee apples
拔丝香蕉	ba-s-shiarng-jiao	glazed toffee bananas
什锦水果盘	sh-jin shwee-guo-pan	fresh fruit arranged on a mountain of ice
甜汤	tian-tarng	sweet soup *made from beans and rock sugar*
汤圆	tarng-yüan	sweet dumplings filled with bean paste, sesame seeds and sugar served in a soup
八宝饭	ba-bao-fan	Eight-Treasure rice pudding *steamed glutinous rice with red bean paste, lotus seeds, and preserved fruit*

Travel

Safety	65	**Taxi [Cab]**	84
Arrival	66	**Transportation**	85
Plane	68	**Car rental**	86
Train	72	**Gas [Petrol] station**	87
Long-distance bus		**Breakdown**	88
[Coach]	78	**Car parts**	90
Subway [Metro]	80	**Accidents**	92
Ferry	81	**Legal matters**	93
Bicycle/Motorbike	83	**Asking directions**	94
Hitchhiking	83	**Road signs**	96

ESSENTIAL

1/2/3 ticket(s) to ...	买一张 / 两张 / 三张去 ... 的票
	mai yee-jarng/liarng-jarng/san-jarng chü ... de piao
To ..., please.	请给一张去 ... 的票。
	ching gay yee-jarng chü ... de piao
one-way [single]	单程 *dan-chung*
round-trip [return]	往返 *warng-fan*
How much ...?	..., 多少钱? *... duo-shao chian?*

Independent travel in China is not easy. Spur-of-the-moment journeys are almost impossible as tickets can rarely be bought immediately before departure. In order to be assured seating, you need to reserve your tickets well in advance.

Safety 安全

Would you accompany me ...?	您能陪我去 ... 吗?
	nin nung pay wo chü ... ma
to the bus stop	公共汽车站 *gong-gong-chee-cher jan*
to my hotel	我住的旅馆 *wo joo de lü-gwan*
I don't want to ... on my own.	我不想一个人 ...
	wo boo-shiarng yee-ge-ren ...
stay here	呆在这儿 *dai dsai jer-r*
walk home	步行回家 *boo-shing hway-jia*

Arrival 抵达后

Every visitor to China must possess a valid passport and a visa issued by the Chinese authorities. Tour groups may be issued group visas – a single document listing the names and particulars of all the participants. The paperwork in this case is handled by the travel agency.

Customs. Before you arrive in China you will have filled out a baggage declaration form listing any valuables (e.g., watches, cameras, electronic items) in your possession. When you leave you may be asked to show that you are taking with you the items listed, except for goods declared as gifts.

It is forbidden to take more than 6000 yuan into China, although there is no limit on the amount of foreign currency.

Local tourist offices. When in China you may need to use one of the many tourist offices to help you book tickets, hotels, flights, etc. Historically CITS (China International Travel Service), CTS (China Travel Service), and CYTS (China Youth Travel Service) catered to different sections of the tourist market. However, today they all seem to be competing with one another, so you may want to check out what each is offering when looking for the best prices and availability.

Head offices (Beijing):
CITS: 601 1122; 2055/fax 601 2013; 512 2068
CTS: 512 9933/fax 512 9008
CYTS: 652 43388/fax 513 4824

Passport control 护照检查

We have a joint passport.	我们是合用护照。 *wo-men sh her-yong hoo-jao*
The children are on this passport.	孩子们用的是这本护照。*hai-ds-men yong de sh jer ben hoo-jao*
I'm here on vacation [holiday]/business.	我是来度假的/办公事的 *wo sh lai doo-jia de/ban gong-sh de*
I'm just passing through.	我只是过境。 *wo j-sh guo-jing*
I'm going to …	我要去 … *wo yao chü …*
I'm …	我是 … *wo sh …*
on my own	一个人来的 *yee-ge-ren lai de*
with my family	跟家人来的 *gen jia-ren lai de*
with a group	随团来的 *swee twan lai de*

WHO ARE YOU WITH? ➤ 120

Customs 验关

I have only the normal allowances.	我只带了正常限额。 *wo j dai le jung-charng shian-er*
It's a gift.	这是礼物。 *jer-sh lee-woo*
It's for my personal use.	这是我的个人用品。 *jer-sh wo-de ger-ren yong-pin*

您有需要申报的物品吗?	Do you have anything to declare?
这件物品要交税。	You must pay duty on this.
这是在哪儿买的?	Where did you buy this?
请打开这只包。	Please open this bag.
你还有其它行李吗?	Do you have any more luggage?

I would like to declare …	我想申报一下 … *wo shiarng shen-bao yee-xia …*
I don't understand.	我听不懂。 *wo ting boo-dong*
Does anyone here speak English?	这儿有人会说英语吗? *jer-r yo-ren hway-shuo ying-yü ma*

护照检查	passport control
过境	border crossing
海关	customs
不需要申报	nothing to declare
申报物品	goods to declare
免税物品	duty-free goods

Duty-free shopping 免税购物

What currency is this in?	这是哪种货币的价格? *jer-sh na-jong huo-bee de jia-ger*
Can I pay in …	我能不能用 … 支付? *wo nung-boo-nung yong … j-foo*
dollars	美元 *may-yüan*
renminbi	人民币 *ren-min-bee*
pounds	英镑 *ying-barng*

Plane 飞机

Flights inside China are handled by several domestic airlines. In recent years domestic air travel has greatly improved. However, you may still find old Soviet-built planes being used, but mostly on routes in outlying areas like Xinjiang and Tibet. On-board service on internal flights varies greatly: refreshments may or may not be served.

Tickets and reservations 票务

When is the ... flight to Shanghai?	去上海的 ... 航班什么时候起飞? *chü sharng-hai de ... harng-ban shen-me sh-ho chee-fay*
first/next/last	头一趟/下一趟/最后一趟 *tou-yee-tarng/ shia-yee-tarng/dswee-ho-yee-tarng*
I'd like 2 ... tickets to Guangzhou.	我要买两张去广州的 ... 机票。 *wo yao mai liarng-jarng chü gwarng-jo de ... jee-piao*
one-way [single]	单程 *dan-chung*
round-trip [return]	往返 *warng-fan*
first class	一等舱 *yee-dung tsarng*
business class	商务舱 *sharng-woo tsarng*
economy class	经济舱 *jing-jee tsarng*
How much is a flight to ...?	去 ... 的机票多少钱? *chü ... de jee-piao duo-shao chian*
Are there any supplements/ reductions?	有没有附加费/折扣? *yo-may-yo foo-jia-fay/jer-ko*
I'd like to ... my reservation for flight number 154.	我想 ... 我的 154 号班机定座。 *wo shiarng ... wo de yee-woo-s hao ban-jee ding-dsuo*
cancel/change/confirm	取消/更改/确认 *chü shiao/ gung-gai/chüe-ren*

Inquiries about the flight 航班查询

What time does the plane leave?	飞机几点起飞? *fay-jee jee-dian chee-fay*
What time will we arrive?	我们几点能到那儿? *wo-men jee-dian nung dao na-r*
What time do I have to check in?	我几点钟得办理登机手续? *wo jee dian-jong day ban-lee dung-jee sho-shü*

Checking in 办理登机手续

Where is the check-in desk for flight ...?	... 趟航班的登机服务台在哪儿? ... tarng harng-ban de dung-jee foo-woo-tai dsa na-r
I have ...	我有 ... wo yo ...
three cases to check in	三个箱子要托运 san-ge shiarng-ds yao tuo-yün
two pieces of hand luggage	两件手提行李 liarng jian sho-tee shing-lee

请出示机票 / 护照。	Your ticket/passport, please.
您要靠窗户的还是靠走道的座位?	Would you like a window or an aisle seat?
吸烟区还是非吸烟区?	Smoking or non-smoking?
请前往候机厅。	Please go through to the departure lounge.
您有几件行李?	How many pieces of baggage do you have?
您的行李超重了。	You have excess baggage.
您必须交付 ... 元的超重费。	You'll have to pay a supplement of ... yuan.
这件行李太重 / 太大, 不能当手提行李。	That's too heavy/large for hand baggage.
这些行李包是您自己打点的吗?	Did you pack these bags yourself?
里面有没有锋利的物品或电器用品?	Do they contain any sharp or electronic items?

到达	arrivals
离境	departures
安全检查	security check
请看管好您的行李	do not leave bags unattended

BAGGAGE ➤ 71

Information 查询

Is there any delay on flight …?	…航班有没有晚点? … harng-ban yo-may-yo wan-dian
How late will it be?	晚点了多少? wan-dian le duo-shao
Has the flight from … landed?	从 … 来的班机已经降落了吗? tsong … lai de ban-jee yee-jing jiarng-luo le ma
Which gate does flight … leave from?	… 号班机从第几号登机口登机? … hao ban-jee tsong dee-jee-hao dung-jee-ko dung-jee

Boarding/In-flight 登机及飞行

Your boarding card, please.	请出示您的登机牌。 ching choo-sh nin de dung-jee-pai
Could I have a drink/ something to eat, please?	我能不能要点饮料/吃的东西? wo nung-boo-nung yao-dian yin-liao/ ch de dong-shee
Please wake me for the meal.	用餐时请叫醒我。 yong-tsan sh ching jiao-shing wo
What time will we arrive?	我们几点钟能到? wo-men jee-dian-jong nung dao
An air sickness bag, please.	请给我一个晕机袋。 ching gay wo yee-ge yün-jee-dai

Arrival 到达

Where is/are (the) …?	… 在哪儿? … dsai na-r
currency exchange	外汇兑换处 wai-hway dwee-hwan-choo
buses	公共汽车 gong-gong-chee-cher
exit	出口 choo-ko
taxis	出租车 choo-dsoo-cher
Is there a bus into town?	有没有去市区的公共汽车? yo-may-yo chü sh-chü de gong-gong-chee-cher
How do I get to the … hotel?	去 … 宾馆怎么走? chü … bin-gwan dsen-me dso

70

Baggage 行李

Tipping is officially discouraged, although it is becoming more acceptable, particularly in the coastal cities.

Porter! Excuse me!	师傅! 劳驾!	*sh-foo! lao-jia*
Could you take my luggage to ...?	能不能把我的行李搬上 ... ?	*nung-boo-nung ba wo de shing-lee ban sharng ...*
a taxi/bus	出租汽车 / 公共汽车	*choo-dsoo-chee-cher/gong-gong-chee-cher*
Where is/are (the) ...?	哪儿有 ... ?	*na-r yo ...*
luggage carts [trolleys]	手推车	*sho-twee-cher*
baggage check [left-luggage office]	行李寄存处	*shing-lee jee-tswun-choo*
baggage reclaim	行李认领	*shing-lee ren-ling*
Where is the luggage from flight ...?	... 号班机在哪儿取行李?	*... hao ban-jee dsai na-r chü shing-lee*

Loss, damage, and theft 丢失、损坏与失窃

I've lost my baggage.	我的行李丢了。	*wo de shing-lee dio le*
My baggage has been stolen.	我的行李被人偷了。	*wo de shing-lee bay ren tou le*
My suitcase was damaged.	我的箱子损坏了。	*wo de shiarng-ds swun-hwai le*
Our baggage has not arrived.	我们的行李没有到。	*wo-men de shing-lee may-yo dao*

您的行李是什么样的?	What does your baggage look like?
您有行李认领牌吗?	Do you have the claim check [reclaim tag]?
您的行李 ...	Your luggage ...
有可能被运到 ... 了。	may have been sent to ...
可能今天晚些时候到。	may arrive later today
请明天再来吧。	Please come back tomorrow.
请拨这个号码询问您的行李是否到了。	Call this number to check if your baggage has arrived.

POLICE ➤ 152; COLOR ➤ 143

Train 火车

There is an extensive rail network covering every province, except Tibet, and trains provide the backbone of the Chinese transportation system. The safety record is good, though you may get your luggage stolen, or your pocket picked. However, be warned: the Chinese have a habit of throwing rubbish out of train windows even going through stations, so watch you don't get hit.

There are no classes; instead there are hard seats and sleepers, and soft seats and sleepers.

Hard seat car. Usually the seat is padded, but this form of travel is noisy and often very crowded. It might be bearable for a day trip, but is not recommended for longer journeys.

Hard sleeper. Generally comfortable as only a set number of people are allowed per car. Sheets and pillows are provided. The best bunk is the middle one since the lower one is used by all and sundry as a seat during the day, and the top one has little headroom and gets very hot and smoky from cigarettes. Lights and speakers go out and off between 9:00 and 10:00 p.m. And if you are at the end of the car in a top bunk where the speakers are located you'll get a rude shock at 6 a.m. or thereabouts! Note: It is hard to get these sleepers at short notice.

Soft seat car. Comfortable, and overcrowding is not permitted. Smoking is also prohibited. Soft seats are about the same as a hard sleeper.

Soft sleeper. Four comfortable bunks in a closed compartment often with air conditioning. Speakers have a volume control and can even be turned off! Soft sleepers cost nearly as much as flying (on some routes more). Recently the demand for soft sleepers has increased, so once again don't rely on getting a berth at short notice.

Foreigners pay two and a half times the Chinese price for plane and train tickets. At present on buses there is no double-pricing rule, with the exception of western China. There are no official discounts for tourists other than for foreign students studying in the P.R.C., and certain foreigners authorized to live and work in China (these groups hold "white" and "red" cards which authorize them to pay the local Chinese price).

For plane tickets, if you do happen to get a Chinese-priced ticket and it is discovered, the ticket will be confiscated and no refund given. For train tickets there is a thriving black-market industry. However, you may be buying a worthless piece of cardboard and in some cities, notably Beijing and Guangzhou, the authorities have clamped down hard and will fine foreigners using black-market tickets.

To the station 去火车站

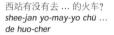

How do I get to the train station?
去火车站怎么走?
chü huo-cher-jan dsen-me dso

Do trains to ... leave from West Station?
西站有没有去 ... 的火车?
shee-jan yo-may-yo chü ... de huo-cher

How far is it?
离这儿有多远? *lee jer-r yo duo-yüan*

Can I leave my car there?
我能不能把汽车停放在那儿?
wo nung-boo-nung ba chee-cher ting-farng dsai na-r

At the station 在火车站

Where is/are ...?
... 在哪儿? *... dsai na-r*

currency exchange office
外汇兑换处
wai-hway dwee-hwan choo

information desk
问询处 *wen-shün-choo*

baggage check
[left-luggage office]
行李寄存处
shing-lee-jee-tswun-choo

lost and found [lost property office]
失物招领处
sh-woo-jao-ling-choo

platforms
站台 *jan-tai*

snack bar
小吃部
shiao-ch-boo

ticket office
售票处
sho-piao-choo

waiting room
候车室
ho-cher-sh

入口	entrance
出口	exit
通往站台	to the platforms
问讯处	information
预售车票	reservations
进站	arrivals
出站	departures

DIRECTIONS ➤ 94

Tickets and reservations 售票处

Buying a hard-seat ticket at short notice is not normally a problem, but you may not be successful in getting a reserved seat. Buying a ticket for a sleeper can be problematic, even impossible, if you try to do it yourself. If you try and the ticket clerk just says **may-yo**, you need to seek the help of a travel agent at CITS, CTS, CYTS, or your hotel. You will have to pay a service charge, but this is much better than a long journey in hard-seat class! Remember too that there is usually a three-day advance purchase limit.

I'd like a … ticket to Shanghai.	我想买一张去上海的 … 车票。	*wo shiarng mai yee-jarng chü sharng-hai de … cher-piao*
one-way [single]	单程	*dan-chung*
round-trip [return]	往返	*warng-fan*
first/second class	头等 / 二等车厢	*tou-dung/er-dung cher-shiarng*
concessionary	优惠价	*yo-hway-jia*
I'd like to reserve a seat.	我想预订一个座位。	*wo shiarng yü-ding yee-ge dsuo-way*
aisle seat	靠走道的座位	*kao dso-dao de dsuo-way*
window seat	靠窗户的座位	*kao chwarng-hoo de dsuo-way*
Is there a sleeping car [sleeper]?	有卧铺车厢吗?	*yo wo-poo cher-shiarng ma*
I'd like a … berth.	我要一个 … (铺位)	*wo yao yee-ge … (poo-way)*
upper/lower	上铺/下铺	*sharng-poo/shia-poo*

Price 价格

How much is that?	多少钱?	*duo-shao chian*
Is there a discount for …?	… 打不打折扣?	*… da-boo-da jer-ko*
children	儿童	*er-tong*
students	学生	*shüe-shung*

NUMBERS ➤ 216; DAYS OF THE WEEK ➤ 218

Queries 疑问

Do I have to change trains?	我需要换车吗？ *wo shü-yao hwan-cher ma*
Is it a direct train?	这是直达车吗？ *jer sh j-da-cher ma*
You have to change at …	你得在 … 换车。 *nee day dsai … hwan-cher*
How long is this ticket valid for?	这张车票的有效期多长？ *jer-jarng cher-piao de yo-shiao-chee duo-charng*
Can I take my bicycle on to the train?	我能不能把自行车带上车？ *wo nung-boo-nung ba ds-shing-cher dai sharng cher*
Can I return on the same ticket?	我回程也能用同一张票吗？ *wo hway-chung ye nung yong tong-yee-jarng piao ma*
In which car [coach] is my seat?	我的座位在第几号车厢？ *wo de dsuo-way dsai dee-jee-hao cher-shiarng*
Is there a dining car on the train?	列车上有餐车吗？ *lie-cher sharng yo tsan-cher ma*

– wo shiarng mai yee-jarng chü nan-jing de cher-piao.
– *dan-chung hai-sh warng-fan?*
– warng-fan piao.
– *yee-bai-woo-sh yüan.*
– wo shü-yao hwan-cher ma?
– *dsai sharng-hai hwan-cher.*
– shie-shie, dsai-jian.

Train times 列车时刻表

Could I have a timetable, please?	我要买一本时刻表。 *wo yao mai yee-ben sh-ker-biao*
When is the … train to Wuhan?	去武汉的 … 车几点开？ *chü woo-han de … cher jee-dian kai*
first/next/last	头班 / 下一班 / 末班 *tou-ban /shia-yee-ban /muo-ban*

How frequent are trains to ...?	去 ... 的火车每隔多久有一班? *chü ... de huo-cher may ger duo-jio yo yee-ban*
once/twice a day	每天一班 / 两班 *may-tian yee-ban/liarng-ban*
five times a day	每天有五班 *may-tian yo woo-ban*
every hour	每小时一班 *may-shiao-sh yee-ban*
What time do they leave?	几点钟离站? *jee-dian-jong lee-jan*
on the hour	每个小时整点 *may-ge shiao-sh jung-dian*
20 minutes past the hour	每个钟点过二十分 *may-ge jong-dian guo er-sh fen*
What time does the train stop at ...?	火车几点在 ... 停站? *huo-cher jee-dian dsai ... ting-jan*
What time does the train arrive in ...?	火车几点到达 ... 站? *huo-cher jee-dian dao-da ... jan*
How long is the trip [journey]?	全程需要多长时间? *chüan-chung shü-yao duo-charng sh-jian*
Is the train on time?	本次列车正点吗? *ben-ts lie-cher jung-dian ma*

Departures 发车

Which platform does the train to ... leave from?	去 ... 的火车从几号站台上车? *chü ... de huo-cher tsong jee-hao jan-tai sharng-cher*
Where is platform 4?	四号站台在哪儿? *s-hao jan-tai dsai na-r*
over there	在那儿 *dsai na-r*
on the left/right	在左边/右边 *dsai dsuo-bian/yo-bian*
Where do I change for ...?	去 ... 在哪儿换车? *chü ... dsai na-r hwan-cher*
How long will I have to wait for a connection?	中转要等多久? *jong-jwan yao dung duo-jio*

Boarding 上车

Is this the right platform for the train to ...?	这是不是去 ... 的站台? *jer sh-boo-sh chü ... de jan-tai*
Is this the train to ...?	这是不是去 ... 的火车? *jer sh-boo-sh chü ... de huo-cher*
Is this seat taken?	这个座位有人坐吗? *jer-ge dsuo-way yo-ren dsuo ma*
I think that's my seat.	这是我的座位吧。 *jer sh wo-de dsuo-way ba*
Here's my reservation.	请看我的对号票。 *ching kan wo-de dwee-hao-piao*
Are there any seats/berths available?	有没有空座位 / 铺位了? *yo-may-yo kong dsuo-way/poo-way le*
Do you mind if ...?	如果 ... 您没有意见吧? *roo-guo ... nin may-yo yee-jian ba*
I sit here	我坐这儿 *wo dsuo jer-r*
I open the window	我开窗户 *wo kai chwarng-hoo*

On the journey 旅途中

How long are we stopping here for?	我们在这儿要停多久? *wo-men dsai jer-r yao ting duo-jio*
When do we get to ...?	我们什么时候能到 ... ? *wo-men shen-me sh-ho nung dao ...*
Have we passed ...?	火车过了 ... 没有? *huo-cher guo le ... may-yo*
Where is the dining/sleeping car?	餐车 / 卧铺车厢在哪儿? *tsan-cher / wo-poo cher-shiarng dsai na-r*
Where is my berth?	我的铺位在哪儿? *wo de poo-way dsai na-r*
I've lost my ticket.	我的车票丢了。 *wo de cher-piao dio le*

紧急制动	emergency brake
报警	alarm
自动车门	automatic doors

TIME ➤ 221

Long-distance bus [Coach]
长途汽车

Long-distance buses are one of the best means of getting around the country: services are extensive, roads bumpy but passable, and you will see parts of the country that you wouldn't from a train. Bear in mind, however, that the bus-safety record is not good and accidents are frequent, especially on winding mountain roads. Many long-distance buses are equipped with cassette players and videos, and you may find yourself beset with screeching music or "kung-fu" films for the duration of the journey. In recent years night buses have become more frequent. They tend to be more dangerous. On the most popular routes sleeper buses (**wo-poo chee-cher**) have been introduced. These are normally double the price. Some have comfortable reclining seats, and others even have two-tier bunks. In addition, on medium-length routes privately owned minibuses now compete with public buses.

Where is the bus [coach] station?	长途汽车站在哪儿? *charng-too-chee-cher jan dsai na-r*
When's the next bus [coach] to …?	去 … 的下趟车是几点? *chü … de shia tarng cher sh jee-dian*
Which bay does it leave from?	从哪个站台上车? *tsong na-ge jan-tai sharng cher*
Where are the bus stops [coach bays]?	长途车站台在哪儿? *charng-too-che jan-tai dsai na-r*
Does the bus [coach] stop at …?	这趟车在 … 停不停? *jer-tarng cher dsai … ting-boo-ting*
How long does the trip [journey] take?	全程需要多长时间? *chüan-chung shü-yao duo-charng sh-jian*

你上车的车站在那边 / 沿这条路往前走。	You need that stop over there / down the road.
你需要乘 … 路车。	You need bus number …
你需要在 … 换车。	You must change buses at …

公共汽车站	bus stop
招手站	request stop
禁止吸烟	no smoking
紧急出口	(emergency) exit

DIRECTIONS ➤ 94; TIME ➤ 221

Buying tickets 买票

Where can I buy tickets?	在哪儿买票? *dsai na-r mai piao*
A ... ticket to Chongqing, please.	我要买一张去重庆的 ... 票。 *wo yao mai yee-jarng chü chong-ching de ... piao*
one-way [single]	单程 *dan-chung*
round-trip [return]	往返 *warng-fan*
weekly/monthly	周票/月票 *jo-piao/yüe-piao*
How much is the fare to ...?	去 ... 的车票多少钱? *chü ... de cher-piao duo-shao chian*

Traveling 旅行

Is this the right bus/tram to ...?	去 ... 是这车吗? *chü ... sh jer cher ma*
Could you tell me when to get off?	到站时能不能告诉我一下? *dao-jan-sh nung-boo-nung gao-soo wo yee-shia*
Do I have to change buses?	我需要换车吗? *wo shü-yao hwan-cher ma*
How many stops are there to ...?	去 ... 一共有几站? *chü ... yee-gong yo jee-jan*
Next stop, please!	下一站请停车! *shia-yee-jan ching ting cher*

– ching-wen, jer-sh chü sh-way-gwarng-charng de
gong-gong-chee-cher ma?
– dwee, sh ba-loo-cher.
– yee-jarng chü sh-way-gwarng-charng.
– yee-kwai-woo.
– dee jee jan shia-cher?
– tsong jer-lee shoo dee s jan shia-cher.

NUMBERS ➤ 217; DIRECTIONS ➤ 94

Subway [Metro] 地铁

There are subway [metro] systems only in Beijing and Shanghai.

Subway [metro] stations are recognised by the sign 地铁 (**dee-tie**). Station names are written in **pinyin** (the standard system for writing Chinese in Latin script), as well as Chinese characters.

The Beijing subway covers 42 kilometers. The standard ticket price is 2 yuan. The two lines are the Ring Line (hours: 05:00 – 23:00) and Line One (hours: 05.40 – 22.40).

The Shanghai subway covers about 16 kilometers and there are 13 stations. The standard ticket price is 2 yuan. The line is open from 06:00 – 21:00.

General Inquiries 一般查询

Where's the nearest subway [metro] station?	请问，附近哪儿有地铁站？ *ching-wen, foo-jin na-r yo dee-tie jan*
Where do I buy a ticket?	在哪儿买票？ *dsai na-r mai piao*
Could I have a map of the subway [metro]?	我想买一份地铁图。 *wo shiarng mai yee-fen dee-tie too*

Traveling 乘车

Which line should I take for …?	去 … 应该乘哪条地铁线？ *chü… ying-gai chung na-tiao dee-tie-shian*
Is this the right train for …?	这是去 … 的车吗？ *jer sh chü … de cher ma*
Which stop is it for …?	去 … 在哪一站下车？ *chü … dsai na yee jan shia-cher*
How many stops is it to …?	去 … 一共有几站？ *chü … yee-gong yo jee-jan*
Is the next stop …?	下一站是不是 … ？ *shia-yee-jan sh-boo-sh*
Where are we?	我们到哪儿了？ *wo-men dao na-r le*
Where do I change for …?	去 … 在哪儿换车？ *chü … dsai na-r hwan-cher*
What time is the last train to …?	去 … 的最后一班车几点？ *chü … de dswee-ho-yee-ban cher jee-dian*

⊖	往其它路线	to other lines	⊕

NUMBERS ➤ 217; BUYING TICKETS ➤ 74, 79

Ferry 轮渡

Many boat services have fallen victim to improved bus and plane transportation. However, in coastal areas you are most likely to use a boat to reach offshore islands, like Hainan Island in the south. There are also several inland routes worth considering. Perhaps the best known of these is the three-day boat ride along the Yangtze River from Chongqing to Wuhan. There are also a number of popular boat services between Hong Kong and the rest of China.

When is the … car ferry to Hainan?	去海南的 … 汽渡几点开? *chü hai-nan de … chee-doo jee-dian kai*
first/next/last	头班/下一班/末班 *tou-ban/shia-yee-ban/muo-ban*
hovercraft/ship	气垫船 / 轮船 *chee-dian-chwan/ lwun-chwan*
A round-trip [return] ticket for …	要一张去 … 的往返票 *yao yee-jarng chü … de warng-fan piao*
two adults and three children	两张成人票, 三张儿童票 *liarng-jarng chung-ren piao, san-jarng er-tong piao*
I want to reserve a … cabin.	我想预订一个 … 舱。 *wo shiarng yü-ding yee-ge … tsarng*
single/double	单人/双人 *dan-ren/shwarng-ren*

救生带	life preserver [belt]
救生艇	life boat
集合处	muster station
禁止进入汽车舱	no access to car decks

Boat trips 乘船旅行

Is there a …?	有没有 … ? *yo-may-yo …*
boat trip	乘船旅行 *chung-chwan lü-shing*
river cruise	江上航游 *jiarng-sharng harng-yo*
What time does it leave/ return?	什么时间开航 / 返航? *shen-me sh-jian kai-harng/fan-harng*
Where can we buy tickets?	在哪儿买票? *dsai na-r mai piao*

TIME ➤ 221; BUYING TICKETS ➤ 74, 79

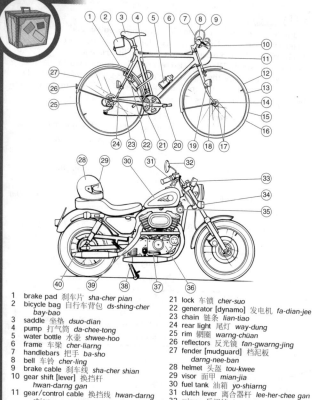

1 brake pad 刹车片 *sha-cher pian*
2 bicycle bag 自行车背包 *ds-shing-cher bay-bao*
3 saddle 坐垫 *dsuo-dian*
4 pump 打气筒 *da-chee-tong*
5 water bottle 水壶 *shwee-hoo*
6 frame 车梁 *cher-liarng*
7 handlebars 把手 *ba-sho*
8 bell 车铃 *cher-ling*
9 brake cable 刹车线 *sha-cher shian*
10 gear shift [lever] 换挡杆 *hwan-darng gan*
11 gear/control cable 换挡线 *hwan-darng shian*
12 inner tube 内胎 *nay-tai*
13 front/back wheel 前/后轮 *chian/ho lwun*
14 axle 轴 *jo*
15 tire [tyre] 车胎 *cher-tai*
16 wheel 车轮 *cher-lwun*
17 spokes 辐条 *foo-tiao*
18 bulb 灯泡 *dung-pao*
19 headlamp 前灯 *chian-dung*
20 pedal 踏板 *ta-ban*

21 lock 车锁 *cher-suo*
22 generator [dynamo] 发电机 *fa-dian-jee*
23 chain 链条 *lian-tiao*
24 rear light 尾灯 *way-dung*
25 rim 辋圈 *warng-chüan*
26 reflectors 反光镜 *fan-gwarng-jing*
27 fender [mudguard] 挡泥板 *darng-nee-ban*
28 helmet 头盔 *tou-kwee*
29 visor 面甲 *mian-jia*
30 fuel tank 油箱 *yo-shiarng*
31 clutch lever 离合器杆 *lee-her-chee gan*
32 mirror 后视镜 *ho-sh-jing*
33 ignition switch 点火开关 *dian-huo kai-gwan*
34 turn [indicator] 转向灯 *jwan-shiarng-dung*
35 horn 喇叭 *la-ba*
36 engine 发动机 *fa-dong-jee*
37 gear shift [lever] 变速杆 *bian-soo gan*
38 kick stand [main stand] 底座 *dee-dsuo*
39 exhaust pipe 排气管 *pai-chee-gwan*
40 chain guard 链条护板 *lian-tiao hoo-ban*

CAR REPAIRS ➤ 89

Bicycle / Motorbike
自行车 / 摩托车

Bicycle riding can be dangerous, especially at night. Many
drivers only use their headlights to flash cyclists to get out of
the way. Other cyclists may swerve in front of you or come
hurtling out of a side street without stopping. If you decide to rent a
bicycle, use the utmost caution.

I'd like to rent a ...	我想租一部 ... *wo shiarng dsoo yee-boo* ...
3-/10-speed bicycle	三挡／十挡的自行车 *san-darng/sh-darng de ds-shing-cher*
moped/motorbike	机动自行车／摩托车 *jee-dong ds-shing-cher/muo-tuo-cher*
How much does it cost per day/week?	租一天／一星期多少钱? *dsoo yee tian/ yee shing-chee duo-shao chian*
Do you require a deposit?	要不要交押金? *yao-boo-yao jiao ya-jin*
The brakes don't work.	刹车不灵。 *sha-cher boo-ling*
There is/are no lights.	没有车灯。 *may-yo cher-dung*
The front/rear tire [tyre] has a flat [puncture].	前／后胎瘪了。 *chian/ho tai bie le*

Hitchhiking 搭便车

Hitchhiking is not officially sanctioned and the same dangers apply as
elsewhere in the world. If you do choose to hitch, then you are well-
advised to do so in pairs, and women should have a male companion.
Hitchhiking in China is rarely free and you will be expected to offer at
least a tip. Some drivers will demand an unreasonable amount. Using the
bus will usually be cheaper and safer.

Where are you heading?	你上哪儿去? *nee sharng na-r chü*
I'm heading for ...	我去 ... *wo chü* ...
Is that on the way to ...?	去 ... 顺路吗? *chü ... shwun-loo ma*
Could you drop me off ...?	能不能让我在 ... 下车? *nung-boo-nung rarng wo dsai ... shia-cher*
here/at ...	这儿／在 ... *jer-r/dsai* ...
at the ... exit	在 ... 路口 *dsai ... loo-ko*
in the center of town	在 市中心 *dsai sh jong-shin*
Thanks for giving me a lift.	谢谢你让我搭你的车。 *shie-shie nee rarng wo da nee de cher*

Taxi [Cab] 出租汽车

You may not be able to find taxis cruising the streets, although this is becoming more common in the big cities, but you can always call a taxi from your hotel. You can hire them for a single trip or on a daily basis – the latter is worth considering if you can split the cost with a group. Some tourist hotels also have minibuses on hand. Taxis often don't use their meters, so negotiate the price before you set off. You can also ask at your hotel reception desk about the price.

Where can I get a taxi?	哪儿能要到出租汽车? *na-r nung yao dao choo-dsoo-chee-cher*
Do you have the number for a taxi?	你有出租汽车公司的电话号码吗? *nee yo choo-dsoo-chee-cher gong-s de dian-hwaa hao-ma ma*
I'd like a taxi ...	我想...要一部出租汽车 *wo shiarng ... yao yee-boo choo-dsoo-chee-cher*
now	现在 *shian-dsai*
in an hour	一小时后 *yee shiao-sh ho*
for tomorrow at 9:00	明天九点钟 *ming-tian jio-dian-jong*
The address I'm going to is ...	我要去的地址是 ... *wo yao chü de dee-j sh ...*

空车   for hire

Please take me to (the) ...	请送我去 ... *ching song wo chü ...*
airport	机场 *jee-charng*
train station	火车站 *huo-cher-jan*
this address	这个地址 *jer-ge dee-j*
How much will it cost?	要多少钱? *yao duo-shao chian*
How much is that?	这趟多少钱? *jer-tarng duo-shao chian*
You said ... yuan.	你说是 ... 块嘛。 *nee shuo sh ... kwai me*
Keep the change.	不用找钱了。 *boo-yong jao-chian le*

– nung dai wo chü huo-cher-jan ma?
– *shing*.
– yao duo-shao-chian?
– ... *kwai. wo-men dao le.*
– shie-shie. boo-yong jao-chian le.

NUMBERS ➤ 217; DIRECTIONS ➤ 94

Transportation 交通工具

Car/Automobile（小）轿车

Outside Beijing and Shanghai, where the idea of drive-away car rental has recently been introduced, it is impossible to rent a car. Even in these two cities it is experimental, expensive, and the process a bureaucratic nightmare, though possible with an international driver's license. In addition, you can only drive within the city limits. Tourists still cannot rent motorbikes or purchase motor vehicles.

Buses 公共汽车

Apart from bicycles, buses are the most common means of getting around in cities. Services are extensive, but buses are normally very crowded. You should also allow plenty of time to reach your destination as traffic is often very slow moving. However, buses are very cheap, rarely more than 2 jiao. Good maps of Chinese cities and bus routes are readily available and are often sold by hawkers outside railway stations. When you get on a bus, point to where you want to go on the map and the conductor, who is seated near the door, will sell you the right ticket.

Bicycle rental 租用自行车

Bicycle rental places catering to foreigners are now found in most popular tourist centers. You may find your hotel rents bicycles, but there are also independent rental places even in towns that do not see many tourists but cater to Chinese travelers. Renting by the hour or by the day is the norm. Rates are typically 2 yuan per hour or 10 – 20 yuan per day. Some hotels, however, may charge ridiculous rates like 10 yuan per hour! Many rental places will ask you to leave some ID; some even want your passport! Give them either a student card, your driver's license, or better still an old expired passport. Before setting off check that your bike is in good working order and that the saddle is high enough. It is also worth tying something onto it – a handkerchief, for example – so that you can recognize it amongst the millions of other bicycles in the bicycle parks.

Bicycle parking. In larger towns and cities use the designated places, generally a roped-off enclosure manned by an attendant. On paying the charge (5 jiao to 1 yuan), you will receive a token. If you don't park in a proper place, you may find your bicycle has been towed away to the police station, and there will be a fine to get it back. Bicycle theft does exist, so keep your bicycle locked and off the streets at night.

Bicycle repair shops. You will find these everywhere. So if you do have a problem with your bicycle it should be easily and cheaply fixed. A simple problem should cost about 5 yuan. However, overcharging foreigners is not unknown, so ask first.

Car rental 租车

It is unlikely that you will be able to/want to rent a car during your stay. For further information ▶ 85 or contact a local tourist office.

Where can I rent a car?	哪里能租到小汽车? *na-lee nung dsoo dao shiao-chee-cher*
I'd like to rent a(n) …	我想租一部 … *wo shiarng dsoo yee-boo …*
2-/4-door car	两门 / 四门小汽车 *liarng-men/s-men shiao-chee-cher*
automatic car	自动排挡车 *ds-dong pai-darng cher*
car with 4-wheel drive	四轮驱动车 *s-lwun chü-dong cher*
car with air conditioning	带空调的车 *dai kong-tiao de cher*
I'd like it for a day/a week.	我想租一天 / 一星期。*wo shiarng dsoo yee-tian/yee-shing-chee*
How much does it cost per day/week?	每天 / 每星期租金是多少? *may-tian/may shing-chee dsoo-jin sh duo-shao*
Is mileage/insurance included?	租金包括不包括里程 / 保险? *dsoo-jin bao-kuo-boo-bao-kuo lee-chung/bao-shian*
Are there special weekend rates?	有没有周末优惠价? *yo-may-yo jo-muo yo-hway-jia*
Can I return the car at …?	我能把车还到 … 吗? *wo nung ba cher hwan dao … ma*
What sort of fuel does it take?	这车用的是哪种燃料油? *jer cher yong de sh na-jong ran-liao-yo*
Where is the high [full]/low [dipped] beam?	大灯的远光 / 近光开关在哪儿? *da-dung de yüan-gwarng/jin-gwarng kai-gwan dsai na-r*
Could I have full insurance?	请给我办全保险。 *ching gay wo ban chüan-bao-shian*

Gas [Petrol] station 加油站

Where's the next gas [petrol] station, please?	请问，下一个加油站在什么地方? *ching-wen, shia-yee-ge jia-yo jan dsai shen-me dee-farng*
Is it self-service?	是自助式吗? *shee ds-joo-sh ma*
Fill it up, please.	请把油箱加满。 *ching ba yo-shiarng jia man*
… liters, please.	请加 … 公升。 *ching jia … gong-shung*
premium [super]/regular	优级 (超级) / 普通 *yo-jee (chao-jee)/poo-tong*
lead-free/diesel	无铅汽油 / 柴油 *woo-chian-chee-yo/chai-yo*
I'm at pump number …	我用的是第 … 号泵 *wo yong de sh dee … hao bung*
Where is the air pump/water?	哪儿能充气/加水? *na-r nung chong-chee/jia-shwee*

每公升价格	price per liter

Parking 停车

Is there a parking lot [car park] nearby?	附近有没有停车场? *foo-jin yo-may-yo ting-cher-charng*
What's the charge per hour/day?	每小时/每天计费是多少? *may shiao-shee/may-tian jee-fay sh duo-shao*
Do you have some change for the parking meter?	您能给我换点停车用的零钱吗? *nin nung gay wo hwan dian ting-cher yong de ling-chian ma*
My car has been booted [clamped]. Who do I call?	我的车被人把轮子锁上了，应该去找谁? *wo de cher bay ren ba lwun-ds suo sharng le, ying-gai chü jao shwee*

NUMBERS ➤ 217; *DIRECTIONS* ➤ 94

Breakdown 抛锚

Where is the nearest garage?	附近有没有修车行？ *foo-jin yo-may-yo shio-cher-harng*
My car broke down.	我的车抛锚了。 *wo de cher pao-mao le*
Can you send a mechanic/tow [breakdown] truck?	能不能派一位修车师傅/牵引车来？ *nung-boo-nung pai yee-way shio-cher sh-foo/chian-yin-cher lai*
I belong to ... recovery service.	我能享受 ... 行车故障援救服务。 *wo nung shiarng-sho ... shing-cher goo-jarng yüan-jio foo-woo*
My registration number is ...	我的车牌号码是 ... *wo de cher-pai hao-ma sh ...*
The car is ...	我的汽车 ... *wo de chee-cher ...*
on the highway [motorway]	在高速公路上 *dsai gao-soo-gong-loo sharng*
2 km from ...	离 ... 两公里远 *lee ... liarng gong-lee yüan*
How long will you be?	我得等多久？ *wo day dung duo-jio*

What is wrong? 出了什么毛病？

My car won't start.	我的车发动不了。 *wo de cher fa-dong boo liao*
The battery is dead.	电瓶没电了。 *dian-ping may dian le*
I've run out of gas [petrol].	没有汽油了。 *may-yo chee-yo le*
I have a flat [puncture].	轮胎打炮了。 *lwun-tai da-pao le*
There's something wrong with ...	... 有毛病 *... yo mao-bing*
I've locked the keys in the car.	我把钥匙锁在车里了。 *wo ba yao-sh suo dsai cher lee le*

Repairs 修理

Do you do repairs?	您这儿修车吗? *nin jer-r shio-cher ma*
Can you repair it?	能修理一下吗? *nung shio-lee yee-shia ma*
Please make only essential repairs.	请修理一下紧要的地方。 *ching shio-lee yee-shia jin-yao de dee-farng*
Can I wait for it?	我能不能在这儿等着? *wo nung-boo-nung dsai jer-r dung je*
Can you repair it today?	今天能修好吗? *jin-tian nung shio-hao ma*
When will it be ready?	什么时候能修好? *shen-me sh-ho nung shio-hao*
How much will it cost?	要多少钱? *yao duo-shao chian*
That's outrageous!	这简直是漫天要价! *jer jian-j sh man-tian yao-jia*
Can I have a receipt for my insurance?	请给我一张发票, 我好转交保险公司。 *ching gay wo yee-jarng fa-piao, wo hao jwan-jiao bao-shian-gong-s*

... 失灵了。	The ... isn't working.
我没有修车需要的零部件。	I don't have the necessary parts.
我得订购零部件。	I will have to order the parts.
我只能凑合着先给你修修。	I can only repair it temporarily.
您的车应该报废了。	Your car is beyond repair.
这车已无法修了。	It can't be repaired.
... 可以修好。	It will be ready ...
今天晚些时候	later today
明天	tomorrow
... 天后	in ... days

DAYS OF THE WEEK ➤ 218; NUMBERS ➤ 217

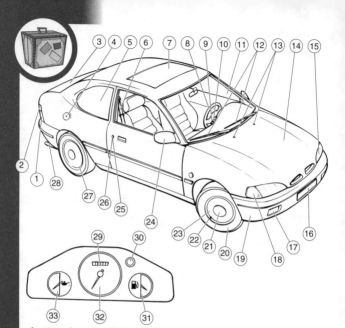

1 taillights [back lights] 尾灯 *way-dung*
2 brakelights 刹车灯 *sha-cher-dung*
3 trunk [boot] 行李箱 *shing-lee-shiarng*
4 gas tank door [petrol cap] 油箱盖 *yo-shiarng-gai*
5 window 车窗 *cher-chwarng*
6 seat belt 安全带 *an-chüan-dai*
7 sunroof 天窗 *tian-chwarng*
8 steering wheel 方向盘 *farng-shiarng-pan*
9 ignition 点火器 *dian-huo-chee*
10 ignition key 点火钥匙 *dian-huo yao-sh*
11 windshield [windscreen] 挡风玻璃 *darng-fung buo-lee*
12 windshield [windscreen] wipers 刮雨器 *gwa-yü-chee*
13 windshield [windscreen] washer 挡风玻璃清洗器 *darng-fung buo-lee ching-shee-chee*
14 hood [bonnet] 引擎罩 *yin-ching jao*

15 headlights 头灯 *tou-dung*
16 license [number] plate 车牌 *cher-pai*
17 fog lamp 雾灯 *woo-dung*
18 turn signals [indicators] 转向灯 *jwan-shiarng-dung*
19 bumper 保险杠 *bao-shian-garng*
20 tires [tyres] 车胎 *cher-tai*
21 hubcap 轮毂盖 *lwun-goo gai*
22 valve 气嘴 *chee-dswee*
23 wheels 车轮 *cher-lwun*
24 outside [wing] mirror 侧翼后视镜 *tser-yee ho-sh-jing*
25 central locking 中控锁 *jong-kong-suo*
26 lock 锁 *suo*
27 wheel rim 轮圈 *lwun-chüan*
28 exhaust pipe 排气管 *pai-chee-gwan*
29 odometer [milometer] 里程表 *lee-chung-biao*
30 warning light 警告灯 *jing-gao-dung*

90

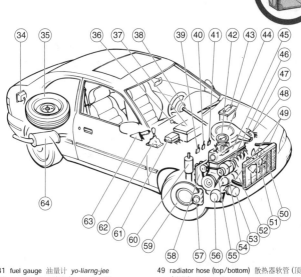

31 fuel gauge 油量计 *yo-liarng-jee*

32 speedometer 速度表 *soo-doo-biao*

33 oil gauge 机油表 *jee-yo biao*

34 backup [reversing] lights 倒车灯 *dao-cher dung*

35 spare wheel 备用轮胎 *bay-yong lwun-tai*

36 choke 手风门 *sho-fung-men*

37 heater 暖气 *nwan-chee*

38 steering column 方向盘轴 *farng-shiarng-pan jo*

39 accelerator 油门 *yo-men*

40 pedal 踏板 *ta-ban*

41 clutch 离合器 *lee-her-chee*

42 carburettor 化油器 *hwaa-yo-chee*

43 battery 电瓶 *dian-ping*

44 alternator 发电机 *fa-dian-jee*

45 camshaft 凸轮轴 *too-lwun-jo*

46 distributor 分配器 *fen-pay-chee*

47 points 接点 *jie-dian*

48 points 接点 *jie-dian*

49 radiator hose (top/bottom) 散热器软管 (顶部/底部) *san-rer-chee rwan-gwan (ding-boo/dee-boo)*

50 radiator 散热器 *san-rer-chee*

51 fan 风扇 *fung-shan*

52 engine 引擎 *yin-ching*

53 oil filter 滤油器 *lü-yo-chee*

54 starter motor 启动马达 *chee-dong ma-da*

55 fan belt 风扇皮带 *fung-shan-pee-dai*

56 horn 喇叭 *la-ba*

57 brake pads 刹车片 *sha-cher pian*

58 transmission [gearbox] 变速箱 *bian-soo-shiarng*

59 brakes 刹车 *sha-cher*

60 shock absorbers 避震器 *bee-jen-chee*

61 fuses 保险丝 *bao-shian-s*

62 gear shift [lever] 排挡杆 *pai-darng-gan*

63 handbrake 手闸 *sho-ja*

64 muffler [silencer] 消音器 *shiao-yin-chee*

Accidents 事故

For police emergencies ☎ 110. For first aid emergencies in
Beijing ☎ 120, ➤ 161.

There has been an accident.	出事故了。 *choo sh-goo le*
It's …	事故出在 … *sh-goo choo dsai …*
on the highway [motorway]	高速公路上 *gao-soo-gong-loo sharng*
near …	靠近 *kao-jin*
Where's the nearest telephone?	附近哪儿有电话? *foo-jin na-r yo dian-hwaa*
Call …	叫 … *jiao …*
the police	警察 *jing-cha*
an ambulance	救护车 *jio-hoo-cher*
a doctor	医生 *yee-shung*
the fire department [brigade]	消防队 *shiao-farng-dwee*
Can you help me, please?	请帮帮我。 *ching barng-barng wo*

Injuries 受伤

There are people injured.	有人受伤了。 *yo-ren sho-sharng le*
No one is hurt.	没人受伤。 *may ren sho-sharng*
He is seriously injured.	他伤得很重。 *ta sharng de hen jong*
She's unconscious.	她昏迷了。 *ta hwun-mee le*
He can't breathe.	他呼吸困难。 *ta hoo-shee kwun-nan*
He can't move.	他动不了。 *ta dong boo liao*
Don't move him.	不要挪动他。 *boo-yao nuo-dong ta*

Legal matters 法律事务

What's your insurance company?
你跟哪家保险公司保的险？
nee gen na-jia bao-shian-gong-s bao de shian

What's your name and address?
你叫什么名字，住哪儿？ *nee jiao shen-me ming-ds, joo na-r*

That car ran into me.
是那辆车撞我的。 *sh na-liarng cher jwarng wo de*

That car was going too fast/too close.
那车开得太快/离我太近。
na cher kai de tai kwai/lee wo tai jin

I had the right of way.
不该我让车。 *boo-gai wo rarng-cher*

I was (only) driving at … kmph.
我只开到每小时 … 公里。 *wo j kai dao may shiao-sh … gong-lee*

I'd like an interpreter.
我想找个翻译。
wo shiarng jao ge fan-yee

I didn't see the sign.
我没看见路标。
wo may kan-jian loo-biao

This person saw it happen.
这人是目击者。
jer-ren sh moo-jee-jer

The registration number was …
车牌号码是 … *cher-pai hao-ma sh …*

请给我看看你的 …	Can I see your …, please?
驾驶执照	driver's license [licence]
保险单	insurance card
汽车注册证	vehicle registration document
这是什么时候发生的?	What time did it happen?
在什么地方发生的?	Where did it happen?
有没有牵涉到其他人?	Was anyone else involved?
有没有目击者?	Are there any witnesses?
你超速了。	You were speeding.
你的车灯不亮。	Your lights aren't working.
你必须 (当场) 付罚金。	You'll have to pay a fine (on the spot).
我们需要你去警察局写份陈述。	We need you to make a statement at the station.

TIME ➤ 221

Asking directions 问路

Excuse me, please.	请问 *ching-wen*
How do I get to ...?	去 ... 怎么走? *chü ... dsen-me dso*
Where is ...?	... 在哪儿? *... dsai na-r*

Can you show me on the map where I am?

您能不能指一下我在地图的什么地方?
nin nung-boo-nung j yee-shia wo dsai dee-too de shen-me dee-farng

I've lost my way.

我迷路了。*wo mee-loo le*

Can you repeat that, please?

请再说一遍好吗?
ching dsai shuo yee-bian hao ma

More slowly, please.

请说慢一点。*ching shuo man-yee-dian*

Thanks for your help.

谢谢您的帮助。
shie-shie nin de barng-joo

Traveling by car 驾车旅行

Is this the right road for ...?

这是去 ... 的路吗?
jer-sh chü ... de loo ma

How far is it to ... from here?

这里离 ... 有多远?
jer-lee lee ... yo duo-yüan

Where does this road lead?

这条路通往哪里?
jer tiao loo tong-warng na-lee

How do I get onto the highway [motorway]?

上高速公路怎么走?
sharng gao-soo-gong-loo dsen-me dso

What's the next town called?

前方是什么城市?
chian-farng sh shen-me chung-sh

How long does it take by car?

开车去要多长时间?
kai-cher chü yao duo-charng sh-jian

– ching-wen, chü huo-cher-jan dsen-me dso?
– dao dee-san ge loo-ko jwan dsuo, ran-ho j dso.
– dee-san ge loo-ko jwan dsuo, hen yüan ma?
– yao sh-fen-jong, boo-shing sh-fen-jong
– shie-shie.
– boo-yong ker-chee.

94

COMMUNICATION DIFFICULTIES ➤ 11

Location 位置

去那儿 ...	It's ...
照直走	straight ahead
左边	on the left
右边	on the right
这条街走到底	at the end of the street
在拐角	on the corner
拐弯就到	around the corner
顺着 ... 的方向	in the direction of ...
在 ... 的对面/在 ... 的后边	opposite .../behind ...
靠近 .../过了 ...	next to .../after ...
沿着 ... 走	Go down the ...
后街/主街	side street/main street
横穿过 ...	Cross the ...
广场/桥	square/bridge
第三个路口转右	Take the third right.
... 转左	Turn left ...
过了第一排交通灯	after the first traffic lights
在第二个十字路口	at the second intersection [crossroad]

By car 开车去

在 ...	It's ... of here.
北边/南边	north/south
东边/西边	east/west
走通往 ... 的道路	Take the road for ...
你走错了。	You're on the wrong road.
你必须回到 ...	You'll have to go back to ...
根据指向 ... 的路标走	Follow the signs for ...

How far? 有多远?

离这儿 ...	It's ...
很近/很远	close/a long way
步行五分钟	5 minutes on foot
开车十分钟	10 minutes by car
沿这条路大约走一百米	about 100 meters down the road
大约十公里远	about 10 kilometers away

TIME ➤ 221; NUMBERS ➤ 217

Road signs 路标

此路不通	access only
改道行使	alternative route
绕道	detour [diversion]
请勿换车道	stay in lane
让车	yield [give way]
低桥	low bridge
单行道	one-way street
封路	road closed
学校	school
请开大灯	use headlights

Town plans 城市规划

机场	airport
公共汽车专用道	bus route
公共汽车站	bus stop
停车场	parking lot [car park]
教堂	church
电影院	movie theater [cinema]
主商业街	main [high] street
旅游信息服务处	information office
地铁站	subway [metro] station
旧城区	old town
公园	park
人行横道线	pedestrian crossing
行人区	pedestrian zone [precinct]
公安局/派出所	police station
邮局	post office
公共建筑	public building
运动场	playing field [sports ground]
车站	station
体育馆	stadium
地下通道	underpass
出租汽车站	taxi stand [rank]
剧场	theater
你在这儿	you are here

DICTIONARY ➤ 169; SIGHTSEEING ➤ 97–107

Sightseeing

Tourist information office	97	Tourist glossary	102
Excursions	98	Who/What/When?	104
Sights	99	Chinese theater	105
Admission	100	Religion	105
Impressions	101	In the countryside	106

China International Travel Service (CITS, also known as **guo-jee lü-shing-sher** or **guo-lü** for short) is responsible for looking after tourists in China. CTS and CYTS offices can help you too ➤ 66.

As well as days packed with sightseeing, your visit to China may well include an evening or two of organized entertainment. Popular spectacles are concerts, acrobat shows, Chinese ballet and opera, the circus, and, of course, banquets.

Tourist information office 旅游信息服务处

Where's the tourist office?	旅游服务处在哪儿? *lü-yo foo-woo-choo dsai na-r*
What are the main points of interest?	主要的游览点有哪些? *joo-yao de yo-lan-dian yo na-shie*
We're here for ...	我们要在这儿停留 ... *wo-men yao dsai jer-r ting-lio ...*
only a few hours	仅仅几小时 *jin-jin jee shiao-sh*
a day	一天 *yee-tian*
a week	一星期 *yee shing-chee*
Can you recommend ...?	你能不能推荐 ... ? *nee nung-boo-nung twee-jian ...*
a sightseeing tour	一种观光游 *yee-jong gwan-gwarng yo*
an excursion	短途旅游 *dwan-too lü-yo*
a boat trip	乘船游览 *chung-chwan yo-lan*
Do you have any information on ...?	您这儿有没有介绍 ... 的资料? *nin jer-r yo-may-yo jie-shao ... de ds-liao*
Are there any trips to ...?	有没有去 ... 的旅游安排? *yo-may-yo chü ... de lü-yo an-pai*

DAYS OF THE WEEK ➤ 218; DIRECTIONS ➤ 94

Excursions
预订短途旅游车票

How much does the tour cost?	这趟旅游多少钱? *jer-tarng lü-yo duo-shao-chian*
Is lunch included?	中饭包括在内吗? *jong-fan bao-kuo dsai-nay ma*
Where do we leave from?	我们从哪儿出发? *wo-men tsong na-r choo-fa*
What time does the tour start?	几点钟开始? *jee dian jong kai-sh*
What time do we get back?	什么时候能回来? *shen-me sh-ho nung hway-lai*
Do we have free time in ...?	我们在 ... 有没有自由活动时间? *wo-men dsai ... yo-may-yo ds-yo huo-dong sh-jian*
Is there an English-speaking guide?	有没有会说英语的导游? *yo-may-yo hway shuo ying-yü de dao-yo*

On tour 旅游途中

Are we going to see ...?	我们去不去看 ... ? *wo-men chü boo chü kan ...*
We'd like to have a look at the ...	我们希望看一看 ... *wo-men shee-warng kan-yee-kan ...*
Can we stop here ...?	我们可以在这儿停一停 ... 吗? *wo-men ker-yee dsai jer-r ting-yee-ting ... ma*
to take photographs	拍照 *pai-jao*
to buy souvenirs	买点纪念品 *mai-dian jee-nian-pin*
for the bathrooms [toilets]	上个厕所 *sharng ge tser suo*
Would you take a photo of us, please?	请给我们拍张照, 好吗? *ching gay wo-men pai jarng jao, hao-ma*
How long do we have here/in ...?	我们在这儿/在 ... 能停留多久? *wo-men dsai jer-r/dsai ... nung ting-lio duo-jio*
Wait! ... isn't back yet.	等一等! ... 还没有回来呢。 *dung-yee-dung! ... hai may-yo hway-lai ne*

98

Sights 风景点

Where is the ...?	... 在哪儿?	dsai na-r
abbey	修道院	shio-dao-yüan
art gallery	美术馆	may-shoo-gwan
battle site	古战场	goo-jan-charng
botanical garden	植物园	j-woo-yüan
castle	城堡	chung-bao
cathedral	大教堂	da-jiao-tarng
cemetery	公墓	gong-moo
church	教堂	jiao-tarng
downtown area	市中心	sh-jong-shin
fountain	喷泉	pen-chüan
Great Hall of the People	人民大会堂	ren-min da-hway-tarng
market	集市	jee-sh
monastery	寺庙	s-miao
museum	博物馆	buo-woo-gwan
old town	旧城区	jio-chung-chü
opera house	歌剧院	ger-jü-yüan
pagoda	宝塔	bao-ta
palace	宫殿	gong-dian
park	公园	gong-yüan
ruins	古迹遗址	goo-jee yee-j
shopping area	商业区	sharng-ye chü
statue	塑像	soo-shiarng
theater	剧场	jü-charng
town hall	市政府大楼	sh-jung-foo da-lo
viewpoint	观光点	gwan-gwarng-dian
war memorial	英雄纪念碑	ying-shiong jee-nian-bay
Can you show me on the map?	你能不能在地图上指给我看?	nee nung-boo-nung dsai dee-too sharng j-gay wo kan

DIRECTIONS ➤ 94

Admission 入口处

Museums are usually open from 9 a.m. to 4 p.m. on weekdays, and most are open between the same hours on Saturdays and Sundays. Most are closed on Mondays. Parks, zoos, and monuments are open between 8 and 9 a.m., closing between 5 and 6 p.m. Most will close for one to three hours in the middle of the day, but are usually open on Sundays.

Is the ... open to the public?	... 对外开放吗？ ... *dwee wai kai-farng ma*
Can we look around?	我们能到处看一看吗？ *wo-men nung* *dao-choo kan-yee-kan ma*
What are the opening hours?	什么时候开门？ *shen-me sh-ho kai-men*
When does it close?	几点关门？ *jee-dian gwan-men*
Is ... open on Sundays?	... 星期天开门吗？ ... *shing-chee-tian kai-men ma*
When's the next guided tour?	下一次有导游带领的参观几点开始？ *shia-yee-ts yo dao-yo dai-ling de tsang-gwan jee-dian kai-sh*
Do you have a guidebook (in English)?	有没有 (英文) 导游册？ *yo-may-yo (ying-wen) dao-yo-tser*
Can I take photos?	我可以拍照吗？ *wo ker-yee pai-jao ma*
Is there access for the disabled?	有没有残疾人专用出入口？ *yo-may-yo* *tsan-jee-ren jwan-yong choo-roo-ko*
Is there an audioguide in English?	有没有英语导游录音？ *yo-may-yo* *ying-yü dao-yo loo-yin*

Paying/Tickets 买票

How much is the entrance fee?	门票多少钱？ *men-piao duo-shao-chian*
Are there any discounts for ...?	... 有没有折扣？ ... *yo-may-yo jer-ko*
children	儿童 *er-tong*
the disabled	残疾人 *tsan-jee-ren*
groups	团体 *twan-tee*
senior citizens	退休人员 *twee-shio ren-yüan*
students	学生 *sh-shung*
1 adult and 2 children, please.	一张成人票，两张儿童票。 *yee-jarng* *chung-ren piao, liarng-jarng er-tong piao*

– wo-yao woo-jarng piao. yo jer-ko ma?
– *yo. er-tong er-sh kwai.*
– liarng-jarng chung-ren piao,
 san-jarng er-tong piao.
– *yee-gong yee-bai-er-sh kwai.*

免费进入	free admission
停止开放	closed
礼品店	gift shop
最迟入门时间下午五点	Latest entry at 5 p.m.
下一趟旅游 ... 点钟出发	next tour at ...
禁止入内	no entry
禁止使用闪光灯	no flash photography
对外开放	open
参观时间	visiting hours

Impressions 感受

It's ...	真是 ... *jen-sh* ...
amazing	不可思议 *boo-ker-s-yee*
awful	糟透了 *dsao tou le*
beautiful	漂亮 *piao-liarng*
bizarre	古怪 *goo-gwai*
boring	没意思 *may-yee-s*
breathtaking	令人赞叹 *ling-ren dsan-tan*
incredible	好极了 *hao-jee le*
lots of fun	很好玩 *hen-hao-wan*
interesting	有意思 *yo-yee-s*
magnificent	宏伟 *hong-way*
romantic	很浪漫 *hen larng-man*
strange	奇特 *chee-ter*
stunning	美极了 *may jee le*
superb	太棒了 *tai barng le*
terrible	很糟糕 *hen dsao-gao*
ugly	丑陋 *cho-lo*
It's good value.	这很划算。*jer hen hwaa-swan*
It's a rip-off.	这是敲竹杠。*jer-sh chiao joo-garng*
I like it.	我挺喜欢的。*wo ting shee-hwan de*
I don't like it.	我不喜欢。*wo boo shee-hwan*

101

天坛	tian-tan	Temple of Heaven (Beijing)
墓地	moo-dee	burial site
颐和园	yee-her-yüan	the Summer Palace (Beijing)
故宫	goo-gong	the Imperial Palace (Beijing)
名胜古迹	ming-shung-goo-jee	historical site
港口	garng-ko	harbor
清真寺	ching-jen-s	mosque
纪念堂	jee-nian-tarng	memorial hall
长城	charng-chung	the Great Wall
博物馆	buo-woo-gwan	museum
纪念碑	jee-nian-bay	monument
亭，凉亭	ting, liarng-ting	pavilion
塔，宝塔	ta, bao-ta	pagoda
园林	yüan-lin	Chinese garden
教堂	jiao-tarng	church
寺庙	s-miao	monastery

陵墓	ling-moo	tomb
建筑	jian-joo	architecture
艺术	yee-shoo	art
书法	shoo-fa	calligraphy
陶瓷	tao-ts	ceramics / pottery
朝代	chao-dai	dynasty
翡翠	fay-tswee	jade
象牙	shiarng-ya	ivory
手工艺品	sho-gong-yee-pin	handicrafts
漆器	chee-chee	lacquerware
画	hwaa	painting
剪纸	jian-j	papercrafts
雕塑	diao-soo	sculpture
纺织品	farng-j-pin	textiles
青铜器	ching-tong-chee	bronzes
木器	moo-chee	woodcrafts

Who/What/When?
谁/什么/什么时候?

What's that building?	那座建筑物是什么? *na dsuo jian-joo-woo sh shen-me*
When was it built?	是什么时候建成的? *sh shen-me sh-ho jian-chung de*
Who was the artist/architect?	是谁画的/设计的? *sh shwee hwaa-de/sher-jee de*
What style is that?	这属于什么建筑风格? *jer shoo-yü shen-me jian-joo fung-ger*

Rulers 统治者

The Chinese claim a history that goes back 5000 years starting with the Xia dynasty. The reign of the emperors came to an end in 1911 when the last imperial dynasty collapsed and the Republic of China came into being under the leadership of Sun Yat-sen. The years between 1911 and 1949 were a bloody period which included civil war, Japanese invasion, World War II. In October 1949, Mao Zedong proclaimed the foundation of the People's Republic of China (P.R.C.), but still China was to suffer under the Cultural Revolution and other dramatic changes. Today China has embarked upon another period of rapid change and development.

What period is that?	那是什么年代? *na-sh shen-me nian-dai*
First emperor of the Qin dynasty, who united China	秦始皇 *chin-sh-hwarng*
Second emperor of the Tang dynasty in its heyday	唐太宗 *tarng-tai-dsong*
First emperor of the Yuan dynasty (Genghis Khan)	元太祖 *yüan-tai-dsoo*
First emperor of the Ming dynasty	明太祖 *ming-tai-dsoo*
Last emperor of the Qing dynasty at the end of the feudal age in China	溥仪 *poo-yee*
Chiarng Kai-shek, generalissimo of Kuomintang	蒋介石 *jiarng-jie-sh*
Mao Zedong (Mao Tse-tung) Chinese communist leader	毛泽东 *mao-dser-dong*

Chinese theater 戏院

Traditional Chinese opera-theater, including the famous Beijing opera, provides spectacular performances combining singing, dance, pantomime, and martial arts. There are over 300 different kinds of opera performed all over China. All have their own traditions and characteristics in terms of costume, setting, music, and performance style. Such performances are well worth a visit, and although you will certainly not understand all of the actors' gestures, let alone the songs and the words, the rhythm, the colors, the mime, and the music will guarantee a memorable experience.

Religion 堂

The Chinese government is officially atheist, yet recently open religious activity has been permitted again. Many temples, some with their own monks and novices, have been allowed to reopen. The most widely practiced religions are Taoism, Buddhism, Islam, Catholicism, and Protestantism. However, only atheists are allowed to become members of the Chinese Communist Party, which precludes large numbers of people.

Buddhism found its way into China in the first century B.C. and spread widely, becoming the most influential religion in China. A branch of Buddhism, Lamaism (also called Tibetan Buddhism), is widespread in Tibet and Inner Mongolia. Islam was introduced to China in the middle of the seventh century, and today there are believed to be 14 million Muslims. Followers of Protestantism and Catholicism are mainly concentrated in large cities like Beijing and Shanghai.

For many Chinese a mixture of Taoism (combining animism with a system of maintaining harmony with the universe), Confucianism (concerning the political and moral aspects of life), and Buddhism (covering the afterlife) best describes a complicated belief system.

Catholic/Protestant church	天主教 / 基督教新教教堂 *tian-joo-jiao/jee-doo-jiao shin-jiao jiao-tarng*
mosque	清真寺 *ching-jen-s*
synagogue	犹太教堂 *yo-tai jiao-tarng*
What time is …?	… 是什么时候? *… sh shen-me sh-ho*
mass/the service	弥撒 / 做礼拜 *mee-sa/dsuo lee-bai*

In the countryside 在乡村

I'd like a map of ...	我想要一份 ... 地图	*wo shiarng yao yee-fen ... dee-too*
this region	本地区 ben-dee-chü	
walking routes	徒步旅行路线	*too-boo lü-shing loo-shian*
cycle routes	自行车旅行 *ds-shing-cher lü-shing*	
How far is it to ...?	到 ... 多远? *dao ... yo duo-yüan*	
Is there a right of way?	有没有优先通行权?	*yo-may-yo yo-shian tong-shing chüan*
Is there a trail / scenic route to ...?	有没有小路或风景优美的道路通往 ... ?	*yo-may-yo shiao-loo huo feng-jing yo-may de dao-loo tong-warng ...*
Can you show me on the map?	你能不能给我在地图上指一下?	*nee nung-boo-nung gay wo dsai dee-too sharng j-yee-shia*
I'm lost.	我迷路了。 *wo mee-loo le*	

Organized walks 有组织的徒步旅行

When does the guided walk / hike start?	由向导带队的徒步旅行什么时候出发?	*yo shiarng-dao dai-dwee de too-boo lü-shing shen-me sh-ho choo-fa*
When will we return?	我们什么时候回来?	*wo-men shen-me sh-ho hway-lai*
Is it a hard course?	这条路难走吗?	*jer-tiao loo nan-dso ma*
gentle / medium / tough	轻松 / 中等 / 难走	*ching-song / jong-dung / nan-dso*
I'm exhausted.	我已精疲力尽了 *wo yee jing-pee-lee-jin le*	
How long are we resting here?	我们在这儿要休息多久?	*wo-men dsai jer-r yao shio-shee duo-jio*
What kind of ... is that?	这是什么 ... ? *jer-sh shen-me ...*	
animal / bird	动物 / 鸟 *dong-woo / niao*	
flower / tree	花 / 树 *hwaa / shoo*	

Geographical features 地理特征

bridge	桥	*chiao*
cave	岩洞	*yan-dong*
cliff	峭壁	*chiao-bee*
farm	农场	*nong-charng*
field	田	*tian*
(foot)path	小道	*shiao-dao*
forest	森林	*sen-lin*
hill	小山	*shiao-shan*
lake	湖	*hoo*
mountain	山	*shan*
mountain pass	山路	*shan-loo*
mountain range	山脉	*shan-mai*
nature reserve	自然保护区	*ds-ran bao-hoo-chü*
panorama	全景	*chüan-jing*
park	公园	*gong-yüan*
peak	山峰	*shan-fung*
picnic area	野餐区	*ye-tsan chü*
pond	池塘	*ch-tarng*
rapids	急流	*jee-lio*
river	江河	*jiarng-her*
sea	海	*hai*
stream	溪流	*shee-lio*
valley	山谷	*shan-goo*
viewpoint	观光点	*gwan-gwarng-dian*
village	村庄	*tswun-jwarng*
vineyard / winery	葡萄园	*poo-tao-yüan*
waterfall	瀑布	*poo-boo*
wood	树林	*shoo-lin*

Leisure

Events	108	Nightlife	112
Tickets	109	Admission	112
Movies [Cinema]	110	Children	113
Theater	110	Sports	114
Opera/Ballet/Dance	111	At the beach	116
Music/Concerts	111	Skiing	117

Events 文娱活动

The Chinese English-language newspaper, *China Daily*, and its weekly publications, *Beijing Weekend* and *Shanghai Star*, can be found at hotels and newsstands in most cities, though with considerable delays inland. They include Chinese and foreign news plus tourist features, sports, and even stock-market reports. A visit to your local CTS office will also provide you with information.

Do you have a program of events?	你们有没有文娱活动时间表? *nee-men yo-may-yo wen-yü huo-dong sh-jian biao*
Can you recommend a good …?	您能不能推荐一个好的 … ? *nin nung-boo-nung twee-jian yee-ge hao de …*
ballet/concert	芭蕾舞/音乐会 *ba-lay-woo/yin-yüe-hway*
movie [film]	电影 *dian-ying*
opera	歌剧 *ger-jü*
Chinese opera-theater	戏院 *shee-yüan*

Availability 票房查询

When does it start?	什么时间开始? *shen-me sh-jian kai-sh*
When does it end?	什么时间结束? *shen-me sh-jian jie-shoo*
Are there any seats for tonight?	还有今晚的票吗? *hai-yo jin-wan de piao ma*
Where can I get tickets?	哪儿能买到票? *na-r nung mai-dao piao*
There are … of us.	我们有 … 个人。 *wo-men yo … ge ren*

Tickets 订票

How much are the seats?	票价多少? *piao-jia duo-shao*
Do you have anything cheaper?	有没有便宜点的? *yo-may-yo piao-yee dian de*
I'd like to reserve ...	我想预订 ... *wo shiarng yü-ding ...*
three tickets for Sunday evening	三张星期天晚上的票 *san-jarng shing-chee-tian wan-sharng de piao*
one ticket for the Friday matinée	一张星期五日场票 *yee-jarng shing-chee woo r-charng piao*

您的信用卡 ... 是什么?	What's your credit card ...?
号码	number
种类	type
失效日期	expiry date
请在 ... 取票	Please pick up the tickets ...
下午 ... 点之前	by ... p.m.
预售票台	at the reservations desk

May I have a program, please?	请给我一份节目单。 *ching gay wo yee-fen jie-moo dan*
Where's the coatcheck [cloakroom]?	衣帽室在哪儿? *yee-mao-sh dsai na-r*

yao mai piao ma?
mai liarng jarng jin-wan de yin-yüe-hwee piao.
hao de.
ker-yee yong shin-yong-ka ma?
ker-yee.
na wo jio yong way-sa-ka ba.
shie-shie ... ching dsai jer-r chian-ds

预售票	advance reservations
售完	sold out
当天票	tickets for today

NUMBERS ➤ 217

109

Movies [Cinema] 电影院

Few travelers in China go to see Chinese films because of the language problem. However, some recent releases have been subtitled into English and have been acclaimed at Western film festivals. You may be lucky enough to track down one of these. Television. Most major hotels will have television sets in every room and will offer their guests closed-circuit television programs and CNN-type news broadcasts. Chinese television and radio broadcast in **putonghua**, standard Chinese speech, as well as in local dialects and minority languages. You may find it interesting (despite the language problem) to watch a little state-run television, where you will find soap operas, news bulletins, Chinese operas, films, sporting events, and even some advertising.

Is there a multiplex theater [cinema] near here?	附近有没有多银幕电影院? *foo-jin yo-may-yo duo-yin-moo dian-ying-yüan*
What's playing at the movies [on at the cinema] tonight?	今晚上映什么电影? *jin-wan sharng-ying shen-me dian-ying*
Is the film dubbed / subtitled?	这部电影有没有配音/字幕? *jer-boo dian-ying yo-may-yo pay-yin/pay ds-moo*
Is the film in the original English?	这电影是不是英文原版? *jer dian-ying sh-boo-sh ying-wen yüan-ban*
A ..., please.	请给我 ...。 *ching gay wo ...*
box [carton] of popcorn	一包爆米花 *yee-bao bao-mee-hwaa*
chocolate ice cream [choc-ice]	一个巧克力冰淇淋 *yee-ge chiao-ker-lee bing-chee-lin*
hot dog	一个热狗 *yee-ge rer-go*
soft drink	一杯软饮料 *yee-bay rwan-yin-liao*
small / regular / large	小/中/大 *shiao/jong/da*

Theater 剧场

What's playing at the ... theater?	... 剧场在上演什么? *... jü-charng dsai sharng-yan shen-me*
Who's the playwright?	编剧是谁? *bian-jü sh shwee*
Do you think I'd enjoy it?	你觉得我会喜欢吗? *nee jüe-de wo hway shee-hwan ma*
I don't know much Chinese.	我汉语懂的不多 *wo han-yü dong-de boo-duo*

Opera/Ballet/Dance
歌剧/芭蕾/舞蹈

Where's the theater?	剧院在哪儿？ *ger-jü-yüan dsai na-r*
Who is the composer/soloist?	作曲家/独唱是谁？ *dsuo-chü-jia/doo-charng sh shwee*
Is formal dress expected?	要不要穿得很庄重？ *yao boo-yao* *chwan de hen jwarng-jong*
Who's dancing?	由哪位舞蹈家表演？ *yo na-way* *woo-dao-jia biao-yan*
I'm interested in contemporary dance.	我对现代舞很感兴趣。 *wo dwee shian-dai-woo hen* *gan-shing-chü*

Music/Concerts 音乐/音乐会

Where's the concert hall?	音乐厅在哪儿？ *yin-yüe-ting dsai na-r*
Which orchestra/band is playing?	是哪个乐团的节目？ *sh na-ge yüe-twan de jie-moo*
What are they playing?	演奏什么乐曲？ *yan-dso shen-me yüe-chü*
Who is the conductor/soloist?	指挥/独奏是谁？ *j-hway/doo-dso sh shwee*
Who is the support band?	哪个乐队伴奏？ *na-ge yüe-dwee ban-dso*
I really like …	我很喜欢 … *wo hen shee-hwan …*
folk music/country music	民间音乐 / 乡村音乐 *min-jian yin-yüe/shiarng tswun yin-yüe*
jazz	爵士乐 *jüe-sh yüe*
karaoke	卡拉OK *ka-la-o-kai*
pop/rock music	流行乐/摇滚乐 *lio-shing-yüe/yao-gwun-yüe*
soul music	爵士灵乐 *jüe-sh lin-yüe*
traditional Chinese music	民乐 *min-yüe*
Have you ever heard of her/him?	你听说过他/她吗？ *nee ting shuo guo ta/ta ma*
Are they popular?	他们很流行吗？ *ta-men hen lio-shing ma*

Nightlife 夜生活

Discos and karaoke bars have become very popular in China and are found in all majore cities. Watch out for over-pricing and rip-offs in karaoke bars though.

What is there to do in the evenings?	晚上有什么事情好做? *wan-sharng yo shen-me sh-ching hao-dsuo*
Can you recommend a …?	你能不能推荐一个 … ? *nee nung-boo-nung twee-jian yee-ge …*
Is there a … in town?	城里有没有 … ? *chung-lee yo-may-yo …*
bar/restaurant	酒吧/餐馆 *jio-ba/tsan-gwan*
casino	赌场 *doo-charng*
discotheque	迪斯科舞场 *dee-s-ker woo-charng*
nightclub	夜总会 *ye-dsong-hway*
What type of music do they play?	那里播放什么样的音乐? *na-lee buo-farng shen-me-yarng de yin-yüe*
How do I get there?	去那儿怎么走? *chū na-r dsen-me-dso*

Admission 入场

What time does the show start?	演出什么时候开始? *yan-choo shen-me sh-ho kai-sh*
Is evening dress required?	需要穿夜礼服吗? *shū-yao chwan ye-lee-foo ma*
Is there a cover charge?	要交服务费吗? *yao-jiao foo-woo-fay ma*
Is a reservation necessary?	需要预订吗? *shū-yao yü-ding ma*
Do we need to be members?	我们需要先成为会员吗? *wo-men shū-yao shian chung-way hway-yüan ma*
Is it customary to dine there?	人们通常在那儿吃饭吗? *ren-men tong-charng dsai na-r ch-fan ma*
How long will we have to stand in line [queue]?	我们排队要排多久? *wo-men pai-dwee yao pai duo-jio*
I'd like a good table.	请给我选一张好桌子 *ching gay wo shüan yee-jarng hao juo-ds*

包括一份免费饮料   includes 1 complimentary drink

Children 儿童

Can you recommend something suitable for the children?
你能不能推荐适合儿童的活动? *nee nung-boo-nung twee-jian sh-her er-tong de huo-dong*

Are there changing facilities here for babies?
这里有没有给婴儿换尿片的地方? *jer-lee yo-may-yo gay ying-er hwan niao-pian de dee-farng*

Where are the bathrooms [toilets]?
厕所在哪儿? *tser-suo dsai na-r*

amusement arcade
游戏厅 *yo-shee-ting*

fairground
游乐场 *yo-ler-charng*

kiddie [paddling] pool
儿童戏水池 *er-tong shee-shwee-ch*

playground
操场 *tsao-charng*

play group
游玩组 *yo-wan dsoo*

zoo
动物园 *dong-woo-yüan*

Baby-sitting 代人照看小孩

Can you recommend a reliable baby-sitter?
你能不能推荐一个可靠的临时保姆? *nee nung-boo-nung twee-jian yee-ge ker-kao de lin-sh bao-moo*

Is there constant supervision?
是不是照看得很周到? *sh-boo-sh jao-kan de hen jo-dao*

Is the staff properly trained?
这些保育员有没有经过正规训练? *jer-shie bao-yü-yüan yo-may-yo jing-guo jung-gway shün-lian*

When can I drop them off?
应该什么时候把他们送来? *ying-gai shen-me s-ho ba ta-men song lai*

I'll pick them up at ...
我 ... 来把他们接走。 *wo ... lai ba ta-men jie dso*

We'll be back by ...
我们 ... 之前回来。 *wo-men ... j-chian hway-lai*

She's 3 and he's 18 months.
女孩三岁，男孩十八个月。 *nü-hai san-swee, nan-hai-sh-ba ge yüe*

Sports 体育

Early risers will no doubt encounter people practising **tai-jee-chūan** (太极拳) on road sides and in parks. This is a physical-philosophical discipline to tone up the body and the mind.

Swimming is also popular with the Chinese. Foreigners wishing to use public swimming pools will need a health certificate from a Chinese clinic showing that they are AIDS free.

Many major hotels will have various facilities (swimming pools, gymnasiums, exercise machines, etc.) for their guests.

Spectating 观看

Is there a soccer [football] game [match] this Saturday?	这个星期六有没有足球赛? *jer-ge shing-chee-lio yo-may-yo dsoo-chio-sai*
Which teams are playing?	哪两个队比赛? *na liarng-ge dwee bee-sai*
Can you get me a ticket?	能不能给我弄一张票? *nung-boo-nung gay wo nong yee-jarng piao*
What's the admission charge?	入场费多少钱? *roo-charng-fay duo-shao-chian*
Where's the racetrack [racecourse]?	赛场在哪儿? *sai-charng dsai na-r*
Where can I place a bet?	在哪儿押注? *dsai na-r ya-joo*
What are the odds on ...?	... 的赔率是多少? *... de pay-lù sh duo-shao*
athletics	田径 *tian-jing*
basketball	篮球 *lan-chio*
cycling	自行车赛 *ds-shing-cher sai*
golf	高尔夫 *gao-er-foo*
horse racing	赛马 *sai-ma*
soccer [football]	足球 *dsoo-chio*
squash	壁球 *bee-chio*
swimming	游泳 *yo-yong*
table tennis	乒乓球 *ping-parng chio*
tennis	网球 *warng-chio*
volleyball	排球 *pai-chio*

114

Playing 参加体育活动

Where's the nearest …?	附近哪儿有 … ? *foo-jin na-r yo …*
golf course	高尔夫球场 *gao-er-foo chio-charng*
sports club	体育俱乐部 *tee-yü jü-ler-boo*
Where are the tennis courts?	网球场在哪儿? *warng-chio-charng* *dsai na-r*
What's the charge per …?	每 … 的收费是多少? *may … de sho-fay sh duo-shao*
day / round / hour	天/轮/小时 *tian/lwun/shiao-sh*
Do I need to be a member?	我需要成为俱乐部会员吗? *wo shü-yao* *chung way jü-ler-boo hway-yüan ma*
Where can I rent …?	哪儿能租到 …? *na-r nung dsoo dao …*
boots	靴子 *shüe-ds*
clubs	球棒 *chio-barng*
equipment	体育用具 *tee-yü yong-jü*
a racket	球拍 *chio-pai*
Can I get lessons?	可以得到指导吗? *ker-yee de-dao* *j-dao ma*
Do you have a fitness room?	你们有没有健身房? *nee-men yo-may-yo jian-shen-farng*
Can I join in?	我可以和你们一起锻炼吗? *wo ker-yee* *her nee-men yee-chee dwan-lian ma*

对不起，订满了。	I'm sorry, we're booked up.
需要交 … 钱的押金。	There is a deposit of …
您要多大尺寸?	What size are you?
要准备一张二寸照片。	You need a passport-size photo.

更衣室	changing room
禁止垂钓	no fishing
无证者止步	permit holders only

At the beach 在海滩

Depending on where you are in China you should pay attention to what the people around you are wearing before going topless or putting on a skimpy bikini or swimming trunks.

While city people may be becoming more used to foreigners and fashions, the Chinese countryside is still conservative – and you may avoid giving offense, or even being harassed, by wearing more modest clothing.

Is the beach pebbly/sandy?	是鹅卵石海滩/沙滩吗? *sh er-lwan-sh hai-tan/sha-tan ma*
Is there a … here?	这里有没有 …? *jer-lee yo-may-yo …*
children's pool	儿童戏水池 *er-tong shee-shwee-ch*
swimming pool	游泳池 *yo-yong-ch*
indoor/open-air	室内/室外 *sh-nay/sh-wai*
Is it safe to swim/dive here?	在这儿游泳/跳水安全吗? *dsai jer-r* *yo-yong/tiao-shwee an-chūan ma*
Is it safe for children?	儿童安全吗? *er-tong an-chūan ma*
Is there a lifeguard?	有没有救生员? *yo-may-yo jio-shung-yüan*
I want to rent a/some …	我想租 … *wo shiarng dsoo …*
deck chair	折叠椅 *jer-die-yee*
jet-ski	滑水快艇 *hwaa-shwee kwai-ting*
motorboat	摩托艇 *muo-tuo-ting*
diving equipment	轻装潜水用具 *ching-jwarng chian-shwee yong-jü*
umbrella [sunshade]	阳伞 *yarng-san*
surfboard	冲浪板 *chong-larng-ban*
water skis	滑水橇 *hwaa-shwee-chiao*
For … hours.	要租 … 小时。 *yao dsoo … shiao-shee*

Skiing 滑雪

Beijing's lakes freeze over during the winter and people often go ice skating. In Harbin, in the north, January temperatures fall very low and ice-boat racing is a popular pastime. North-east China is also the place to go skiing, both downhill and cross-country. However, as Western shoe sizes are generally large, if you want to do any winter sports, it may be wise to take your own equipment.

Is there much snow?	雪多吗?	*shüe duo ma*
What's the snow like?	积雪情况如何?	
	jee-shüe ching-kwarng roo-her	
heavy / icy	大雪 / 冰雪	*da-shüe / bing-shüe*
powdery / wet	粉状雪 / 湿雪	*fen-jwarng shüe / sh-shüe*
I'd like to rent some ...	我想租 ...	*wo shiarng dsoo ...*
poles	雪杖	*shüe-jarng*
skates	溜冰鞋	*lio-bing-shie*
ski boots	滑雪靴子	*hwaa-shüe shüe-ds*
skis	雪橇	*shüe-chiao*
These are too ...	这些太 ...	*jer-shie tai ...*
big / small	大 / 小	*da / shiao*
They're uncomfortable.	穿着不舒服。	*chwan-je boo-shoo-foo*
A lift pass for a day / five days, please.	买一张一天 / 五天有效的登山缆车票。	
	mai yee-jarng yee-tian / woo-tian yo-shiao de dung-shan lan-cher piao	
I'd like to join the ski school.	我想参加滑雪学校。	
	wo shiarng tsan-jia hwaa-shüe shüe-shiao	
I'm a beginner.	我是初学者。	
	wo sh choo-shüe-jer	
I'm experienced.	我已经会了。	
	wo yee-jing hway-le	

缆车	cable car / gondolas
座椅式缆车	chair lift
导索升降缆车	drag lift

Making Friends

Introductions	118	Enjoying your trip?	123
Where are you from?	119	Invitations	124
Who are you with?	120	Encounters	126
What do you do?	121	Telephoning	127

Introductions 互相介绍

The Chinese are often keen to practice their English, though conversation possibilities are restricted because of language problems. However, sign language can help you get along, and a friendly approach normally elicits a similar response.

In some restaurants foreigners are given a separate, special room. If this is the case, don't insist on being seated with the Chinese diners as it would embarrass both staff and customers alike.

Hello, we haven't met.
您好，我们没见过面。
nin hao, wo-men may jian-guo mian

My name is …
我姓 …。
wo shing …

May I introduce …?
我来介绍一下 …
wo-lai jie-shao yee-shia …

Pleased to meet you.
幸会。
shing hway

What's your name?
您贵姓?
nin gway shing

How are you?
身体好吗?
shen-tee hao ma

Fine, thanks. And you?
很好，谢谢。你呢?
hen hao, shie-shie. nee ne

– *nee hao, nee dsen-me-yarng?*
– *hen hao, shie-shie, nee ne?*
– *ye boo-tsuo, shie-shie.*

Where are you from? 你是哪国人?

Where do you come from?	你是哪里人? *nee sh na-lee ren*
Where were you born?	你出生在什么地方? *nee choo-shung dsai shen-me dee-farng*
I'm from ...	我是 ... 人 *wo she ... ren*
Australia	澳大利亚 *ao-da-lee-ya*
Britain	英国 *ying-guo*
Canada	加拿大 *jia-na-da*
England	英格兰 *ying-ger-lan*
Ireland	爱尔兰 *ai-er-lan*
Scotland	苏格兰 *soo-ger-lan*
U.S.	美国 *may-guo*
Wales	威尔士 *way-er-sh*
Where do you live?	你住在哪儿? *nee joo dsai na-r*
What part of ... are you from?	你是 ... 什么地方人? *nee sh ... shen-me dee-farng ren*
Japan	日本 *r-ben*
Korea	韩国 *han-guo*
China	中国 *jong-guo*
We come here every year.	我们每年都到这儿来。 *wo-men may-nian dou dao jer-r lai*
It's my / our first visit.	我 / 我们是第一次来这儿。 *wo/wo-men sh dee-yee-ts lai jer-r*
Have you ever been to ...?	你去没去过 ... ? *nee chü may chü guo ...*
the U.K. / the U.S.	英国 / 美国 *ying-guo/may-guo*
Do you like it here?	你喜欢这里吗? *nee shee-hwan jer-lee ma*
What do you think of the ...?	你认为 ... 怎么样? *nee ren-way ... dsen-me-yarng*
I love the ... here.	我很喜欢这里的 ... *wo hen shee-hwan jer-lee de ...*
I don't really like the ... here.	我不太喜欢这里的 ... *wo boo tai shee-hwan jer-lee de ...*
food / people	吃的东西 / 人 *ch-de-dong-shee/ren*

Who are you with?
你是和谁一起来的?

Who are you with?	你是和谁一起来的? *nee sh her shwee yee-chee lai de*
I'm on my own.	我一个人来的。 *wo yee-ge-ren lai de*
I'm with a friend.	我是跟一位朋友一起来的。 *wo sh gen yee-way pung-yo yee-chee lai de*
I'm with my ...	我是和我的 ... 一起来的。 *wo sh her wo de ... yee-chee lai de*
husband / wife	丈夫/妻子 *jarng-foo/chee-ds*
family	家人 *jia-ren*
children / parents	孩子们/父母 *hai-ds-men/foo-moo*
boyfriend / girlfriend	男朋友/女朋友 *nan-pung-yo/nü-pung-yo*
father / son	父亲/儿子 *foo-chin/er-ds*
mother / daughter	母亲/女儿 *moo-chin/nü-r*
brother / uncle	兄弟/叔叔 *shiong-dee/shoo-shoo*
sister / aunt	姐妹/姨妈 *jie-may/yee-ma*
What's your son's / wife's name?	你儿子/妻子叫什么名字? *nee er-ds/chee-ds jiao shen-me ming-ds*
Are you married?	你结婚了吗? *nee jie-hwun le ma*
I'm ...	我 ... *wo ...*
married / single	已婚/单身 *yee-hwun/dan-shen*
divorced / separated	离婚了/分居了 *lee-hwun le/fen-jü le*
engaged	订婚了 *ding-hwun le*
We live together.	我们生活在一起。 *wo-men shung-huo dsai yee-chee*
Do you have any children?	你们有孩子吗? *nee-men yo hai-ds ma*
We have two boys and a girl.	两个男孩，一个女孩。 *liarng-ge nan-hai, yee-ge nü-hai*
How old are they?	他们多大了? *ta-men duo da le*
They're ten and twelve.	一个十岁，一个十二岁。 *yee-ge sh-swee, yee-ge sh-er swee*

What do you do? 你做什么工作?

What do you do?	你做什么工作? *nee dsuo shen-me gong-dsuo*
What are you studying?	你在学什么科目? *nee dsai shüe shen-me ker-moo*
I'm studying ...	我是学 ... 的。 *wo sh shüe ... de*
I'm in ...	我是 ... *wo sh ...*
business	经商的 *jing-sharng de*
engineering	搞工程的 *gao gong-chung de*
retail	搞零售的 *gao ling-sho de*
sales	搞销售的 *gao shiao-sho de*
Who do you work for ...?	你的雇主是谁? *nee de goo-joo sh shwee*
I work for ...	我的雇主是 ... *wo de goo-joo sh ...*
I'm (a/an) ...	我是 ... *wo sh ...*
accountant	会计师 *kwai-jee-sh*
housewife	家庭主妇 *jia-ting joo-foo*
student	学生 *shüe-shung*
retired	退休了 *twee-shio le*
self-employed	个体户 *ger-tee-hoo*
between jobs	待业人员 *dai-ye-ren-yüan*
What are your interests/ hobbies?	你有什么业余爱好? *nee yo shen-me ye-yü ai-hao*
I like ...	我喜欢 ... *wo shee-hwan ...*
music	音乐 *yin-yüe*
reading	读书 *doo-shoo*
sports	体育 *tee-yü*
I play ...	我参加 ... 活动。 *wo tsan-jia ... huo-dong*
Would you like to play ...?	你喜欢 ... 吗? *nee shee-hwan ... ma*
cards	打牌 *da-pai*
chess	下棋 *shia-chee*

What weather! 瞧这天气!

What a lovely day!	天气真好!	*tian-chee jen-hao*
What awful weather!	天气真糟糕!	*tian-chee jen dsao-gao*
It's cold/hot today!	今天真冷/真热!	
	jin-tian jen lung/jen rer	
Is it usually this warm?	通常都这么暖吗?	
	tong-charng do jer-me nwan ma	
Do you think it's going to … tomorrow?	你认为明天会 … 吗?	
	nee ren-way ming-tian hway … ma	
be a nice day	是个好天	*sh ge hao-tian*
rain	下雨	*shia-yü*
snow	下雪	*shia-shüe*
What is the weather forecast for tomorrow?	明天的天气预报怎么说?	*ming-tian de tian-chee yü-bao dsen-me shuo*
It's …	是 …	*sh …*
cloudy	多云	*duo-yün*
foggy	有雾	*yo-woo*
frosty	有霜	*yo-shwarng*
icy	结冰	*jie-bing*
stormy	雷雨	*lay-yü*
windy	大风	*da-fung*
It's raining.	下雨了。	*shia-yu le*
It's snowing.	下雪了。	*shia-shüe le*
It's sunny.	阳光灿烂。	*yarng-gwarng tsan-lan*
Has the weather been like this for long?	这种天气持续很久了吗?	*jer-jong tian-chee ch-shü hen-jio le ma*
What's the pollen count?	空气中花粉含量是多少?	*kong-chee jong hwaa-fen han-liarng sh duo-shao*
high/medium/low	高/中等/低	*gao/jong-dung/dee*
Will it be good weather for skiing?	有关滑雪的天气预报怎么说?	*yo-gwan hwaa-shüe de tian-chee yü-bao dsen-me shuo*

天气预报	weather forecast

122

Enjoying your trip? 游玩得开心吗?

你们是来度假的吗?	Are you on vacation?
你们是怎么来的的?	How did you get/travel here?
你们住在哪儿?	Where are you staying?
你们在这儿有多久了?	How long have you been here?
你们要住多久?	How long are you staying?
你们已经做了些什么?	What have you done so far?
你们下一步要上哪儿去?	Where are you going next?
你们度假玩得愉快吗?	Are you enjoying your vacation?

I'm here on ...	我来这儿 ... *wo lai jer-r ...*
a business trip	办公事 *ban gong-sh*
vacation [holiday]	度假 *doo-jia*
We came by ...	我们是坐 ... 来的。 *wo-men sh dsuo ... lai de*
train/bus/plane	火车/公共汽车/飞机 *huo-cher/gong-gong-chee-cher/fay-jee*
car/ferry	小轿车/轮渡 *shiao-jiao-cher/lwun-doo*
I have a rental car.	我租了一部车。 *wo dsoo-le yee-boo cher*
We're staying ...	我们住在 ... *wo-men joo-dsai ...*
in an apartment	一套公寓房里 *yee-tao gong-yü-farng lee*
at a hotel/campsite	旅馆里/露营地 *lü-gwan lee/loo-ying-dee*
with friends	朋友家里 *pung-yo jia-lee*
Can you suggest ...?	你能不能推荐 ... ? *nee nung-boo-nung twee-jian ...*
things to do	可做的事情 *ker dsuo de sh-ching*
places to eat	吃饭的地方 *ch-fan de dee-farng*
places to visit	旅游点 *lü-yo dian*
We're having a great/terrible time.	我们这次的旅游太愉快了/太糟糕了。 *wo-men jer-ts de lü-yo tai yü-kwai le/tai dsao-gao le*

Invitations 邀请

Would you like to have dinner with us on …?	… 您能不能来和我们一起吃饭? … *nin nung-boo-nung lai her wo-men yee-chee ch-fan*
May I invite you to lunch?	我想请你吃午饭, 可以吗? *wo shiarng ching nee ch-woo-fan, ker-yee ma*
Can you come for a drink this evening?	今晚跟我们一起去喝一杯, 好吗? *jin-wan gen wo-men yee-chee chü her-yee-bay, hao-ma*
We are having a party. Can you come?	我们要开一个晚会, 你能来吗? *wo-men yao kai yee-ge wan-hway, nee nung lai ma*
May we join you?	我插进来行吗? *wo cha jin-lai shing-ma*
Would you like to join us?	你想和我们一起来吗? *nee shiarng her wo-men yee-chee lai ma*

Going out 外出

What are your plans for …?	你 … 打算干什么? *nee … da-swan gan shen-me*
today / tonight	今天 / 今晚 *jin-tian/jin-wan*
tomorrow	明天 *ming-tian*
Are you free this evening?	今晚你有空吗? *jin-wan nee yo-kong ma*
Would you like to …?	想不想去 … ? *shiarng-boo-shiarng chü …*
go dancing	跳舞 *tiao-woo*
go for a drink	喝一杯 *her-yee-bay*
go out for a meal	出去吃饭 *choo-chü ch-fan*
go for a walk	出去散散步 *choo-chü san-san-boo*
go shopping	逛逛商店 *gwarng gwarng sharng-dian*
I'd like to go to …	我想去 … *wo shiarng chü …*
I'd like to see …	我想看 … *wo shiarng kan …*
Do you enjoy …?	你喜欢 … 吗? *nee shee-hwan … ma*

Accepting/Declining 接受 / 拒绝

Great. I'd love to.	太好了。我一定来。 *tai-hao le. wo yee-ding lai*
Thank you, but I'm busy.	谢谢，可是我没空。 *shie-shie, ker-sh wo may-kong*
May I bring a friend?	我能带个朋友一起来吗? *wo nung dai-ge pung-yo yee-chee lai ma*
Where shall we meet?	我们在哪儿见? *wo-men dsai na-r jian*
I'll meet you ...	我在 ... 跟你会面。 *wo dsai ... gen nee hway-mian*
in front of your hotel	你的旅馆门口 *nee de lü-gwan men-ko*
I'll call for you at 8.	我八点来接你。 *wo ba-dian lai jie nee*
Could we make it a bit later/earlier?	能不能早一点/迟一点? *nung-boo-nung dsao yee-dian/ch yee-dian*
How about another day?	换个日子怎么样? *hwan-ge r-ds dsen-me-yarng*
That will be fine.	那行。 *na shing*

Dining out/in 外出 / 在家吃饭

You may find yourself in a situation where a Chinese person does you a great kindness, such as offers you a seat on a crowded train, lets you borrow a bicycle, or acts as a personal tour guide. In such situations a gift is appropriate and will generally be much appreciated. Many Chinese people study English and will appreciate books and magazines in English. Stamps also make good gifts as stamp collecting is a very popular hobby. Foreign coins and postcards may be of interest too. And a photograph of you and your family will also go down well.

Let me buy you a drink.	我来给你买一杯。 *wo lai gay nee mai yee-bay*
Do you like ...?	你喜欢不喜欢 ...? *nee shee-hwan boo shee-hwan ...*
What are you going to have?	你想要什么? *nee shiarng yao shen-me*
That was a lovely meal.	这顿饭吃得很舒服。 *jer-dwun fan ch-de hen shoo-foo*

TIME ➤ 221

Encounters 交朋友

Do you mind if …?	… 你介意吗?
	… nee jie-yee ma
I sit here/I smoke	我坐这儿/我抽烟
	wo dsuo jer-r/wo cho-yan
Can I get you a drink?	我能给你要一杯饮料吗?
	wo nung gay nee yao yee-bay yin-liao ma
I'd love to have some company.	我很高兴能有人作伴。
	wo hen gao-shing nung yo-ren dsuo-ban
Why are you laughing?	你笑什么? *nee shiao shen-me*
Is my Chinese that bad?	我汉语说得很糟糕吗?
	wo han-yü shuo de hen dsao-gao ma
Shall we go somewhere quieter?	我们要不要换个安静点的地方? *wo-men yao-boo-yao hwan ge an-jing dian de dee-farng*
Leave me alone, please!	请你走吧!
	ching nee dso ba
You look great!	你真漂亮!
	nee jen piao-liarng
Would you like to come back with me?	你愿不愿意和我一道回去? *nee yüan-boo-yüan-yee her wo yee-dao hway-chü*
I'm not ready for that.	我看这不妥当。
	wo kan jer boo tuo-darng
I'm afraid we have to leave now.	不早了, 我们得走了。
	boo dsao le, wo-men day dso le
Thanks for the evening.	谢谢你今晚的陪同。
	shie-shie nee jin-wan de pay-tong
It was great.	我很开心。 *wo hen kai-shin*
Can I see you again tomorrow?	明天我能跟你再见面吗?
	ming-tian wo nung gen nee dsai jian-mian ma
See you soon.	回见。 *hway-jian*
Can I have your address?	能把你的地址给我吗?
	nung ba nee de dee-j gay wo ma

SAFETY ➤ 65

Telephoning 打电话

China's telephone system is undergoing a major overhaul – including the addition of card phones. Most hotel rooms are now equipped with phones, and you can make both international and domestic calls from your hotel room. Local calls are usually free. You can also use street-corner public pay phones or privately run phone booths to make local calls. And long-distance domestic calls can also be made from phone booths, but not usually international calls. For international calls use your hotel or a main telecommunications office – and arrange the call in advance. You will be charged by the minute and given a receipt. Hotels often levy a 30% surcharge on long-distance calls. In telecommunications offices you are normally required to pay a deposit. For international directory assistance ☎ 115.

Can I have your telephone number?	能把你的电话号码告诉我吗? *nung ba nee-de dian-hwaa hao-ma gao-soo wo ma*
Here's my number.	我的号码给你。 *wo-de hao-ma gay nee*
Please call me.	请给我打电话。 *ching gay wo da dian-hwaa*
I'll give you a call.	我会给你打电话的。 *wo hway gay nee da dian-hwaa de*
Where's the nearest telephone booth?	附近哪儿有电话亭? *foo-jin na-r yo dian-hwaa-ting*
May I use your phone?	我可以用一下您的电话吗? *wo ker-yee yong-yee-shia nin de dian-hwaa ma*
It's an emergency.	我有急事儿。 *wo yo jee-sh-er*
I'd like to call someone in England.	我想打个电话去英国。 *wo shiarng da ge dian-hwaa chü ying-guo*
What's the area [dialling] code for …?	… 的地区号是多少? *… de dee-chü hao sh duo-shao*
I'd like a phonecard, please.	请给一张电话卡。 *ching gay yee-jarng dian-hwaa ka*
What's the number for Information [Directory Enquiries]?	要查询台应该拨什么号码? *yao cha-shün-tai ying-gai buo shen-me hao-ma*
I'd like the number for …	请告诉我 … 的号码。 *ching gao-soo wo … de hao-ma*
I'd like to call collect [reverse the charges].	我想要对方付款。 *wo shiarng yao dwee-farng foo-kwan*

Speaking 通话

Hello. This is …	喂，我是 … *way, wo sh …*
I'd like to speak to …	请找一下 … *ching jao yee-shia …*
Extension …	分机号码是 … *fen-jee hao-ma sh …*
Speak louder, please.	请大点声说 *ching da dian shung shuo*
Speak more slowly, please.	请慢点说。 *ching man-dian shuo*
Could you repeat that, please.	请您再说一遍。 *ching nin dsai shuo yee-bian*
I'm afraid he's/she's not in.	对不起，他/她不在。 *dwee-boo-chee, ta/ta boo dsai*
You have the wrong number.	你拨错号码了。 *nee buo tsuo hao-ma le*
Just a moment.	请等一等。 *ching dung-yee-dung*
Hold on, please.	请稍等。 *ching shao-dung*
When will he/she be back?	他/她什么时候回来？ *ta/ta shen-me sh-ho hway-lai*
Will you tell him/her that I called?	能不能告诉他/她我来过电话？ *nung-boo-nung gao-soo ta/ta wo lai-guo dian-hwaa*
My name is …	我叫 … *wo jiao …*
Would you ask him/her to phone me?	您能不能请他/她给我回个电话？ *nin nung-boo-nung ching ta/ta gay wo hway ge dian-hwaa*
I must go now.	我得挂了。 *wo day gwaa le*
Nice to speak to you.	很高兴能跟您说话。 *hen gao-shing nung gen nin shuo-hwaa*
I'll be in touch.	我会保持联系的。 *wo hway bao-ch lian-shee de*
Bye.	再见。 *dsai-jian*

Stores & Services

Stores and services	130	**Hairdresser**	147
Opening hours	132	**Household articles**	148
Service	133	**Jeweler**	149
Preference	134	**Newsstand [News-**	
Decision	135	**agent]/Tobacconist**	150
Paying	136	**Photography**	151
Complaints	137	**Police**	152
Repairs/Cleaning	137	**Lost property/Theft**	153
Bank/Changing		**Post office**	154
money	138	**Souvenirs**	156
Pharmacy	140	**Gifts**	156
Toiletries	142	**Music**	157
Clothing	143	**Toys and games**	157
Color	143	**Antiques**	157
Size	146	**Supermarket/**	
Health and beauty	147	**Minimart**	158

China is undergoing a consumer revolution. More and more stores in the big cities look like those in Hong Kong. However, it is probably still best to look for electronic items in Hong Kong and Singapore. Department stores in cities like Beijing, Shanghai, and Guangzhou offer a wide selection of goods. Friendship stores, originally set up to provide foreigners with luxury items and souvenirs, are today a bit of an anachronism. However, they are still useful places to look for souvenirs.

ESSENTIAL

I'd like ...	我要 ... *wo yao* ...
Do you have ...?	你们有没有 ... ? *nee-men yo-may-yo* ...
How much is that?	那个多少钱? *na-ge duo-shao-chian*
Thank you.	谢谢. *shie-shie*

营业	open
休息	closed
大减价	sale

Stores and services 商店与服务

Where is ...? ... 在哪儿?

Where's the nearest ...?	附近哪儿有 ... ? *foo-jin na-r yo ...*
Where's there a good ...?	哪儿有好一点的 ... ? *na-r yo hao-yee-dian de ...*
Where's the main shopping mall [centre]?	主要的购物中心在哪儿? *joo-yao de go-woo jong-shin dsai na-r*
Is it far from here?	离这儿远吗? *lee jer-r yüan ma*
How do I get there?	去那儿怎么走? *chü na-r dsen-me dso*

Stores 商店

antique store	古玩店 *goo-wan-dian*
bakery	面包店 *mian-bao-dian*
bank	银行 *yin-harng*
bookstore	书店 *shoo-dian*
butcher	肉店 *ro-dian*
camera store	照相器材店 *jao-shiarng chee-tsai dian*
cigarette kiosk [tobacconist]	香烟店 *shiarng-yan-dian*
clothing store [clothes shop]	服装店 *foo-jwarng-dian*
department store	百货商店 *bai-huo-sharng-dian*
drugstore	杂货店 *dsa-huo-dian*
fish store [fishmonger]	水产品店 *shwee-chan-pin-dian*
florist	花店 *hwaa-dian*
gift store	礼品店 *lee-pin-dian*
greengrocer	蔬菜店 *shoo-tsai-dian*
health food store	保健食品店 *bao-jian sh-pin-dian*
jeweler	珠宝店 *joo-bao-dian*
liquor store [off-licence]	酒类专卖店 *jio-lay jwan-mai-dian*

market	集市	*jee-sh*
newsstand [newsagent]	报摊	*bao-tan*
pastry store	点心店	*dian-shin-dian*
pharmacy	药店	*yao-dian*
produce store [grocer]	副食品店 *foo-sh-pin-dian*	
record [music] store	音像店 *yin-shiarng-dian*	
shoe store	鞋店	*shie-dian*
souvenir store	纪念品商店 *jee-nian-pin sharng-dian*	
sporting goods store	体育用品店 *tee-yyong-pin dian*	
supermarket	超级市场	*chao-jee-sh-charng*
toy store	玩具店	*wan-jü-dian*

Services 服务业

clinic	多科诊所 *duo-ker jen-suo*	
dentist	牙医	*ya-yee*
doctor	医生	*yee-shung*
dry cleaner	干洗店 *gan-shee-dian*	
hairdresser/barber	美发厅/理发店 *may-fa-ting/ lee-fa-dian*	
hospital	医院	*yee-yüan*
laundromat	洗衣店 *shee-yee-dian*	
optician	眼镜店 *yan-jing-dian*	
police station	公安局/派出所 *gong-an-jü/pai-choo-suo*	
post office	邮局	*yo-jü*
travel agency	旅行社	*lü-shing-sher*

Opening hours 营业时间

Department stores are normally open from 9 a.m. to 7 p.m. (8 p.m. in summer) seven days a week. Local stores sometimes stay open later.

When does the ... open/close?	... 什么时候开门/关门? ... *shen-me sh-ho kai-men/gwan-men*
Are you open in the evening?	你们晚上营业吗? *nee-men wan-sharng ying-ye ma*
Do you close for lunch?	你们中午休息吗? *nee-men jong-woo shio-shee ma*
Where is the ...?	... 在哪儿? *... dsai na-r*
cashier [cash desk]	付款柜台 *foo-kwan gway-tai*
escalator	自动扶梯 *ds-dong-foo-tee*
elevator [lift]	电梯 *dian-tee*
store directory [guide]	商店示意图 *sharng-dian sh-yee-too*
first [ground (*Brit.*)] floor	一楼 *yee-lo*
second [first (*Brit.*)] floor	二楼 *er-lo*
Where's the ... department?	... 部在哪儿? *... boo dsai na-r*

营业时间	business hours
午休	closed for lunch
全天营业	open all day
入口	entrance
自动扶梯	escalator
出口	exit
紧急出口/安全门	emergency/fire exit
电梯	elevator [lift]
楼梯	stairs

Service 服务

Can you help me?	你能帮个忙吗? *nee-nung barng ge marng ma*
I'm looking for …	我想找 … *wo shiarng jao …*
I'm just browsing.	我只是随便看看。 *wo j-sh swee-bian kan-kan*
It's my turn.	轮到我了。 *lwun dao wo le*
Do you have any …?	你们有没有 …? *nee-men yo-may-yo …*
I'd like to buy …	我想买 …。 *wo shiarng mai …*
Could you show me …?	能不能让我看一下 …? *nung-boo-nung rarng wo kan yee-shia*
How much is this/that?	这/那多少钱? *jer/na duo-shao-chian*
That's all, thanks.	没别的了, 谢谢。 *may bie de le, shie-shie*

您好, 女士/先生。	Good morning/afternoon, madam/sir.
有人关照您了吗?	Are you being served?
您想买点什么?	What would you like?
就这些吗?	Is that everything?
还要别的什么吗?	Anything else?

– *nin shiarng mai shen-me?*
– *boo-mai shen-me, j-sh swee-bian kan-kan.*
– *may-wen-tee.*
– *ching wen yee-shia.*
– *lai le, nin shiarng yao shen-me?*
– *na-ge duo-shao chian?*
– *rarng wo cha-yee-cha … liarng-bai woo-sh yüan.*

顾客服务台	customer service
自选	self-service
减价优惠	clearance

Preference 喜好

I want something …	我想要 … *wo shiarng yao* …
It must be …	必须是 … *bee-shü sh* …
big / small	大的 / 小的 *da-de/shiao-de*
cheap / expensive	便宜的 / 贵的 *pian-yee de/gway-de*
dark / light (color)	深色的 / 浅色的 *shen-ser de/chian-ser de*
light / heavy	轻的 / 重的 *ching-de/jong-de*
oval / round / square	椭圆的 / 圆的 / 方的 *tuo-yüan de/yüan de/farng de*
genuine / imitation	真的 / 仿制的 *jen de/farng-j de*
I don't want anything too expensive.	太贵的我不要。 *tai-gway de wo boo-yao*
In the region of … yuan.	… 元左右。 *… yüan dsuo-yo*

您要哪种 … ?	What … would you like?
颜色 / 形状	color / shape
质量 / 数量	quality / quantity
您要哪种类型的?	What sort would you like?
您想买哪种价格档次的?	What price range are you thinking of?

Do you have anything …?	你们有没有 …? *nee-men yo-may-yo* …
larger / smaller	大点的 / 小点的 *da-dian de/shiao-dian de*
better quality / cheaper	质量好点的 / 更便宜点的 *j-liarng hao-dian de/gung pian-yee dian de*
Can you show me …?	我能不能看看 …? *wo nung-boo-nung kan-kan* …
that / this one	那个 / 这个 *na-ge/jer-ge*
these / those ones	这些 / 那些 *jer-shie/na-shie*
the one in the window / display case	橱窗里的 / 陈列柜里的 *choo-chwarng lee de/chen-lie-gway lee de*
some others	其它的 *chee-ta de*

COLORS ➤ 143

Conditions of purchase 购货条件

Is there a guarantee?	有没有保用证？ *yo-may-yo bao-yong jung*
Are there any instructions with it?	有没有使用说明？ *yo-may-yo sh-yong shuo-ming*

Out of stock 缺货

对不起，我们店里没有。	I'm sorry, we haven't any.
我们缺货。	We're out of stock.
想不想看看别的牌子/ 另外一种？	Can I show you something else/ a different sort?
想要我们替您订购吗？	Shall we order it for you?

Can you order it for me?	你能不能为我订一个？ *nee nung-boo-nung way wo ding yee-ge*
How long will it take?	需要多久才能到货？ *shü-yao duo-jio tsai-nung dao-huo*
Is there another store that sells …?	还有哪家商店能买到 …？ *hai-yo na-jia sharng-dian nung mai dao …*

Decision 拿主意

That's not quite what I want.	我想要的不是这个。 *wo shiarng yao de boo-sh jer-ge*
No, I don't like it.	这个我不喜欢。 *jer-ge wo boo shee-hwan*
That's too expensive.	太贵了。*tai-gway le*
I'd like to think about it.	我再考虑一下。*wo dsai kao-lü yee-shia*
I'll take it.	我买了。*wo mai le*

– *nee-hao, wo sharng mai yee-jian*
  mian-mao-shan.
– *hao-de, yao shen-me yan-ser de?*
– *yao chung ser de. kwan-song yee-dian de.*
– *jer-jian dsen-me-yarng? yee-bai-woo-sh kwai …*
– *hmm, jer boo-sh wo shiarng yao de, shie-shie le.*

Paying 付款

Credit cards are accepted in more and more tourist areas; look out for the familiar emblems in hotels, restaurants and department stores. A 4% commission is charged on credit card purchases. Traveler's checks [cheques] are accepted at currency exchange counters of hotels and stores almost everywhere in China.

Where do I pay?	在哪儿付款? *dsai na-r foo-kwan*
How much is that?	这多少钱? *jer duo-shao chian*
Could you write it down, please?	请您写下来, 好吗? *ching nin shie-shia-lai, hao-ma*
Do you accept traveler's checks [cheques]?	你们收不收旅行支票? *nee-men sho-boo-sho lü-shing j-piao*
I'll pay by ...	我用 ... 支付 *wo yong ... j-foo*
cash	现金 *shian-jin*
credit card	信用卡 *shin-yong-ka*
I don't have any smaller change.	我没有零钱。 *wo may-yo ling-chian*
Sorry, I don't have enough money.	对不起, 我钱不够。 *dwee-boo-chee, wo chian boo-go*

你用什么方式支付?	How are you paying?
签帐请求没批准。	This transaction has not been approved / accepted.
这张信用卡失效了。	This card is not valid.
你有没有其它证件让我看看?	May I have further identification?
有没有面值小一点的钱?	Do you have any smaller change?

Could I have a receipt, please?	请给个收据。 *ching gay ge sho-jü*
I think you've given me the wrong change.	你好象找错钱了。 *nee hao-shiarng jao tsuo chian le*

付款处	Please pay here.
行窃必究	Shoplifters will be prosecuted.

136

Complaints 投诉

This doesn't work.	这个失灵了。 *jer-ge sh-ling le*
Can you exchange this, please?	请给换一个。 *ching gay hwan yee-ge*
I'd like a refund.	我要求退款。 *wo yao-chio twee-kwan*
Here's the receipt.	收据给你。 *sho-jü gay-nee*
I don't have the receipt.	我没有收据。 *wo may-yo sho-jü*
I'd like to see the manager.	我要见你们的经理。 *wo yao jian nee-men de jing-lee*

Repairs/Cleaning 修理/清洗

Hotels provide quick and efficient laundry and dry-cleaning services. Laundry is usually returned within 24 hours, but dry-cleaning may take an extra day in all but the biggest hotels.

This is broken. Can you repair it?	这个坏了。你们能修吗? *jer-ge hwai le, nee-men nung shio ma*
Do you have … for this?	你们有没有合适的 …? *nee-men yo-may-yo her-sh de …*
a battery	电池 *dian-ch*
replacement parts	备用零件 *bay-yong ling-jian*
There's something wrong with …	… 出毛病了 *… choo-mao-bing le*
Can you … this?	你们能不能给 …? *nee-men nung-boo-nung gay …*
clean	清洗一下 *ching-shee yee-shia*
press	熨一熨 *yün-yee-yün*
patch	补一补 *boo-yee-boo*
Could you alter this?	能不能改一改? *nung-boo-nung gai-yee-gai*
When will it be ready?	什么时候能取? *shen-me sh-ho nung-chü*
This isn't mine.	这不是我的。 *jer boo-sh wo de*
There's … missing.	… 不见了。 *… boo-jian le*

TIME ➤ 221; DATE ➤ 219

Bank/Currency exchange
银行/外币兑换处

Banks in hotels are open from 7:30 or 8 a.m. to around 7 p.m. with a break for lunch. In large hotels exchange facilities stay open later. The Chinese currency is called **RMB** (**renminbi**), or "People's Money" ➤ 139. Foreign currency and traveler's checks [cheques] may be exchanged in hotels and Friendship stores with a passport. Remember to keep your exchange receipts in case you want to convert any leftover **RMB** when leaving the country.

各类业务	all transactions
外币兑换	currency exchange
营业/休息	open/closed
出纳员	cashiers

Where's the nearest …?	附近哪儿有 …? *foo-jin na-r yo …*
bank	银行 *yin-harng*
currency exchange office [bureau de change]	外币兑换处 *wai-bee dwee-hwan-choo*

Changing money 兑换外币

Can I exchange foreign currency here?	这儿能兑换外币吗? *jer-r nung dwee-hwan wai-bee ma*
I'd like to change some dollars/pounds into renminbi.	我想用美元/英镑换些人民币。 *wo shiarng yong may-yüan/ying-barng hwan shie ren-min-bee*
I want to cash some traveler's checks [cheques].	我想用旅行支票兑些现金。 *wo shiarng yong lü-shing-j-piao dwee shie shian-jin*
What's the exchange rate?	兑换率是多少? *dwee-hwan-lü sh duo-shao*
How much commission do you charge?	你们收多少手续费? *nee-men sho duo-shao sho-shü-fay*
Could I have some small change, please?	请给我一些零钱。 *ching gay wo yee-shie ling-chian*
I've lost my traveler's checks. These are the numbers.	我的旅行支票丢了。这是支票号码。 *wo de lü-shing-j-piao dio le. jer-sh j-piao hao-ma*

Security 查验身分

我能看看 ... 吗?	Could I see ...?
您的护照	your passport
您的身分证件	some identification
您的银行卡	your bank card
您的地址是什么?	What's your address?
您住在哪儿?	Where are you staying?
请填一下这张表。	Fill out this form, please.
请在这儿签名。	Please sign here.

ATMs [Cash machines] 自动提款机

Can I withdraw money on my credit card here?
这儿可以用信用卡取钱吗?
jer-r ker-yee yong shin-yong-ka chü-chian ma

Where are the ATMs [cash machines]
哪儿有自动提款机?
na-r yo ds-dong tee-kwan jee

Can I use my ... card in the cash machine?
我能用 ... 卡从提款机中取钱吗?
wo nung yong ... ka tsong tee-kwan-jee jong chü-chian ma

The cash machine has eaten my card.
提款机把我的卡吃进去了。
tee-kwan-jee ba wo-de ka ch-jin-chü le

自动提款机	automated teller (ATM) [cash machine]

Currency	The Chinese currency is **RMB (renminbi)**. The monetary unit is the **yuan** (元), which is divided into **jiao** and **fen**.
1 yuan = 10 jiao	1 元 = 10 角
1 jiao = 10 fen	1 角 = 10 分

Pharmacy 药店

It is difficult or impossible to find many Western items in Chinese pharmacies. So be sure to take any essential medications with you. To avoid problems at customs, make sure all medication is clearly marked and in its original prescription bottle.

Where's the nearest pharmacy?	附近哪儿有药店? *foo-jin na-r yo yao-dian*
What time does the pharmacy open/close?	药店什么时候开门/关门? *yao-dian shen-me sh-ho* *kai-men/gwan-men*
Can you make up this prescription for me?	请您按这张处方给我配药。 *ching nin an jer-jarng choo-farng* *gay wo pay-yao*
Shall I wait?	是不是等一会就行? *sh-boo-sh dung-yee-hway jio shing*
I'll come back for it.	我回头来取。 *wo hway-tou lai-chü*

Dosage instructions 剂量说明

How much should I take?	我一次服多少? *wo yee-ts foo duo-shao*
How often should I take it?	几小时服一次? *jee shiao-sh foo yee-ts*
Is it suitable for children?	这儿童能服吗? *jer er-tong nung foo ma*

服 …	Take …
… 片	… tablets
… 汤匙	… teaspoons
饭前/饭后	before/after meals
用凉开水送服	with cooled boiled water
整个	whole
上午/夜里	in the morning/at night
连续服用 … 天	for … days

DOCTOR ➤ 161

仅供外用	for external use only
不可内服	not to be taken internally

Asking advice 请教药剂师

What would you recommend for …?	… 您建议吃点什么药? … nin jian-yee ch-dian shen-me yao
a cold	感冒 gan-mao
a cough	咳嗽 ker-so
diarrhea	痢疾 lee-jee
a hangover	酒后不适症 jio-ho boo-sh-jung
hay fever	花粉病 hwaa-fen-bing
insect bites	蚊叮虫咬 wen-ding chong-yao
a sore throat	嗓子疼 sarng-ds tung
sunburn	晒伤 shai-sharng
motion [travel] sickness	晕车 yün-cher
an upset stomach	肠胃不适 charng-way boo-sh
Can I get it without a prescription?	不要医生处方也能买吗? boo-yao yee-shung choo-farng ye-nung mai ma

Over-the-counter treatment 无需医生处方的常用药

Can I have …?	请给我一点 … ching gay wo yee-dian …
antiseptic cream	消毒药膏 shiao-doo yao-gao
aspirin	阿斯匹林 a-s-pee-lin
gauze [bandages]	绷带 bung-dai
condoms	避孕套 bee-yün-tao
cotton [cotton wool]	脱脂棉 tuo-j-mian
insect repellent	驱蚊剂 chü-wen-jee
painkillers	止痛片 j-tong-pian
vitamin tablets	维生素片 way-shung-soo-pian

Toiletries 化妆品

I'd like some ...	我想买点 ... *wo shiarng mai dian ...*
after-shave	须后水 *shü-ho-shwee*
after-sun lotion	日光浴后护肤液 *r-gwarng-yü ho hoo-foo-ye*
deodorant	除汗臭剂 *choo-han-cho jee*
razor blades	刀片 *dao-pian*
sanitary napkins [towels]	卫生巾 *way-shung-jin*
soap	香皂 *shiarng-dsao*
sun block	防晒膏 *farng-shai-gao*
sunscreen	防晒霜 *farng-shai-shwarng*
factor ...	系数 ... *shee shoo ...*
tampons	月经棉塞 *yüe-jing mian-sai*
tissues	纸面巾 *j-mian-jin*
toilet paper	卫生纸 *way-shung-j*
toothbrush	牙刷 *ya-shwaa*
toothpaste	牙膏 *ya-gao*

Haircare 护发用品

comb	梳子 *shoo-ds*
conditioner	护发素 *hoo-fa-soo*
hair mousse/gel	摩斯 *muo-s*
hair spray	喷发定型剂 *pen-fa ding-shing-jee*
shampoo	洗发膏 *shee-fa-gao*

For the baby 婴儿用品

baby food	婴儿食品 *ying-er sh-pin*
baby wipes	婴儿擦洗巾 *ying-er tsa-shee-jin*
diapers [nappies]	尿片 *niao-pian*
sterilizing solution	消毒液 *shiao-doo-ye*

Clothing 服装

You will find all manner of clothing, much very reasonably priced, for sale in the Friendship stores, street markets (be prepared to bargain), and local department stores. In the chic, expensive boutiques that are springing up in the large cities you will find famous brand-name items from international fashion houses – at a price.

女装	ladieswear
男装	menswear
童装	childrenswear

General 一般用语

| I'd like … | 我要 … *wo yao …* |
| Do you have any …? | 你们有没有 …? *nee-men yo-may-yo …* |

Color 颜色

I'm looking for something in …	我想要 … 的。 *wo shiarng yao … de*
beige	米色 *mee-ser*
black / white	黑色/白色 *hay-ser/bai-ser*
blue / green	蓝色/绿色 *lan-ser/lü-ser*
brown	棕色 *dsong-ser*
gray	灰色 *hway-ser*
orange	橘黄色 *jü-hwarng-ser*
purple	紫色 *ds-ser*
red / pink	红色/粉红色 *hong-ser/fen-hong-ser*
yellow	黄色 *hwarng-ser*
light …	浅 … *chian …*
dark …	深 … *shen …*
I want a darker/lighter shade.	我要更深/更浅一点的。 *wo yao gung shen / gung chian yee-dian de*
Do you have the same in …?	有没有跟这个一样但颜色是 … 的? *yo-may-yo gen jer-ge yee-yarng dan yan-ser sh … de*

belt	皮带 *pee-dai*
bikini	比基尼 (三点式)游泳衣 *bee-jee-nee (san-dian-sh)* yo-yong-yee*
blouse	女衬衫 *nü-chen-shan*
bra	胸罩 *shiong-jao*
briefs	短内裤 *dwan-nay-koo*
cap	帽子 *mao-ds*
coat	外衣 *wai-yee*
dress	连衣裙 *lian-yee-chün*
handbag	手提包 *sho-tee-bao*
hat	帽子 *mao-ds*
jacket	夹克衫 *jia-ker-shan*
jeans	牛仔裤 *nio-dsai-koo*
leggings	绑腿 *barng-twee*
pants (U.S.)	长裤 *charng-koo*
pantyhose [tights]	裤袜 *koo-waa*
raincoat	雨衣 *yü-yee*
scarf	围巾 *way-jin*
shirt	衬衫 *chen-shan*
shorts	短裤 *dwan-koo*
skirt	裙子 *chün-ds*
socks	袜子 *wa-ds*
stockings	长统袜 *charng-tong-wa*
suit	西服 *shee-foo*
sweater	套衫 *tao-shan*
sweatshirt	棉毛衫 *mian-mao-shan*
swimming trunks/swimsuit	游泳裤/游泳衣 *yo-yong-koo/yo-yong-yee*
T-shirt	T 恤衫 *tee-shü-shan*
tie	领带 *ling-dai*
trousers	长裤 *charng-koo*
underpants	内裤 *nay-koo*
with long/short sleeves	长袖/短袖 *charng-shio/dwan-shio*
with a V-/round neck	V 型领/圆领 *vee-shing-ling/yüan-ling*

Shoes 鞋类

boots	靴子	*shüe-ds*
flip-flops	人字拖鞋	*ren-ds tuo-shie*
running [training] shoes	运动鞋	*yün-dong-shie*
sandals	凉鞋	*liarng-shie*
shoes	鞋	*shie*
slippers	拖鞋	*tuo-shie*

Walking / Hiking gear 行走/远足用具

knapsack	背包	*bay-bao*
hiking boots	长途行走靴	*charng-too shing-dso-shüe*
waterproof jacket / anorak	防水夹克衫	*farng-shwee jia-ker-shan*
windbreaker [cagoule]	连帽防风衣	*lian-mao farng-fung-yee*

Fabric 织物

I want something in …	我想要 … 的。	*wo shiarng yao … de*
cotton	棉	*mian*
denim	牛仔布料	*nio-dsai-boo-liao*
lace	花边	*hwaa-bian*
leather	皮革	*pee-ger*
linen	亚麻布	*ya-ma-boo*
wool	毛	*mao*
Is this …?	这是不是 …?	*jer-sh-boo-sh …*
pure cotton	纯棉的	*chwun-mian de*
synthetic	人造的	*ren-dsao de*
Is it hand / machine washable?	可以手洗/用洗衣机洗吗?	*ker-yee sho-shee/yong shee-yee-jee shee-ma*

只能干洗	dry clean only
只能手洗	handwash only
不可熨烫	do not iron
不褪色	colorfast

Does it fit? 是否合身?

Can I try this on?	我可以试穿吗? *wo ker-yee sh-chwan ma*
Where's the fitting room?	试衣间在哪儿? *sh-yee jian dsai na-r*
It fits well. I'll take it.	正合身。我买了。 *jung her-sh. wo mai le*
It doesn't fit.	这不合身。 *jer boo her-shen*
It's too…	太 … *tai*
short/long	短/长 *dwan/charng*
tight/loose	紧/松 *jin/song*
Do you have this in size …?	这个有没有 … 号的? *jer-ge yo-may-yo … hao de*
What size is this?	这是什么尺寸的? *jer-sh shen-me ch-tswun de*
Could you measure me, please?	请给我量一量尺寸。 *ching gay wo liarng-yee-liarng ch-tswun*
I don't know Chinese sizes.	我不熟悉中国的尺寸。 *wo boo shoo-shee jong-guo de ch-tswun*

Size 尺寸

Clothing sizes in China are still being standardized, and do not correspond to those in the West. In Friendship stores, and places where clothes are made for export, you will find sizes given as small, medium, and large. However, you may find these are of a smaller cut than you would find at home.

Chinese measurements combine two factors, one of which is height. For example, a jacket may be sized 165-88, i.e., for a person 1 meter, 65 centimeters tall, who has an 88-centimeter chest measurement.

When buying shoes the safest way is to try them on, if you can find any large enough – U.S. 7 $\frac{1}{2}$/U.K. 6 is considered large!

extra large (XL)	特大号
large (L)	大号
medium (M)	中号
small (S)	小号

1 centimeter (cm.) = 0.39 in.	1 inch = 2.54 cm.
1 meter (m.) = 39.37 in.	1 foot = 30.5 cm.
10 meters = 32.81 ft.	1 yard = 0.91 m.

Health and beauty 保健与美容

I'd like a ...	我想做一下 ... *wo shiarng dsuo yee-shia ...*
facial	美容 *may-rong*
manicure	修指甲 *shio-j-jia*
massage	按摩 *an-muo*
waxing	热蜡脱毛 *rer-la tuo-mao*

Hairdresser/Hairstylist 美发厅

The larger hotels usually have a hairdresser and a barber. The service is good and cheap by Western standards. The treatment may also include a scalp and neck massage, which is most relaxing. Tipping is not permitted.

I'd like to make an appointment for ...	我想约个时间来 ... *wo shiarng yüe ge sh-jian lai ...*
Can you make it a bit earlier/later?	能不能早点/迟点? *nung-boo-nung dsao-dian/ch-dian*
I'd like a ...	我要 ... *wo yao ...*
cut and blow-dry	剪短吹干 *jian-dwan chwee-gan*
shampoo and set	洗头加定型 *shee-tou jia ding-shing*
trim	修一修 *shio-yee-shio*
I'd like my hair ...	请把我的头发 ... *ching ba wo-de tou-fa ...*
highlighted	用浅色染一染 *yong chian-ser ran-yee-ran*
permed	烫一烫 *tarng-yee-tarng*
Don't cut it too short.	不要剪得太短。 *boo-yao jian-de tai dwan*
A little more off the ...	... 再多去掉一点。 *... dsai duo chü-diao yee-dian*
back/front	后面/前面 *ho-mian/chian-mian*
neck/sides	脖子上/两边 *buo-ds-sharng/liarng-bian*
top	头顶 *tou-ting*
That's fine, thanks.	这样很好, 谢谢。 *jer-yarng hen-hao, shie-shie*

Household articles 日常家用品

I'd like a(n)/some … 我要 … wo yao …

adapter	电源转接器	dian-yüan jwan-jie-chee
alumin(i)um foil	铝箔	lü-buo
bottle opener	开瓶器	kai-ping-chee
can [tin] opener	开罐头刀	kai-gwan-tou-dao
clothes pins [pegs]	衣夹	yee-jia
corkscrew	瓶塞钻	ping-sai dswan
light bulb	灯泡	dung-pao
matches	火柴	huo-chai
paper napkins	纸巾	j-jin
plastic wrap [cling film]	保鲜纸	bao-shian-j
plug	插头	cha-tou
scissors	剪刀	jian-dao
screwdriver	螺丝刀	luo-s-dao

Cleaning items 洗涤用品

bleach	漂白剂	piao-bai-jee
detergent [washing powder]	洗衣粉	shee-yee-fen
dish cloth	擦碗碟巾	tsa-die-jin
dishwashing [washing-up] liquid	餐具洗涤剂	tsan-jü shee-dee-jee
garbage [refuse] bags	垃圾袋	la-jee-dai
sponge	海绵	hai-mian

Crockery / Cutlery 碗碟 / 餐具

cups / glasses	杯子	bay-ds
knives / forks	刀 / 叉	dao/cha
spoons	调羹	tiao-gung
mugs	茶杯	cha-bay
plates	盘子	pan-ds
bowls	碗	wan
chopsticks	筷子	kwai-ds

Jeweler 珠宝店

Could I see ...?	我能看看 ... 吗?
	wo nung kan-kan ... ma
this/that	这个 / 那个 *jer-ge / na-ge*
It's in the window/display cabinet.	在橱窗 / 陈列柜里。
	dsai choo-chwarng / chen-lie gway lee
alarm clock	闹钟 *nao-jong*
battery	电池 *dian-ch*
bracelet	手镯 *sho-juo*
brooch	胸针 *shiong-jen*
chain	手链 *sho-lian*
clock	钟 *jong*
earrings	耳环 *er-hwan*
necklace	项链 *shiarng-lian*
ring	戒指 *jie-j*
watch	手表 *sho-biao*

Materials 材料

Is this real silver/gold?	这是真银 / 真金的吗?
	jue-sh jen-yin / jen-jin de ma
Is there a certificate for it?	有没有凭证? *yo-may-yo ping-jung*
Do you have anything in ...?	你们有没有 ... 的?
	nee-men yo-may-yo ... de
copper	铜 *tong*
crystal	水晶 *shwee-jing*
cut glass	雕花玻璃 *diao-hwaa buo-lee*
diamond	钻石 *dswan-shee*
enamel	珐琅 *fa-larng*
gold	金 *jin*
gold-plate	镀金 *doo-jin*
pearl	珍珠 *jen-joo*
platinum	白金 *bai-jin*
silver	银 *yin*
silver-plate	镀银 *doo-yin*
stainless steel	不锈钢 *boo-shio-garng*

Newsstand [Newsagent] / Tobacconist 报刊店 / 香烟专卖店

The *China Daily* is China's official English-language newspaper and is available in most major cities. In Shanghai you will also find the *Shanghai Star*. In large cities it is also possible to find English-language magazines like *Time*, *Newsweek*, *The Far Eastern Economic Review,* and *The Economis*t, as well as European magazines and newspapers like the *International Herald Tribune*. Hotels are the best source for these, though Friendship stores may also stock copies. Outside the major cities, however, English-language books and magazines are not readily available. So it is wise to bring your own.

Do you sell English-language books / newspapers?	你们出售英文书刊 / 报纸吗? *nee-men choo-sho ying-wen shoo-kan/bao-j ma*
I'd like (a) …	我要买 … *wo yao mai …*
book	书 *shoo*
candy [sweets]	糖果 *tarng-guo*
chewing gum	口香糖 *ko-shiarng-tarng*
chocolate bar	一条巧克力 *yee-tiao chiao-ker-lee*
cigarettes (packet of)	(一包) 香烟 *yee-bao shiarng-yan*
cigars	雪茄烟 *sh-jia-yan*
dictionary	词典 *ts-dian*
English-Chinese	英汉 *ying-han*
envelopes	信封 *shin-fung*
guidebook of …	… 的导游手册 *… de dao-yo sho-tser*
lighter	打火机 *da-huo-jee*
magazine	杂志 *dsa-j*
map	地图 *dee-too*
map of the town	市区图 *sh-chü-too*
road map of …	… 公路图 *… gong-loo too*
matches	火柴 *huo-chai*
newspaper	报纸 *bao-j*
American / English	美国 / 英国 *may-guo/ying-guo*
paper / pen	纸 / 笔 *j/bee*
stamps	邮票 *yo-piao*
tobacco	烟丝 *yan-s*

Photography 照相器材

I'm looking for a … camera.	我想买一部 … 照相机。 *wo-shiarng mai yee-boo … jao-shiarng-jee*
automatic	自动 *ds-dong*
compact	袖珍式 *shio-jen-sh*
disposable	一次性 *yee-ts-shing*
SLR	单镜反射式 *dan-jing fan-sher-sh*
I'd like a(n) …	我要买 … *wo yao mai …*
battery	电池 *dian-ch*
camera case	照相机护套 *jao-shiarng-jee hoo-tao*
electronic flash	闪光灯 *shan-gwarng-dung*
filter	滤色镜 *lü-ser-jing*
lens	镜头 *jing-tou*
lens cap	镜头盖 *jing-tou-gai*

Film / Processing 胶卷 / 冲洗胶卷

I'd like a … film.	我要一个 … 胶卷。 *wo yao yee-ge … jiao-jüan*
black and white	黑白 *hay-bai*
color	彩色 *tsai-ser*
24/36 exposures	24 张 / 36 张的 *er-sh-s jarng / san-sh-lio jarng de*
I'd like this film developed, please.	请给我冲洗这个胶卷。 *ching gay wo chong-shee jer-ge jiao-jüan*
Would you enlarge this, please?	可以把这张放大吗? *ker-yee ba jer-jarng farng-da ma*
How much do … exposures cost?	冲洗一卷 … 张的胶卷多少钱? *chong-shee yee-jüan … jarng de jiao-jüan duo-shao-chian*
When will the photos be ready?	什么时候能取? *shen-me sh-ho nung chü*
I'd like to collect my photos.	我来取照片。 *wo lai chü jao-pian*
Here's the receipt.	给你收据。 *gay nee sho-jü*

151

Police 警察

Armed police wear green uniforms and peaked caps displaying the national insignia of China. Tourists often confuse the police with members of the air force, whose uniform is identical except for the cap, which has a red star.

Where's the nearest police station?	附近哪儿有公安局/派出所? *foo-jin na-r yo gong-an-jü/pai-choo-suo*
Does anyone here speak English?	这儿有人会说英语吗? *jer-r yo-ren hway-shuo ying-yü ma*
I want to report a(n) …	我要报告一起 … *wo yao bao-gao yee-chee …*
accident/attack	事故/行凶案 *sh-goo / shing-shiong-an*
mugging/rape	抢劫/强奸案 *chiarng-jie / chiarng-jian-an*
My child is missing.	我的孩子失踪了。 *wo de hai-ds sh-dsong le*
Here's a photo of him/her.	这是她/他的照片。 *jer-sh ta / ta de jao-pian*
Someone's following me.	有人跟踪我。*yo-ren gen-dsong wo*
I need an English-speaking lawyer.	我需要一位会说英语的律师。*wo shü-yao yee-way hway shuo ying-yü de lü-sh*
I need to make a phone call.	我要打个电话。 *wo yao da-ge dian-hwaa*
I need to contact the … Consulate.	我需要跟 … 领事馆联系。 *wo shü-yao gen … ling-sh-gwan lian-shee*
American/British	美国/英国 *may-guo / ying-guo*

你能不能描述一下他/她什么样?	Can you describe him/her?
男的/女的	male/female
有胡须/没有胡须	with beard/without beard
红头发/头发花白	red-headed/gray [grey] haired
长头发/短头发/秃顶	long/short hair/balding
身高大约 …	approximate height …
年龄 … (左右)	aged (approximately) …
他/她穿的是 …	He/She was wearing …

CLOTHES ➤ 144; COLOR ➤ 143

Lost property/Theft 丢失财物 / 失窃

I want to report a theft.	我要报告一起偷窃案。 *wo yao bao-gao yee-chee* *tou-chie-an*
My car's been broken into.	我的汽车被人撬开了东西。 *wo de chee-cher bay-ren chiao-kai tou le* *dong-shee*
I've been robbed/mugged.	我被人抢劫了。*wo bay-ren chiarng-jie le*
I've lost my …	我的 … 丢了。 *wo de … dio le*
My … has been stolen.	我的 … 被人偷掉了。 *wo de … bay-ren tou-diao le*
bicycle	自行车 *ds-shing-cher*
camera	照相机 *jao-shiarng-jee*
rental car	租来的汽车 *dsoo-lai de chee-cher*
credit cards	信用卡 *shin-yong-ka*
handbag	手提包 *sho-tee-bao*
money	钱 *chian*
passport	护照 *hoo-jao*
purse/wallet	钱包 *chiao-bao*
ticket	票 *piao*
watch	手表 *sho-biao*
What shall I do?	我该怎么办呢？*wo gai dsen-me-ban ne*
I need a police report for my insurance claim.	我需要一份保险索赔用的警察证明。 *wo shü-yao yee-fen bao-shian suo-pay* *yong de jing-cha jung-ming*

丢失了什么？	What's missing?
什么东西被抢 / 偷走了？	What's been taken?
什么时候被偷的？	When was it stolen?
事情是什么时候发生的？	When did it happen?
你现在住在哪儿？	Where are you staying?
是从哪儿被偷走的？	Where was it taken from?
当时你在哪儿？	Where were you at the time?
我们正在给你找个翻译。	We're getting an interpreter for you.
我们要调查这件事。	We'll look into the matter.
请填一下表。	Please fill out this form.

Post office 邮局

As well as local post offices, there are branch post offices in nearly all major tourist hotels where you can send postcards, letters, and packages (the contents will be checked by the post office staff before mailing, so don't seal it until it has been checked). Hotel branches are open from 8 a.m. to 6 p.m. Monday through Saturday, and on Sunday mornings from 8 a.m. to noon. Cheaper hotels normally allow you to mail letters from the front desk. Both the international and domestic postal services are efficient and reliable. However, you may find that postal rates differ from one post office to another.

General queries 一般询问

Where is the post office?	邮局在哪儿? *yo-jü dsai na-r*
What time does the post office open/close?	邮局什么时候开门 / 关门? *yo-jü shen-me sh-ho kai-men / gwan-men*
Does it close for lunch?	午休时间关门吗? *woo-shio sh-jian gwan-men ma*
Where's the mailbox [postbox]?	哪儿有邮筒? *na-r yo yo-tong*
Is there any mail for me?	有我的信件吗? *yo wo de shin-jian ma*

Buying stamps 买邮票

A stamp for this postcard, please.	请给我一张寄明信片的邮票。 *ching gay wo yee-jarng jee ming-shin-pian de yo-piao*
A ...yuan stamp, please.	请给我一张 ... 元的邮票。 *ching gay wo yee-jarng ... yüan de yo-piao*
What's the postage for a letter to ...?	寄到 ... 的信邮资是多少? *jee dao ... de shin yo-ds sh duo-shao*

– nee hao, wo shiarng jee jer-shie ming-shing-pian
    chü may-guo.
        – jee jarng?
        – jio-jarng.
– na jio-sh liarng yüan chung jio: yee gong sh-ba yüan.

Sending packages 寄包裹

I want to send this package [parcel] by …	这个包裹请寄 … *jer-ge bao-guo ching jee …*
airmail	航空 *harng-kong*
special delivery [express]	特快专递 *ter-kwai jwan-dee*
registered mail	挂号 *gwaa-hao*
It contains …	里面装了 … *lee-mian jwarng le …*

请填一下海关申报表。	Please fill out the customs declaration.
包裹值多少钱?	What's the value?
里面装了什么?	What's inside?

Telecommunications 电讯

Phonecards come in denominations of 20, 50, and 100 yuan, but can only be used in the province you buy them. There are also cards that can be used throughout China, which cost 200 yuan, called **chüan-guo-ka**. Most major hotels have a business center with telephone, fax, and telex services, and probably photocopiers, typewriters, and even computers.

I'd like a phonecard, please.	请给我一张电话磁卡。 *ching gay wo yee-jarng dian-hwaa-ts-ka*
20/50/100 yuan, please.	20/50/100 元的。 *er-sh/woo-sh/yee-bai yüan de*
Do you have a photocopier?	你们有复印机吗? *nee-men yo foo-yin-jee ma*
I'd like to send a message …	我想送一份 … *wo shiarng song yee-fen …*
by e-mail/fax	电子邮件 / 传真 *dian-ds yo-jian / chwan-jen*
What's your e-mail address?	你的电子邮件地址是什么? *nee de dian-ds yo-jian dee-j sh shen-me*
Can I access the Internet here?	这里能联上因特网吗? *jer-lee nung lian-sharng yin-ter-warng ma*
What are the charges per hour?	每小时收费多少? *may shiao-sh sho-fay duo-shao*

包裹	packages
邮件待领处	general delivery [poste restante]
邮票	stamps
电报	telegrams

Souvenirs 纪念品

You will have no difficulty finding any number of souvenirs and presents to take home. There is something for everybody and in every price range. However, a word of warning, there is a thriving counterfeiting industry in operation – selling cheap forgeries: coins, cassette players, watches, cigarettes, as well as expensive ones: jade and antiques. So take care – and with antiques get an official certificate of verification.

cheongsam*	旗袍	chee-pao
vase	花瓶	hwaa-ping
silk	丝绸	s-cho
porcelain	陶瓷	tao-ts
handicrafts	手工艺品	sho-gong-yee-pin
four treasures of the study**	文房四宝	wen-farng-s-bao
jade jewelry	翡翠首饰	fay-tswee sho-sh
fans	工艺扇	gong-yee-shan
tea	茶	cha

* a close-fitting woman's dress with a hight neck and slit skirt

** an ink slab, ink stick, calligraphy brush, and paper

Gifts 礼品

bottle of wine	一瓶酒	yee-ping-jio
box of Chinese sweets	盒装水果糖	her-jwarng shwee-guo-tarng
calendar	挂历	gwaa-lee
key ring	钥匙圈	yao-sh-chüan
postcard	明信片	ming-shin-pian
souvenir guidebook	纪念品说明册	jee-nian-pin shuo-ming tser
tea towel	茶巾	cha-jin
T-shirt	T 恤衫	tee-shü-shan

Music 音乐

I'd like a ...	我要买 ... *wo yao mai ...*
cassette	一盒磁带 *yee-her ts-dai*
compact disc	一张 CD 唱盘 *yee-jarng see-dee charng-pan*
record	一张唱片 *yee-jarng charng-pian*
videocassette	一盘录像带 *yee-pan loo-shiarng-dai*
Who are the popular native singers/bands?	本国有哪些流行歌星和乐队? *ben-guo yo na-shie lio-shing ger-shing her yüe-dwee*

Toys and games 玩具和游戏

I'd like a toy/game ...	我想买一个 ... 玩具 / 游戏。 *wo shiarng mai yee-ge ...* *wan-jü/yo-shee*
for a boy	男孩的 *nan-hai wan-de*
for a 5-year-old girl	5 岁女孩玩的 *woo-swee nü-hai wan-de*
ball	球 *chio*
chess set	象棋 *shiarng-chee*
doll	洋娃娃 *yarng wa-wa*
electronic game	电子游戏机 *dian-ds yo-shee-jee*
pail and shovel [bucket and spade]	小桶和铲子 *shiao-tong her chan-ds*
teddy bear	玩具熊 *wan-jü-shiong*

Antiques 古董

How old is this?	这个有多少年代了? *jer-ge yo duo-shao nian-dai le*
Do you have anything of the ... dynasty?	你们有没有 ... 朝的古董? *nee-men yo-may-yo ... chao de goo-dong*
Can you send it to me?	你们能给我送来吗? *nee-men nung gay wo song-lai ma*
Will I have problems with customs?	过海关会有问题吗? *guo-hai-gwan hway yo wen-tee ma*
Is there a certificate of authenticity?	有没有证书说明这是正宗的? *yo-may-yo jung-shoo shuo-ming jer-sh jung-dsong de*

Supermarket/Minimart
超级市场 / 小型集市

In major cities you will find Western-style supermarkets selling a limited variety of goods, many imported. Most Chinese shop in the markets for fresh meat, fish, fruit, and vegetables. Rice, noodles, and other staples are sold at "grain" stores. In addition, there are small grocery stores selling all manner of other provisions. These stores are always called **nan-bay-huo-sharng-dian** (literal meaning: *goods-from-the-south-and-the-north store*).

At the supermarket 在超级市场

Excuse me. Where can I find (a) …?	请问，哪里有 … ？ *ching-wen, na-lee yo …*
Do I pay for this here or at the checkout?	这件东西是在这儿付钱还是在付款台付钱？ *jer-jian dong-shee sh dsai jer-r foo-chian hai-sh dsai foo-kwan-tai foo-chian*
Where are the carts [trolleys]/baskets?	哪儿有手推车 / 篮子？ *na-r yo sho-twee-cher/lan-ds*
Is there a … here?	这儿有没有 … ？ *jer-r yo-may-yo …*
delicatessen/pharmacy	熟食部 / 药房 *shoo-sh-boo/yao-farng*

洗涤用品	cleaning products
乳制品	dairy products
鲜鱼	fresh fish
鲜肉	fresh meat
新鲜农产品	fresh produce
冷冻食品	frozen foods
禽类	poultry
罐头水果 / 蔬菜	canned foods
酒类	wines and spirits
面包和糕点	bread and cakes

Weights and measures

- **1 kilogram** or **kilo (kg)** = 1000 grams **(g)**; **100 g** = 3.5 oz.; **1 kg** = 2.2 lb.; 1 oz. = **28.35 g**; 1 lb. = **453.60 g**
- **1 litre (l)** = 0.88 imp. quart or 1.06 U.S. quart; 1 imp. quart = **1.14 l** 1 U.S. quart = **0.951 l**; 1 imp. gallon = **4.55 l**; 1 U.S. gallon = **3.8 l**

Food hygiene 食品卫生

启封后请于 ... 天内食用	eat within ... days of opening
冰箱内存放	keep refrigerated
可用微波炉加热	microwaveable
食用前须加热	reheat before eating
适合素食者	suitable for vegetarians
保鲜期至 ...	use by ...

At the minimart 在小型集市

I'd like some of that/those.	我想要一点那个/那种。 *wo shiarng yao yee-dian na-ge/na-jong*
I'd like (a) ...	我要 ... *wo yao*
this one/these	这个/这些 *jer-ge/jer-shie*
that one/those	那个/那些 *na-ge/na-shie*
to the left/right	左边的/右边的 *dsuo-bian de/yo-bian de*
over there/here	在那里/在这里 *dsai na-lee/dsai jer-lee*
bag of chips [crisps]	一包炸土豆片 *yee-bao ja too-dou-pian*
bottle of wine	一瓶酒 *yee-ping-jio*
cake	蛋糕 *dan-gao*
can [tin] of cola	一罐可乐 *yee-gwan ker-ler*
carton of milk	一盒牛奶 *yee her jio-nai*
half-dozen eggs	六个鸡蛋 *lio-ge jee-dan*
half-kilo of tomatoes	半公斤西红柿 *ban gong-jin shee-hong-sh*
jar of jam	一瓶果酱 *yee-ping guo-jiarng*
kilo of apples	一公斤苹果 *yee gong-jin ping-guo*
liter of milk	一公升牛奶 *yee gong-shung nio-nai*
... slices of ham	... 片火腿肉 *... pian huo-twee-ro*
100 grams of nuts	100 克炒货 *yee-bai-ker chao-huo*
That's all thanks.	就这些，谢谢。 *jo jer-shie, shie-shie*

– ching gay wo ban gong-jin dou-foo.
– *sh jer-jong ma?*
– sh de.
– *hao … hai yao shen-me?*
– hai yao lio pian huo-twee.
– *gay nin.*

Provisions/Picnic 食物 / 野餐

butter	黄油	*hwarng-yo*
cheese	干酪	*gan-lao*
cookies [biscuits]	饼干	*bing-gan*
eggs	鸡蛋	*jee-dan*
grapes	葡萄	*poo-tao*
ice cream	冰淇淋	*bing-chee-lin*
instant coffee	速溶咖啡	*soo-rong-ka-fay*
(loaf of) bread	大面包	*da-mian-bao*
margarine	人造黄油	*ren-dsao hwarng-yo*
milk	牛奶	*nio-nai*
potato chips [crisps]	炸土豆片	*ja too-dou-pian*
rolls	小面包	*shiao-mian-bao*
sausages	香肠	*shiarng-charng*
five-spice seasoned beef	五香牛肉	*woo-sharng nio-ro*
tea bags	茶包	*cha-bao*
beer	啤酒	*pee-jio*
soft drink	软饮料	*rwan yin-liao*
wine	葡萄酒	*poo-tao-jio*

In the large tourist hotels in the major cities you will find a selection of Western-style breads and cakes available. Elsewhere you will see what look like soft bread rolls, but these may not appeal to the Western palate being sweetish and often rather dry in texture. Typical Chinese bread products include steamed buns (**man-tou**), clay-oven bread (**shao-bing**), and fried bread rolls (**yo-bing**), the last of which you will find for sale at street stalls and in local restaurants.

Health

Doctor/General	161	Gynecologist	167	
Accident and injury	162	Hospital		167
Symptoms	163	Optician		167
Health conditions	163	Dentist		168
Doctor's inquiries	164	Payment and		
Parts of the body	166	insurance		168

You will not normally be required to produce proof of vaccination upon entry unless you have previously traveled to, or through, regions where such diseases as cholera and yellow fever are endemic.

No special health difficulties face the visitor to China. However, if you plan to visit a malaria zone, you need to begin treatment before your trip. Be sure to take with you any essential medications, as it is difficult or impossible to find many items in Chinese pharmacies.

Should you require medical care in China, your guide, hotel receptionist, or the local CITS office will make arrangements. Foreign tourists treated in a Chinese hospital must pay a registration fee plus the cost of any medicine prescribed. There is a separate, additional charge in case of hospitalization. Make sure you are properly covered by your travel/health insurance.

Warning: In the extreme event of an emergency blood transfusion, those with Rh-negative blood should be warned that Chinese blood banks do not store Rh-negative blood. Consult your doctor about this before you go.

Doctor/General 医生 / 一般用语

Where can I find a hospital/dental office [surgery]?	医院/牙科诊所在哪儿? *yee-yüan/ya-ker jen-suo dsai na-r*
Where's there a doctor/dentist who speaks English?	哪儿有会说英语的医生/牙医? *na-r yo hway shuo ying-yde yee-shung/ya-yee*
Could the doctor come to see me here?	医生能不能来这儿为我看病? *yee-shung nung-boo-nung lai jer-r way wo kan-bing*
Can I make an appointment for …?	我想预约个 … 的时间。 *wo shiarng yü-yüe ge … sh-jian*
today/tomorrow	今天 / 明天 *jin-tian / ming-tian*
as soon as possible	尽可能早 *jin ker-nung dsao*
It's urgent?	是急诊吗? *sh jee-jen ma*
I've got an appointment with Doctor …	我约好了要见 … 大夫。 *wo yüe-hao le yao jian … dai-foo*

TIME ➤ 221; DATE ➤ 218

Accident and injury 出事故、受伤

My ... is hurt/injured.	我的 ... 受伤了。 *wo de ... sho-sharng le*
husband/wife	丈夫/妻子 *jarng-foo/chee-ds*
son/daughter	儿子/女儿 *er-ds/nü-r*
friend	朋友 *pung-yo*
baby	婴儿 *ying-er*
He/She is ...	他/她 ... *ta / ta ...*
unconscious	昏迷了 *hwun-mee le*
(seriously) injured	受了(重)伤 *sho le (jong) sharng*
He/She is bleeding (heavily).	他/她在(大)出血。 *ta/ta dsai (da) choo-shüe*
I've got a/an ...	我 ... *wo ...*
blister	起了个水泡 *chee-le ge shwee-pao*
boil	长了个疖子 *jarng le ge jie-ds*
bruise	碰伤了 *pung-sharng le*
burn	被烧伤了 *bay shao-sharng le*
cut	被割伤了 *bay ger-sharng le*
graze	皮肤被擦伤了 *pee-foo bay tsa-sharng le*
insect bite	被虫咬了 *bay chong yao le*
lump	起了个疙瘩 *chee-le ge ger-da*
rash	出了疹子 *choo-le jen-ds*
sting	被黄蜂叮了 *bay hwarng-fung ding le*
strained muscle	拉伤了肌肉 *la-sharng le jee-ro*
swelling	起了个肿块 *chee-le ge jong-kwai*
wound	受伤了 *sho-sharng le*
My ... hurts.	我 ... 疼。 *wo ... tung*

Symptoms 短期症状

I've been feeling ill for … days.	我已经有 … 天不舒服了。 *wo jee-jing yo … tian boo-shoo-foo le*	
I feel faint.	我感觉四肢无力。 *wo gan-jüe s-j woo-lee*	
I feel feverish.	我感觉在发烧。 *wo gan-jüe dsai fa-shao*	
I've been vomiting.	我呕吐过。 *wo o-too guo*	
I've got diarrhea.	我得了痢疾。 *wo de-le lee-jee*	
It hurts here.	这里疼。 *jer-lee tung*	
I have (a/an) …	我 … *wo …*	
backache	腰痛 *yao-tong*	
cold	感冒了 *gan-mao le*	
cramps	肚子绞痛 *doo-ds jiao-tong*	
earache	耳朵痛 *er-duo tong*	
headache	头痛 *tou-tong*	
sore throat	嗓子疼 *sarng-ds tung*	
stiff neck	脖子僵直 *buo-ds jiarng-jee*	
stomachache	胃疼 *way-tung*	
sunstroke	中暑了 *jong-shoo le*	

Health conditions 健康状况

I have arthritis.	我有关节炎。 *wo yo gwan-jie-yan*
I have asthma.	我有哮喘病。 *wo yo shiao-chwan-bing*
I am …	我 … *wo …*
deaf	耳聋 *er-long*
diabetic	有糖尿病 *yo tarng-niao-bing*
epileptic	有癫痫病 *yo dian-shian-bing*
handicapped	有残疾 *yo tsan-jee*
(… months) pregnant	怀孕 (… 个月) 了 *hwai-yün (… ge yüe) le*
I have a heart condition.	我心脏不好。 *wo shin-jarng boo-hao*
I have high blood pressure.	我有高血压。 *wo yo gao-shüe-ya*
I had a heart attack … years ago.	… 年前我心脏病发作过一次。 *… nian chian wo shin-dsarng-bing fa-dsuo guo yee-ts*

163

Doctor's inquiries 医生问诊

这种感觉已经有多久了?	How long have you been feeling like this?
是不是第一次出现这种现象?	Is this the first time you've had this?
你有没有服用其它药?	Are you taking any other medication?
你对什么过敏吗?	Are you allergic to anything?
你打过破伤风预防针吗?	Have you been vaccinated against tetanus?
你胃口怎么样?	Is your appetite OK?

Examination 检查

我来给您量量体温 / 血压。	I'll take your temperature/ blood pressure.
请把袖子卷起来。	Roll up your sleeve, please.
请把衣服脱到腰部。	Please undress to the waist.
请躺下来。	Please lie down.
把嘴张开。	Open your mouth.
深呼吸。	Breathe deeply.
请咳嗽一下。	Cough, please.
哪儿疼?	Where does it hurt?
这儿疼吗?	Does it hurt here?

Diagnosis 诊断

我要你拍张X光。	I want you to have an X-ray.
我要一点你的血样/便样/尿样。	I want a specimen of your blood/stools/urine.
我要介绍你去看专科。	I want you to see a specialist.
我要介绍你去医院检查。	I want you to go to hospital.
折断了/扭伤了。	It's broken/sprained.
脱臼了/拉伤了。	It's dislocated/torn.

你患了 ...	You've got (a/an) ...
阑尾炎	appendicitis
膀胱炎	cystitis
流感	flu
食物中毒	food poisoning
骨折	fracture
胃炎	gastritis
痔疮	hemorrhoids
疝	hernia
... 发炎	inflammation of ...
麻疹	measles
肺炎	pneumonia
坐骨神经痛	sciatica
扁桃腺炎	tonsilitis
肿瘤	tumor
性病	venereal disease
这里发炎了。	It's infected.
这病会传染。	It's contagious.

Treatment 治疗

我给你一点 ...	I'll give you ...
消毒剂	an antiseptic
止痛片	a painkiller
我给你开 ...	I'm going to prescribe ...
一个疗程的抗生素	a course of antibiotics
一些栓剂	some suppositories
你对某些药物过敏吗?	Are you allergic to any medication?
... 吃一片。	Take one pill ...
每隔 ... 小时	every ... hours
一天 ... 次	... times a day
饭前 / 饭后	before/after each meal
疼痛时服用	in case of pain
连服 ... 天	for ... days
回去后去看医生。	Consult a doctor when you get home.

Parts of the body 身体部位

	appendix	阑尾	*lan-way*
	arm	臂	*bee*
	back	背部	*bay*
	bladder	膀胱	*parng-gwarn*
bone		骨	*goo*
breast		乳房	*roo-farng*
chest		胸	*shiong*
ear		耳朵	*er-duo*
eye		眼睛	*yan-jing*
face		脸	*lian*
finger		手指	*sho-j*
foot		脚	*jiao*
gland		腺	*shian*
hand		手	*sho*
head		头	*tou*
heart		心脏	*shin-dsarng*
jaw		下巴	*shia-ba*
joint		关节	*gwan-jie*
kidney		肾	*shen*
knee		膝盖	*shee-gai*
leg		腿	*twee*
lip		唇	*chwun*
liver		肝	*gan*
mouth		嘴	*dswee*
muscle		肌肉	*jee-ro*
neck		颈	*jing*
nose		鼻子	*bee-ds*
rib		肋骨	*lay-goo*
shoulder		肩	*jian*
skin		皮肤	*pee-foo*
stomach		胃	*way*
thigh		大腿	*da-twee*
throat		嗓子	*sarng-ds*
thumb		拇指	*moo-j*
toe		脚趾	*jiao-j*
tongue		舌	*sher*
tonsils		扁桃体	*bian-tao-tee*
vein		静脉	*jing-mai*

Gynecologist 妇科

I have …   我 …。 *wo …*

abdominal pains   肚子痛 *doo-ds tong*

period pains   有痛经毛病
                                          yo tong-jing mao-bing

a vaginal infection   有阴道炎 *yo yin-dao-yan*

I haven't had my period for   我已有 … 月没来月经了。
… months.   *wo jee-jing yo … yüe may lai yüe-jing le*

I'm on the Pill.   我在服用避孕药。
                                          wo dsai foo-yong bee-yün-yao

Hospital 医院

Please notify my family.   请告诉我家人。
                                          ching gao-soo wo jia-ren

I'm in pain.   我很疼痛。 *wo hen tung-tong*

I can't eat/sleep.   我不能吃饭/睡觉。
                                          wo boo-nung ch-fan/shwee-jiao

When will the doctor come?   医生什么时候能来?
                                          yee-shung shen-me sh-ho nung lai

Which ward is … in?   … 在哪个病房? *dsai na-ge bing-farng*

I'm visiting …   我来探望 … *wo lai tan-warng …*

Optician 眼镜店

I'm near- [short-] sighted/   我眼睛近视/远视。
far- [long-] sighted.   *wo yan-jing jin-sh/yüan-sh*

I've lost …   我丢了 … *wo dio le*

one of my contact lenses   一片隐形眼镜
                                          yee-pian yin-shing yan-jing

my glasses/a lens   眼镜/一个镜片
                                          yan-jing/yee-ge jing-pian

Could you give me a   您能给我配一个吗?
replacement?   *nin nung gay wo pay yee-ge ma*

Dentist 牙医

I have toothache.	我牙痛。
	wo ya-tong
This tooth hurts.	这个牙很痛。
	jer-ge ya hen tong
I've lost a filling / tooth.	我补牙的填料掉了 / 掉了一颗牙齿。
	wo boo-ya de tian-liao diao le /
	diao le yee-ker ya-ch
Can you repair this denture?	你能把这个假牙修一下吗? *nee nung ba*
	jer-ge jia-ya shio yee-shia ma
I don't want it extracted.	我不想把它拔掉。
	wo boo-shiarng ba ta ba-diao

我要给你打一针 / 作局部麻醉。	I'm going to give you an injection / an anesthetic.
你的牙需要补一补 / 装个假齿冠。	You need a filling / cap (crown).
这颗牙非拔不可了。	I'll have to take it out.
我只能临时给你补一补。	I can only fix it temporarily.
… 小时内不要吃东西。	Don't eat anything for … hours.

Payment and insurance 付帐和保险

How much do I owe you?	收多少钱?
	sho duo-shao chian
I have insurance.	我有保险。
	wo yo bao-shian
Can I have a receipt for my insurance?	请给我一张健康保险索赔用的收据。
	ching gay wo yee-jarng jian-karng bao-shian suo-pay yong de sho-jü
Would you fill out this insurance form, please?	请填一下这份健康保险单。
	ching tian yee-shia jer-fen jian-karng bao-shian-dan

Dictionary
English - Chinese

Most terms in this dictionary are either followed by an example or cross-referenced to pages where the word appears in a phrase. The notes below provide some basic grammar guidelines.

Nouns and adjectives

There are no articles (a, an, the), singular or plural, in Chinese. Whether the noun is singular or plural is judged from the context, or by a number modifying the noun.

Adjectives precede the noun and, if they comprise a single character, are generally preceded by the adverb **hen** (literal meaning: *very*).

Verbs

Chinese verbs are even more invariable than English ones, with no differences between singular and plural forms.

wo shüe-shee	I learn
nee shüe-shee	you learn (singular)
ta* shüe-shee	he/she/it learns
wo-men shüe-shee	we learn
nee-men shüe-shee	you learn (plural)
ta-men shüe-shee	they learn

* Although written differently, the characters are all pronounced the same (**ta**).

Past tense

The suffix **le** is placed after the verb to show that the action has been completed.

wo may-tian dou <u>ch</u> dsao-fan	I eat breakfast everyday.
jin-tian wo <u>ch</u> le dsao-fan	I ate breakfast today.

The suffix **guo** after a verb is used to show that an action happened in the past, but without a specific reference to a particular point in time.

wo <u>chü-guo</u> jong-guo	I have been to China.

Future tense

The future tense has exactly the same form as the present. To indicate the future nature of an action, an adverb or adverbial phrase is needed.

wo shüe-shee han-yü	I learn Chinese.
<u>ming-nian</u> wo yao shüe han-yü	I'm going to learn Chinese next year.

A

a few 几个 jee-ger 15

a little 一点点 yee-dian-dian 15

a lot 很多 hen-duo 15

a piece of ... 一块... yee-kwai... 40

a.m. 上午 sharng-woo

abbey 修道院 shio-dao-yüan 99

about (approximately) 大约 da-yüe 15

above (place) 在 ... 上方 dsai ... sharng-farng 12

abroad 在国外 dsai guo-wai

accept, to 接受 jie-sho 136

accessories 装饰品 jwarng-sh-pin 144

accident 事故 sh-goo 92, 152

accidentally 不小心 boo-shiao-shin 28

accommodation 住宿 joo-soo 123

accompany, to 陪伴 pay-ban 65

acne 痤疮 tsuo-chwarng

acrylic 丙纶 bing-lwun

actor/actress 演员 yan-yüan

adapter 电源转接器 dian-yüan jwan-jie-chee 148

address 地址 dee-j 84, 126

adjoining room 靠在一起的房间 kao-dsai-yee-chee de farng-jian 22

admission charge 入场费 roo-charng-fay 114

adult 成人 chung-ren 81, 100

after (place) 过了 ... guo-le ... 95; (time) ... 之后 ... j-ho 13

after-shave 须后水 shü-ho-shwee 142

after-sun lotion 日晒后护肤油 r-shai ho hoo-foo-yo 142

afternoon, in the 下午 shia-woo 221

aged, to be 年龄 nian-ling 152

ago ... 前 ... chian 221

agree: I don't agree 我不同意 wo boo tong-yee

air conditioning 空调 kong-tiao 22, 25

air mattress 充气床垫 chong-chee chwarng-dian 31

air pump 气泵 chee-bung 87

airmail 航空 harng-kong 155

airport 机场 jee-charng 96

aisle seat 靠走道座位 kao dso-dao dsuo-way 74

alarm clock 闹钟 nao-jong 149

alcoholic (drink) 酒精饮料 jio-jing yin-liao

all 所有/全部 suo-yo/chüan-boo

allergic, to be 过敏 guo-min 164, 165

allergy 过敏症 guo-min-jung

allowance 允许定额 yün-shü ding-er 67

almost 几乎 jee-hoo

alone 独自 doo-ds

already 已经 yee-jing 28

also 也 ye

alter, to 更改 gung-gai 137

alumin(i)um foil 铝箔纸 lü-buo-j 148

always 总是 dsong-sh 13

am: I am 我是 wo sh

amazing 不可思议 boo-ker-s-yee 101

ambassador 大使 da-sh

ambulance 救护车 jio-hoo-cher 92

American (adj) 美国 may-guo 150, 152

American (person) 美国人 may-guo-ren

amount 数目/一笔钱 shoo-moo/ yee-bee chian 42

amusement arcade 娱乐厅 yü-ler-ting 113

anaesthetic 麻醉剂 ma-dswee-jee

and 和/以及 her/yee-jee

animal 动物 dong-woo 106

anorak 防水夹克衫 farng-shwee jia-ker-shan 145

another 另一个 ling-yee-ge 21

another (day/time) 另一(天/个时间) ling yee (tian/yee-ge sh-jian) 125

antacid 解酸药 jie-swan-yao

antibiotics 抗生素 karng-shung-soo 165

antifreeze 防冻剂 farng-dong-jee

antique 古董 goo-dong 157;
~ **store** 古玩店 goo-wan-dian 130

antiseptic 抗菌的 karng-jün de 165;
~ **cream** 消毒药膏 shiao-doo yao-gao 141

any 任何 ren-her

anyone: does anyone speak English? 有人会说英语吗? yo-ren hway shuo ying-yü ma

anything cheaper 有更便宜的吗 yo gung-pian-yee de ma 21

anything else? 还要什么? hai-yao shen-me

apartment 公寓房间 gong-yü farng-jian 28, 123

apologize: I apologize 抱谦 bao-chian

appendicitis 阑尾炎 lan-way-yan 165

appendix 阑尾 lan-way 166

appetite 胃口 way-ko 164

appointment 预约 yü-yüe 161;
to make an ~ 约个时间 yüe-ge sh-jian 147

approximately 大约 da-yüe 152

April 四月 s-yüe 218

architect 建筑师 jian-joo-sh 104

are there ...? 有没有 ...? yo-may-yo ... 17

area code 地区号 dee-chü hao 127

arm 臂膀 166

around (time) ... 前后 ... chian-ho 13

arrive, to 到达 dao-da 68, 70, 71

arrive in, to 到达 dao-da 76

art gallery 美术馆 may-shoo gwan 99

arthritis, to have 患关节炎 hwan-gwan-jie-yan 163

artificial sweetener 人造糖 ren-dsao-tarng 38

artist 艺术家 yee-shoo-jia 104

ashtray 烟灰缸 yan-hway-garng 39

ask: I asked for ... 我要了... wo yao le ... 41

aspirin 阿斯匹林 a-s-pee-lin 141

asthma, to have 患哮喘病 hwan shiao-chwan-bing 163

at (place) 在 dsai 12

at last! 终于... jong-yü ... 19

at least 至少 j-shao 23

athletics 田径 tian-jing 114

attack 行凶案 shing-shiong-an 152

attractive 有吸引力的 yo shee-yin-lee de

August 八月 ba-yüe 218

aunt 婶子 shen-ds 120

Australia 澳大利亚 ao-da-lee-ya 119

Australian (person) 澳大利亚人 ao-da-lee-ya-ren

authentic: is it authentic? 这是真货吗? jer-sh jen-huo ma

authenticity 正宗 jung-dsong 157

ATM/cash machine 自动提款机 ds-dong tee-kwan-jee 139

automatic (car) 自动排挡汽车 ds-dong pai-darng chee-cher 86;
~ **camera** 自动照相机 ds-dong jao-shiarng-jee 151

automobile 汽车 chee-cher

autumn 秋天 chio-tian 219

avalanche 雪崩 shüe-bung

awful 很坏的/糟透的 hen-hwai de/dsao-tou de 101, 122

B **baby** 婴儿 ying-er 39, 113, 162; **~ food** 婴儿食品 ying-er sh-pin 142; **~ wipes** 婴儿擦洗巾 ying-er tsa-shee-jin 142; **~-sitter** 临时保姆 lin-sh bao-moo 113

back *(of head)* 后部 ho-boo 147

back *(of body)* 背部 bay-boo 166

back by, to be ... ...之前回来 ... j-chian hway-lai 113

backache 腰痛 yao-tung 163

backpacking 背包旅行 bay-bao lü-shing

bad 坏的 hwai de 14

baggage 行李 shing-lee 32, 71; **~ check** 行李存放处 shing-lee tswun-farng-choo 71, 73; **~ reclaim** 行李认领 shing-lee ren-ling 71

bakery 面包店 mian-bao-dian 130

balcony 阳台 yarng-tai 29

ball 球 chio 157

ballet 芭蕾 ba-lay 108, 111

band *(musical)* 乐队 yüe-dwee 111, 157

bandages 绷带 bung-dai 141

bank 银行 yin-harng 130, 138

bar *(hotel)* 酒吧 jio-ba 26, 112

barber 理发师 lee-fa-sh

basement 地下室 dee-shia-sh

basket 篮子 lan-ds 158

basketball 篮球 lan-chio 114

bath 浴缸y garng 21

bath towel 浴巾 yü-jin 27

bathroom 卫生间 way-shung-jian 26, 29

battery *(car)* 电瓶 dian-ping 88

battery 电池 dian-ch 137, 149, 151

battle site 古战场 goo-jan-charng 99

be back, to 回来 hway-lai 135

be, to 是 sh 17

beach 海滩 hai-tan 116

beard 胡子 hoo-ds

beautiful 漂亮 piao-liarng 14, 101

because ... 因为 ... yin-way ... 15

because of ... 因为 ... yin-way ... 15

bed 床 hwarng 21

bed and breakfast 房价包早餐 farng-jia bao dsao-tsan 24

bedding 床褥 chwarng-roo 29

bedroom 卧室 wo-sh 29

beer 啤酒 pee-jio 40; **~ garden** 园林雅座 yüan-lin ya-dsuo 35

before ... ... 之前 ... j-chian 13, 165, 221

begin, to 开始 kai-sh

beginner 初学者 choo-shüe-jer 117

beige 米色 mee-ser 143

belong: this belongs to me 这是我的 jer-sh wo-de

belt 皮带 pee-dai 144

berth 铺位 poo-way 74, 77

best 最好的 dswee-hao-d

better 更好 gung-hao 14

better quality 好点的 hao-dian de 134

between *(time)* ... 之间 ... j-jian 221

between jobs 待业人员 dai-ye-ren-yüan 121

bib 围嘴 way-dswee

bicycle 自行车 ds-shing-cher 75, 83, 153; **~ hire** 租自行车 dsoo ds-shing-cher 83

bidet 坐浴盆 dsuo-yü-pen

big 大 da 14, 117, 134

bigger 大点的 da dian de 24

bikini 比基尼 bee-jee-nee 144

bill 帐单 jarng-dan 32, 42

bin liner 垃圾塑料袋 la-jee soo-liao-dai

binoculars 双筒望远镜 shwarng-tong warng-yüan-jing

bird 鸟 niao 106

birthday 生日 shung-r 219

biscuits 饼干 bing-gan 160

bite (insect) 虫咬 chong-yao

bitten: I've been bitten by a dog 我被狗咬了 wo bay go yao le

bitter (taste) 苦 koo 41

bizarre 古怪 goo-gwai 101

black 黑色 hay-ser 143; **~ and white film (camera)** 黑白胶卷 hay-bai jiao-jüan 151; **~ coffee** 不加奶咖啡 boo jia nai ka-fay 40

bladder 膀胱 parng-gwarng 166

blanket 毯子 tan-ds 27

bleach 漂白剂 piao-bai-jee 148

bleeding 出血 choo-shüe 162

blinds 窗帘 chwarng-lian 25

blister 水泡 shwee-pao 162

blocked, to be 堵塞了 doo-ser le 25

blood 血 shüe 164; **~ group** 血型 shüe-shing; **~ pressure** 血压 shüe-ya 164; **high ~ pressure** 高血压 gao-shüe-ya 163

blouse 女衬衫 nü chen-shan 144

blow-dry 吹干 chwee-gan 147

blue 蓝色 lan-ser 143

boarding card 登机牌 dung-jee-pai 70

boat 船 chwan 81; **~ trip** 乘船旅行 chung-chwan lü-shing 81, 97

boil (medical) 烫伤 tarng-sharng 162

boiled: boiled water 开水 kai-shwee

boiler 锅炉 guo-loo 29

bone 骨 goo 166

book 书 shoo 150

book, to 预订 yü-ding 21

booking 预订 yü-ding 22

bookstore 书店 shoo-dian 130

booted, to be 车轮被锁 cher-lwun bay suo 87

boots 靴子 shüe-ds 115, 145

boring 没意思 may ye-s 101

born: I was born in 我出生于 wo choo-shung yü

borrow: may I borrow your ...? 我能借您的 ... 吗? wo nung jie nin-de ... ma

botanical garden 植物园 jee-woo-yüan 99

bottle 瓶 ping 37, 159; **~ of wine** 一瓶葡萄酒 yee-ping poo-tao-jio 156; **~-opener** 开瓶器 kai-ping-chee 148

bottled (beer) 瓶装(啤酒) ping-jwarng (pee-jio) 40

bowel 大肠 da-charng

bowls 碗 wan 148

boy 男孩 nan-hai 120, 157

boyfriend 男朋友 nan-pung-yo 120

bra 胸罩 shiong-jao 144

bracelet 手镯 sho-juo 149

bread 面包 mian-bao 38

break, to 打破 da-po 28

break down, to (of car) (汽车)抛锚 (chee-cher) pao-mao 28, 88

breakdown (of car) (汽车)抛锚 (chee-cher) pao-mao 88

breakdown truck 牵引车 chian-yin-cher 88

breakfast 早餐 dsao-tsan 26, 27

breast 乳房 roo-farng 166

breathe, to 呼吸 oo-shee 92, 164

breathtaking 令人赞叹 ling-ren dsan-tan 101

bridge 桥 chiao 107

briefs (clothing) 短内裤 dwan-nay-koo 144

brilliant 好极了 hao-jee le 101

bring, to (a friend) 带(朋友) dai (pung-yo) 125

British (adj) 英国 ying-guo 152

British (person) 英国人 ying-guo-ren

brochure 宣传册 shüan-chwan tser

broken 坏了 hwai le 137

A-Z

broken, to be 破了 po-le 25; *(of a bone)* 骨折了 goo-jer le 164

bronchitis 支气管炎 j-chee-gwan-yan

brooch 胸针 shiong-jen 149

brother 兄弟 shiong-dee 120

brown 棕色 dsong-ser 143

browse, to 随便看看 swee-bian kan-kan 133

bruise 擦伤 tsa-sharng 162

bucket 小桶 shiao-tong 157

building 建筑物 jian-joo-woo

built, to be 被修建 bay-shio-jian 104

bulletin board 布告牌 boo-gao-pai 26

bureau de change 外币兑换处 wai-bee dwee-hwan-choo 138

burger 汉堡包 han-bao-bao 40

burn *(injury)* 烧伤 shao-sharng 162

bus 公共汽车 gong-gong-chee-cher 70, 78; **~ route** 公共汽车专用道 gong-gong-chee-cher jwan-yong dao 96; **~ station** 长途汽车站 charng-too-chee-cher jan 78; **~ stop** 公共汽车站 gong-gong-chee-cher jan 65, 96

business 商务/公务 sharng-woo/gong-woo 121; **on ~** 因公 yin gong 66; **~ class** 商务舱 sharng-woo tsarng 68, **~ trip** 出差 choo-chai 123

busy, to be *(occupied)* 没空 may-kong 125

butane gas 天然气 tian-ran chee 30, 31

butcher 肉店 ro-dian 130

butter 黄油 hwarng-yo 38, 160

button 钮扣 nio-ko

buy, to 买 mai 125

by *(near)* 靠近 kao-jin 36; *(time)* 不迟于/ ...之前 boo-ch-yü/... j-chian 13, 221; **~ bus** 坐公共汽车 dsuo gong-gong-chee-cher 123; **~ car** 开车 kai cher 17, 94, 123;

~ credit card 用信用卡 yong shin-yong-ka 17; **~ ferry** 坐轮渡 dsuo lwun-du 123; **~ plane** 坐飞机 dsuo fay-jee 123; **~ train** 坐火车 dsuo huo-cher 123

bye! 再见! dsai-jian

C

cabin 舱 tsarng 81

cable TV 有线电视 yo-shian-dian-sh 22

café 咖啡馆 ka-fay-gwan 35

cagoule 连帽防风衣 lian-mao farng-fung-yee 145

cake 糕点 gao-dian 40

calendar 挂历 gwaa-lee 156

call, to *(phone)* 打电话 da dian-hwaa 127, 128

call collect, to 打对方付钱的电话 da dwee-farng foo-chian de dian-hwaa 127

call, to 叫 jiao 92, 94

camera 照相机 jao-shiarng-jee 151, 153; **~ case** 照相机护套 jao-shiarng-jee hoo-tao 151; **~ store** 照相器材店 jao-shiarng chee-tsai-dian 130

camp, to 露营 loo-ying

campbed 折叠床 jer-die-chwarng 31

camping 露营 loo-ying 30

camping equipment 露营用具 loo-ying yong-jü 31

campsite 露营地 loo-ying-dee 30, 123

can *(tin)* 罐 gwan 159

can I ...? 我能不能 wo nung-boo-nung ... 18

can I have ...? 请给我 ..., 好吗? ching gay wo ..., hao-ma 18

can you help me? 您能不能帮我一下? nin nung-boo-nung barng wo yee-shia 18

can you recommend ...? 你能不能推荐一家 ... ? nee nung-boo-nung twee-jian yee-jia ... 112

can opener 开罐头刀 kai-gwan-tou dao 148

Canada 加拿大 jia-na-da 119

Canadian (person) 加拿大人 jia-na-da-ren

cancel, to (reservation) 取消 chü shiao 68

cancer 癌症 ai jung

candles 蜡烛 la-joo 148

candy 糖果 tarng-guo 150

cap 帽子 mao-ds 144

cap (dental) 假齿冠 jia-ch-gwan 168

car 车/汽车/小汽车 cher/chee-cher/shiao-chee-cher 86, 88, 153; (part of train) 车厢 cher-shiarng 75, 77; **by ~** 开车 kai-cher 95; **~ ferry** 汽渡 chee-doo 81; **~ hire** 租车 dsoo-cher 86; **~ park** 停车场 ting-cher-charng 26, 87, 96

carafe 瓶 ping 37

caravan 活动住房 huo-dong-joo-farng 30

cards (playing) 打牌 da-pai 121

carpet (rug) 地毯 dee-tan

carrier bag 购物袋 go-woo-dai

carry-cot 手提婴儿床 sho-tee ying-er-chwarng

carton 纸盒 j-her 159

carts (shopping) 手推车 sho-twee-cher 158

cases 箱子 shiarng-ds 69

cash 现金 shian-jin 17, 136

cash machine 提款机 tee-kwan-jee 139

cash, to 换现金 hwan-shian-jin 138

cashier [cash desk] 付款柜台 foo-kwan-gway-tai 132

casino 赌场 doo-charng 112

cassette 磁带 ts-dai 157

castle 城堡 chung-bao 99

catch, to (bus) 赶上 gan-sharng

cathedral 大教堂 da-jiao-tarng 99

Catholic 天主教 tian-joo-jiao 105

cave 岩洞 yan-dong 107

CD CD唱盘 see-dee charng-pan

CD-player CD唱盘机 see-dee charng-pan-jee

cemetery 公墓 gong-moo 99

center of town 市中心 sh-jong-shin 21

central heating 中央暖气系统 jong-yarng nwan-chee shee-tong

ceramics 陶瓷 tao-ts

certificate 凭证/证书 ping-jung/jung-shoo 149, 157

chain 手链 sho-lian 149

chair-lift 座椅式缆车 dsuo-yee-sh lan-cher 117

change (coins) 零钱 ling-chian 87, 136

change, to (baby) 换(尿片) hwan (niao-pian) 39

change, to (train/bus) 换车 hwan-cher 75, 76, 79, 80

change, to (money) 兑换 dwee-hwan 138

change, to (reservation) 更改 gung-gai 68

changing facilities 换尿片的地方 hwan niao-pian de dee-farng 113

chapel 小教堂 shiao-jiao-tarng 99

charcoal 木炭 moo-tan 31

charge 收费 sho-fay 30, 115, 155

charter flight 包机航班 bao-jee harng-ban

cheap 便宜 pian-yee 14, 134

cheaper 更便宜 gung-pian-yee 21, 24, 109, 134

check book 支票簿 j-piao-boo

check in, to 办理登机手续 ban-lee dung-jee sho-shü 68

A-Z

check out, to *(hotel)* 退房 结帐 twee-farng jie-jarng
check-in desk 登机服务台 dung-jee foo-woo-tai 69
checkout *(supermarket)* 付款台 foo-kwan-tai 158
cheers! 干杯! gan-bay
cheese 奶酪 nai-lao 160
chemist 药店 yao-dian 130
cheque book 支票簿 j-piao-boo
chess 棋 chee 121
chess set 象棋 hiarng-chee 157
chest *(body)* 胸 shiong 166
chewing gum 口香糖 ko-shiarng-tarng 150
child 孩子 hai-ds 152
child's seat *(high chair)* 儿童座椅 er-tong dsuo-yee 39; ~ seat *(in car)* 儿童座椅 er-tong dsuo-yee 86; ~minder 照顾孩子的人 jao-goo hai-ds de ren
children 儿童/孩子们 er-tong/hai-ds-men 22, 24, 39, 66, 74, 81, 100, 113, 120
China 中国 jong-guo 119
Chinese *(cuisine)* 中菜 jong-tsai 35
Chinese *(language)* 汉语 han-yü 11, 110, 126
Chinese *(person)* 中国人 jong-guo-ren
choc-ice 巧克力冰淇淋 chiao-ker-lee bing-chee-lin 110
chocolate *(flavor)* 巧克力味 chiao-ker-lee way 40; ~ bar 一条巧克力 yee-tiao chiao-ker-lee 150; ~ ice cream 巧克力冰淇淋 chiao-ker-lee bing-chee-lin 110
chopsticks 筷子 kwai-ds 148
Christmas 圣诞节 shung-dan-jie 219
church 教堂 jiao-tarng 96, 99, 105
cigarette kiosk 香烟店 shiarng-yan dian 131
cigarettes 香烟 shiarng-yan 150
cigars 雪茄 shüe-jia 150

cinema 电影院 dian-ying-yüan 96, 110
clamped, to be 车轮被锁 cher-lwun bay suo 87
clean 干净 gan-jing 14, 39, 41
clean, to 清洗 ching-shee 137
cliff 峭壁 chiao-bee 107
cling film 保鲜纸 bao-shian-j 148
clinic 多科诊所 duo-ker jen-suo 131
cloakroom 衣帽室 yee-mao-sh 109
clock 钟 jong 149
close *(near)* 很近 hen-jin 95
close, to 关门 gwan-men 100, 132, 140
clothes 服装 foo-jwarng 144
clothes pins [pegs] 衣服夹 yee-foo-jia 148
clothing store 服装店 foo-jwarng-dian 130
cloudy, to be 多云 duo-yün 122
clubs *(golf)* 球棒 chio-barng 115
coach 长途汽车 charng-too-chee-cher 78; *(part of train)* 车厢 cher-shiarng 75, 77; ~ bay 汽车站台 chee-cher jan-tai 78; ~ station 长途汽车站 charng-too-chee-cher jan 78
coast 海岸 hai-an
coat 外衣 wai-yee 144
coatcheck 衣帽室 yee-mao-sh 109
coathanger 衣架 yee-jia
cockroach 蟑螂 jarng-larng
code *(area, dialling)* 号码 hao-ma
coffee 咖啡 ka-fay 40
coin 硬币 ying-bee
cold 冷 lung 14, 122
cold *(flu)* 感冒 gan-mao 141, 163
cold *(food)* 凉了 liarng le 41
collapse: he's collapsed 他晕倒了 ta yün-dao le
collect, to 取 chü 151
color 颜色 yan-ser 134, 143

176

color film 彩色胶卷 tsai-ser jiao-j n 151

comb 梳子 shoo-ds 142

come back, to (for collection) 回头 (来取) hway-tou (lai-chü) 140

commission 手续费 sho-shü fay 138

compact camera 袖珍式照相机 shio-jen-sh jao-shiarng-jee 151

compact disk CD 唱盘 see-dee charng-pan 157

company (business) 公司 gong-s

company (companionship) 作伴 dsuo-ban 126

compartment (train) 车厢 cher-shiarng

complaint, to make a 抱怨 bao-yüan 137

composer 作曲家 dsuo-chü-jia 111

computer 电脑 dian-nao

concert 音乐会 yin-yüe-hway 108, 111

concert hall 音乐厅 yin-yüe-ting 111

concession 优惠 yo-hway

conditioner 护发素 hoo-fa-soo 142

condoms 避孕套 bee-yün-tao 141

conductor 指挥 j-hway 111

confirm, to 确认 chüe-ren 22, 68

confirmation 确认 chüe-ren 22

congratulations! 恭喜你! gong-shee nee

connection 中转 jong-jwan 76

constipation 便秘 bian-bee

Consulate 领事馆 ling-sh-gwan 152

consult, to 看(医生) kan (yee-shung) 165

contact lens(es) 隐形眼镜 yin-shing yan-jing 167

contact, to 找 ... 联系 jao ... lian-shee 28

contagious, to be 会传染 hway chwan-ran 165

contain, to 装了 jwarng le 155

contemporary dance 现代舞 shian-dai-woo 111

contraceptive 避孕药 bee-yün-yao

cook (chef) 厨师 choo-sh

cook, to 烹调 pung-tiao

cooker 炉子 loo-ds 28, 29

cookies 饼干 bing-gan 160

cooking (cuisine) 烹调 pung-tiao

coolbox 冰盒 bing-her

copper 铜 tong 149

copy 副本 foo-ben

corkscrew 瓶塞钻 ping-sai-dswan 148

corner 拐角 gwai-jiao 95

correct 正确 jung-chüe

cosmetics 化妆品 hwaa-jwarng-pin

cot (child's) 幼儿床 yo-er-chwarng 22

cottage 乡村别墅 shiarng-tswun bie-shoo 28

cotton [wool] 棉球 mian-chio 141

cotton (material) 棉 mian 145

cough 咳嗽 ker-so 141

cough, to 咳嗽 ker-so 164

could I have ...? 我能不能要 ... ? wo nung-boo-nung yao ... 18

country (nation) 国家 guo-jia

country music 乡村音乐 sharng-tswun yin-yüe 111

courier (guide) 导游 dao-yo

course (meal) 道 dao

cousin 堂表亲 tarng-biao-chin

cover charge 服务费 foo-woo-fay 112

craft shop 工艺品商店 gong-yee-pin sharng-dian

cramps 绞痛 jiao-tong 163

creche 托儿所 tuo-er-suo

credit card 信用卡 shin-yong-ka 42, 136, 139, 153

crib (child's) 幼儿床 yo-er-chwarng 22

A-Z

crisps 炸土豆片 ja too-dou-pian 160

crockery 陶器 tao-chee 29

cross, to (road) 横穿 hung-chwan 95

crossroad 十字路口 sh-ds-loo-ko 95

crowded 拥挤 yong-jee 31

crown (dental) 假齿冠 jia-ch-gwan 168

cruise (n) 乘船游览 chung-chwan yo-lan

crutches 拐杖 gwai-jarng

crystal 水晶 shwee-jing 149

cup 杯子 bay-ds 39

cupboard 橱柜 choo-gway

cups/glasses 杯子 bay-ds 148

currency 货币 huo-bee 67, 138

currency exchange 外汇兑换处 wai-hway dwee-hwan-choo 70, 73, 138

curtains 窗帘 chwarng-lian

customs 海关 hai-gwan 67, 157

customs declaration 海关申报表 hai-gwan shen-bao-biao 155

cut 割伤 ger-sharng 162

cut and blow dry 剪短吹干 jian-dwan chwee-gan 147

cut glass 雕花玻璃 diao-hwaa buo-lee 149

cutlery 餐具 tsan-jü 29

cycle route 自行车旅行线路 ds-shing-cher lü-shing shian-loo 106

cycling 自行车赛 ds-shing-cher sai 114

cystitis 膀胱炎 parng-gwarng-yan 165

D **daily** 每天 may-tian

damaged, to be 被损坏 bay swun-hwai 28, 71

Damn! 该死的! gai-s-de 19

damp (n/adj) 潮湿 chao-sh

dance (performance) 舞蹈 woo-dao 111

dancing, to go 跳舞 tiao-woo 124

dangerous 危险的 way-shian de

dark 深色的 shen-ser de 14, 24, 134, 143

darker 更深的 gung-shen de 143

daughter 女儿 nü-r 120, 162

dawn, at 清晨，早晨 ching-chen, dsao-chen 221

day 天 tian 97, 122

day ticket 当天有效票 darng-tian yo-shiao piao

day trip 一日游 yee-r-yo

dead (battery) 没有电了 may-yo dian le 88

deaf, to be 耳聋 er-long 163

December 十二月 sh-er-yüe 218

deck chair 折叠椅 jer-die-yee 116

declare, to 申报 shen-bao 67

deduct, to (money) 扣除 ko-choo

deep 深的 shen de

deep freeze 速冻 soo-dong

defrost, to 解冻 jie-dong

degrees (temperature) 度 doo

delay 晚点 wan-dian 70

delicatessen 熟食店 sho-sh-dian 130, 158

delicious 好吃 hao-ch 14

deliver, to 送货 song-huo

denim 牛仔布料 nio-dsai-boo-liao 145

dental floss 牙线 ya-shian

dentist 牙医 ya-yee 131, 161, 168

dentures 假牙 jia-ya 168

deodorant 除汗臭香水 choo-han-cho shiarng-shwee 142

depart, to (train, bus) 出发 choo-fa

department (in store) 部 boo 132

department store 百货商店 bai-huo-sharng-dian 130

departure lounge 候机厅 ho-jee-ting

deposit 押金 ya-jin 24, 83

describe, to 描述 miao-shoo 152

destination 目的地 moo-dee-dee

details 详情 shiarng-ching

detergent 洗涤剂 shee-dee-jee

develop, to (photos) 冲洗 chong-shee 151

diabetes 糖尿病 tarng-niao-bing

diabetic, to be 患糖尿病 hwan-tarng-niao-bing 39, 163

diagnosis 诊断 jen-dwan 164

dialling code 地区号 dee-chü hao 127

diamond 钻石 dswan-sh 149

diapers 尿片 niao-pian 142

diarrhea 痢疾 lee-jee 141, 163

dice 色子 shai-ts

dictionary 词典 ts-dian 150

diesel 柴油 chai-yo 87

diet: I'm on a diet 我在节食 wo dsai jie-sh

difficult 困难 kwun-nan 14

dining car 餐车 tsan-cher 75, 77

dining room 餐厅 tsan-ting 26, 29

dinner jacket 晚礼服 wan-lee-foo

dinner, to have 吃饭 ch-fan 124

direct (of train, etc.) 直达 j-da 75

direct, to 指路 j-loo 18

direction, in the ... 方向 dsai ... farng-shiarng 95

director (of company) 董事 dong-sh

directory (telephone) 电话簿 dian-hwaa-boo

Directory Enquiries 查询台 cha-shün-tai 127

dirty 不干净 boo-gan-jing 14, 28

disabled 残疾人 tsan-jee-ren 22, 100

discotheque 迪斯科舞场 dee-s-ker woo-charng 112

dish (meal) 菜 tsai 37

dish cloth 擦碟巾 tsa-die-jin 148

dishwashing liquid 餐具洗涤剂 tsan-jü shee-dee-jee 148

dislocated, to be 脱臼 tuo-jio 164

display cabinet 陈列柜 chen-lie-gway 134, 149

disposable camera 一次性照相机 yee-ts-shing jao-shiarng-jee 151

distilled water 蒸馏水 jung-lio-shwee

disturb: don't disturb 请勿打扰 ching-woo da-rao

dive, to 潜水 chian-shwee 116

diving equipment 轻装潜水用具 ching-jwarng chian-shwee yong-jü 116

divorced, to be 离婚了 lee-hwun le 120

dizzy: I feel dizzy 我头昏 wo tou-hwun

do you accept ...? 你们收不收 ... ? nee-men sho-boo-sho ... 136

do you have ...? 你们有没有...? nee-men yo-may-yo ... 37

do: things to do 可做的事 ker dsuo de sh 123

doctor 医生 yee-shung 92, 131, 161, 167

doctor's office [surgery] 诊所 jen-suo 161

doll 洋娃娃 yarng-wa-wa 157

dollar 美元 may-yüan 67, 138

door 门 men 25, 29

dosage 剂量 jee-liarng 140

double 双人 shwarng-ren 81; ~ **bed** 双人床 shwarng-ren-chwarng 21; ~ **room** 双人房间 shwarng-ren farng-jian 21

downstairs (在) 楼下 (dsai) lo-shia 12

downtown area 市中心 sh-jong-shin 99

dozen 打 da 159, 217

draft [draught] (beer) 散装(啤酒) san-jwarng (pee-jio) 40

dress 连衣裙 lian-yee-chün 144

A-Z

drink, to 喝 her 70
drink (n) 一杯饮料 yee-bay yin-liao 124, 125, 126
drinking water 饮用水 yin-yong-shwee 30
drive, to 行驶 shing-sh 93
driver 司机 s-jee
drop someone off, to 让某人下车 rarng mo-ren shia-cher 83, 113
drowning: someone is drowning 有溺水了 yo-ren nee-shwee le
drugstore 杂货店 dsa-huo-dian 130
drunk 醉 dswee
dry cleaner 干洗店 gan-shee-dian 131
dry-clean, to 干洗 gan-shee
dubbed, to be 配音 pay-yin 110
dummy (U.K.) 橡皮奶头 shiarng-pee nai-tou
during 在 ... 期间 dsai ... chee-jian
dustbins 垃圾箱 la-jee-shiarng 30
duty-free shopping 免税购物 mian-shwee go-woo 67
duvet 羽绒被 yü-rong-bay

E **e-mail** 电子邮件 dian-ds yo-jian 155; **~ address** 电子邮件地址 dian-ds yo-jian dee-j 155
ear 耳朵 er-duo 166; **~ drops** 滴耳药水 dee er yao-shwee; **~ache** 耳朵痛 er-duo-tong 163
earlier 早一点 dsao-yee-dian 125, 147
early 早/提前 dsao/tee-chian 13, 14, 221
earrings 耳环 er-hwan 149
east 东 dong 95
easy 容易 rong-yee 14
eat, to 吃/吃饭 ch/ch-fan 41, 167; **places to ~** 吃饭的地方 ch-fan de dee-farng 123

economy class 经济舱 jing-jee tsarng 68
eggs 鸡蛋 jee-dan 160
elastic (adj) 有弹性的 yo tan-shing de
electric outlets 电源插座 dian-yüan cha-dsuo 30
electric shaver 电动剃须刀 dian-dong tee-shü-dao
electricity meter 电表 dian-biao 28
electronic flash 闪光灯 shan-gwarng-dung 151
electronic game 电子游戏 dian-ds yo-shee 157
elevator 电梯 dian-tee 26, 132
else: something else 其它事物 chee-ta sh-woo
embassy 大使馆 da-sh-gwan
emerald 翡翠 fay-tswee
emergency 紧急事情 jin-jee sh-ching 127; **~ exit** 紧急出口 jin-jee choo-ko
empty 空 kong 14
enamel 珐琅 fa-larng 149
end, to 结束 jie-shoo 108
engaged, to be 订婚了 ding-hwun le 120
engine 引擎 yin-ching
engineering 工程 gong-chung 121
England 英格兰 ying-ger-lan 119
English (language) 英语 ying-yü 11, 67, 110, 150, 152, 161
English (person) 英格兰人 ying-ger-lan-ren
English-speaking 会说英语的 hway shuo ying-yü de 98, 152
enjoy, to 喜欢 shee-hwan 110
enlarge, to (photos) 放大 farng-da 151
enough 够了/够 go-le/go 15, 42, 136
ensuite bathroom 卫生套间 way-shung tao-jian
entertainment guide 娱乐指南 yü-ler j-nan
entrance fee 入门费 roo-men-fay 100

entry visa 入境签证
  roo-jing chian-jung
envelope 信封 shin-fung 150
epileptic, to be 患有癫痫病
  hwan-yo dian-shian-bing 163
equipment (*sports*) 体育用具
  tee-yü yong-jü 115
error 错误 tsuo-woo
escalator 自动扶梯
  ds-dong foo-tee 132
essential 关键的 gwan-jian de 89
E.U. 欧洲联盟 o-jo lian-mung
Eurocheque 欧洲通用支票
  o-jo tong-yong j-piao
evening dress 夜礼服 ye-lee-foo 112
evening, in the 晚上 wan-sharng 221
events 文娱活动
  wen-yü huo-dong 108
every day 每天 may-tian; **~ hour** 每
  小时 may shiao-sh 76; **~ week** 每星
  期 may shing-chee 13
examination (*medical*) 检查 jian-cha
example, for 例如 lee-roo
except 除了 choo-le
excess baggage 超重行李
  chao-jong shing-lee 69
exchange rate 兑换率
  dwee-hwan-l 138
exchange, to 换/兑换
  hwan/dwee-hwan 138
excluding meals 不包括吃饭
  boo bao-kuo ch-fan 24
excursion 短途旅游
  dwan-too lü-yo 97
excuse me (*apology*) 对不起
  dwee-boo-chee 10; (*attention*) 请问
  ching-wen 10, 94
exhausted, to be 筋疲力尽
  jin-pee-lee-jin 106
exit 出口处 choo-ko-choo 70
expected, to be 需要 shü-yao 111
expensive 贵 gway 14, 134

exposure (*photos*)
  张 jarng 151
express 特快 ter-kwai
  155
extension 分机号码 fen-
  jee hao-ma 128
extra (*adj*) 额外的
  er-wai de 27
extracted, to be (*tooth*) 拔牙
  ba-ya 168
eye 眼睛 yan-jing 166

F **fabric** 织物 jee-woo 145
  face 脸 lian 166
facial 面部按摩 mian-boo
  an-muo 147
facilities 设备 sher-bay 22, 30
factor ... 系数 ... shee-shoo ... 142
faint, to feel 四肢无力
  s-jee woo-lee 163
fairground 游乐场
  yo-ler-charng 113
fall (*season*) 秋天 chio-tian 219
family 家人 jia-ren 66, 120, 167
famous 著名的 joo-ming de
fan 电风扇 dian-fung-shan 25
far 远 yüan 95
far-sighted 远视 yüan-sh 167
far: how far is it? 有多远?
  yo duo-yüan 73
fare 车费 cher-fay 79
farm 农场 nong-charng 107
fast 快 kwai 93
fast food 快餐 kwai-tsan 40;
  ~ food restaurant 快餐馆
  kwai-tsan-gwan 35
fast, to be (*clock*) 快 kwai 221
fat 脂肪 j-farng 39
father 父亲 foo-chin 120
faucet 水龙头
  shwee-long-tou 25

faulty: this is faulty 这个失灵了 jer-ge sh-ling le

favorite [favourite] 最喜爱的 dswee shee-ai de

fax machine 传真机 chwan-jen-jee 155

February 二月 er-yüe 218

feed, to 喂饭 way-fan 39

feeding bottle 奶瓶 nai-ping

feel ill, to 感觉不舒服 gan-jüe boo-shoo-foo 163

female 女的 nü-de 152

ferry 轮渡 lwun-doo 81

feverish, to feel 发烧 fa-shao 163

few 没几个 may-jee-ger 15

fiancé(e) 未婚夫(妻) way-hwun-foo (chee)

field 田 tian 107

fifth 第五 dee-woo 217

fight (brawl) 吵架 chao-jia

fill in, to 填 tian 155

fill out, to (a form) 填 tian 168

filling (dental) 补牙的填料 boo-ya de tian-liao 168

film 电影 dian-ying 108, 110

film (camera) 胶卷 jiao-jüan 151

filter 滤色镜 lü-ser-jing 151

find, to 找到 jao-dao 18

fine (good) 行 shing 19

fine: Fine, thank you. 很好，谢谢你。hen-hao, shie-shie ne 118

finger 手指 sho-j 166

fire alarm 火警报警器 huo-jing bao-jing-chee; **~ department [brigade]** 消防队 shiao-farng-dwee 92; **~ escape** 太平梯 tai-ping-tee; **~ extinguisher** 灭火器 mie-huo-chee; **~: There's a fire!** 失火啦! sh-huo-la; **~wood** 木柴 moo-chai

first 第一 dee-yee 68, 75, 217

first class 一等舱/一等车厢 yee-dung tsarng / yee-dung cher-shiarng 68, 74

fish restaurant 鱼餐馆 yü san-gwan 35

fish store [fishmonger] 鱼店 yü-dian 130

fit, to (clothes) 合身 her-shen 146

fitting room 试衣间 sh-yee jian 146

fix, to 修 shio 168

flashlight 手电筒 sho-dian-tong 31

flat (bicycle) 瘪了 bie le 83

flat (tire) 打炮 da-pao 88

flavor 风味 fung-way

flea 跳蚤 tiao-dsao

flight 航班 harng-ban 68, 70; **~ number** 航班号 harng-ban hao 68

flip-flops 人字拖鞋 ren-ds tuo-shie 145

floor (level) 楼层 lo-tsung 132

florist 花店 hwaa-dian 130

flour 面 mian 39

flower 花 hwaa 106

flu 流感 lio-gan 165

flush: the toilet won't flush 厕所抽水不灵了 tser-suo cho-shwee boo-ling le

fly (insect) 苍蝇 tsarng-ying

foggy, to be 有雾 yo-woo 122

folk art 民间艺术 min-jian yee-shoo; **~ music** 民间音乐 min-jian yin-yüe 111

follow, to 沿着 yan-jer 95

follow, to (pursue) 跟踪 gen-dsong 152

food 食物 sh-woo 39, 41; **~ poisoning** 食物中毒 sh-woo-jong-doo 165

food (cuisine) 吃的东西 ch-de-dong-shee 119

foot 脚 jiao 166

football 足球 dsoo-chio 114

footpath 小道 shiao-dao 107

for *(direction to a place)* 去 chü 94

for *(time)* 连续 lian-shü 13; **~ a day** 租用一天 dsoo-yong yee-tian 86; **~ a week** 租用一星期 dsoo-yong yee-shing-chee 86

forecast 预报 yü-bao 122

foreign currency 外币 wai-bee 138

forest 森林 sen-lin 107

forget, to 忘记了 warng-jee le 42

fork 叉子 cha-ds 39, 41, 148

form 表(格) biao (ger) 23, 155, 168

formal dress 正规衣服 jung-gway yee-foo 111

fortnight 两个星期 liarng-ge shing-chee

fortunately 幸好 shing-hao 19

fountain 喷泉 pen-chüan 99

four-door car 四门车 s-men cher 86; **~-wheel drive** 四轮驱动 s-lwun chü-dong 86

fourth 第四 dee-s 217

foyer *(hotel, theater)* 门厅 men-ting

fracture 骨折 goo-jer 165

frame *(glasses)* 眼镜架 yan-jing-jia

free *(available)* 空 kong 36

free *(not busy)* 有空 yo-kong 124

free *(of charge)* 免费 mian-fay 69

freezer 冷冻柜 lung-dong-gway 29

frequent: how frequent? 每隔多久有一班? may ger duo-jo yee yee-ban 76

frequently 频繁 pin-fan

fresh 新鲜 shin-shian 41

Friday 星期五 shing-chee-woo 218

fried 炸 ja

friend 朋友 pung-yo 162

friendly 友善 yo-shan

fries 炸土豆条 ja-too-dou-tiao 38, 40

frightened, to be 害怕 hai-pa

from 从 ... 来 tsong ... lai 12

from *(come from)* 来自 lai-ds 119

from ... to *(time)* 从 ... 到 ... tsong ... dao ... 13, 221

front 前面 chian-mian 147

front door 前门 chian-men 26

frosty, to be 有霜 yo-shwarng 122

frying pan 炒锅 chao-guo 29

fuel *(gasoline/petrol)* 燃料油 **(汽油)** ran-liao-yo (chee-yo) 86

full 满 man 14

full board *(American Plan [A.P.])* 吃住全包 ch-joo chüan-bao 24

full insurance 全保险 chüan-bao-shian 86

fun, to have 玩得开心 wan-de kai-shin

furniture 家具 jia-jü

fuse 保险丝 bao-shian-s 28; **~ box** 保险丝盒 bao-shian-s her 28

G **game** 比赛 bee-sai 114

game *(toy)* 游戏机 yo-shee-jee 157

garage 修车行 shio-cher-harng 88

garbage bags 垃圾袋 la-jee-dai 148

garden 花园 hwa-yüan

gas: I smell gas! 有煤气味! yo may-chee way; **~ bottle** 煤气罐 may-chee-gwan 28; **~ station** 加油站 jia-yo jan 87

gasoline 汽油 chee-yo 87, 88

gastritis 胃炎 way-yan 165

gate *(airport)* 登机口 dung-jee-ko 70

gauze 纱带 bung-dai 141

genuine 真的 jen-de 134, 157

get off, to 下车 shia-cher 79

get to: how do I get to ...? 去 ... 怎么走? chü ... dsen-me dso 70, 73, 77, 94

get, to *(find)* 到 dao 84

gift 礼品 lee-pin 67, 156;
~ **store** 礼品店 lee-pin-dian 130

girl 女孩 nü-hai 120, 157;
~**friend** 女朋友 nü-pung-yo 120

give, to 给 gay

gland 淋巴 lin-ba 166

glass 杯子 bay-ds 37, 39

glasses (optical) 眼镜 yan-jing 167

glossy finish (photos) 光面 gwarng-mian

glove 手套 sho-tao

go, to 去 chü 18

go: let's go! 我们走吧! wo-men dso ba

go, to (to take out) 不在店里吃 boo dsai dian-lee ch 40

go away! 走开! dso-kai

go back, to (turn around) 回头 hway-tou 95

go for a walk, to 出去散散步 choo-chü san-san-boo 124

go on! 接着来! jie-jer lai 19

go out, to (in evening) 出去玩 choo-chü wan

go shopping, to 逛逛商店 gwarng-gwarng sharng-dian 124

goggles 护目镜 hoo-moo-jing

gold 金 jin 149; ~**-plate** 镀金 doo-jin 149

golf 高尔夫 gao-er-foo 114;
~ **course** 高尔夫球场 gao-er-foo chio-charng 115

good 好 hao 14, 35, 42; ~ **afternoon** 你好 nee-hao 10; ~ **evening** 你好 nee-hao 10; ~ **morning** 你早 nee-dsao 10: ~ **night** 晚安 an-an 10; ~**bye** 再见 dsai-jian 10

good value, to be 很划算 hen hwaa-swan 101

grade (fuel) 级别 jee-bie 87

gram 克 ker 159

grandparents 祖父母 dsoo-foo-moo

grapes 葡萄 poo-tao 160

grass 草 tsao

gray 灰色 hway-ser 143

graze 擦伤 tsa-sharng 162

great (excellent) 太好了 tai-hao le 19, 125

green 绿色 lü-ser 143

greengrocer 蔬菜店 shoo-tsai-dian 130

grilled 烧烤 shao-kao

grocer [grocery store] 食品杂货店 sh-pin dsa-huo-dian 130

ground (earth) 露营地 loo-ying-dee 31

groundcloth [groundsheet] 铺地防湿布 poo-dee farng-sh-boo 31

group 团体 twan-tee 66, 100

guarantee 保用证 bao-yong-jung 135

guide (tour) 导游 dao-yo 98

guidebook 导游册 dao-yo-tser 150

guided tour 有导游的游览 yo dao-yo de yo-lan

guitar 吉他 jee-ta

gum 牙床 ya-chwarng

guy rope 拉绳 la-shung 31

gynocologist 妇科医生 foo-ker yee-shung 167

H

hair 头发 tou-fa 147; ~ **mousse/gel** 摩斯 muo-s 142; ~ **spray** 喷发定型剂 pen-fa ding-shing-jee 142; ~**cut** 理发 lee-fa; ~**dresser** 美发厅 may-fa-ting 131, 147; ~**stylist** 美发师 may-fa-sh 147

half, a 半 ban 217; ~ **board** (Modified American Plan [M.A.P.]) 吃住半包 ch-joo ban-bao 24; ~ **past** ... 半 ... ban 220

hammer 小锤子 shiao chwee-ds 31

hand 手 sho 166; **~ luggage** 手提行李 sho-tee shing-lee 69; **~ washable** 可以手洗 ker-yee sho-shee 145; **~bag** 手提包 sho-tee-bao 144, 153

handicapped, to be 有残疾 yo tsan-jee 163

handicrafts 手工艺品 sho-gong-yee-pin

handkerchief 手帕 sho-pa

hanger (clothes) 衣架 yee-jia 27

hangover 酒后不适 jio-ho boo-sh 141

harbor 港湾 garng-wan

hat 帽子 mao-ds 144

have, to 要 yao 18, 125; **~: I'll have ...** 我要 … wo yao ... 37

have, to (hold stock of) 有 yo 133

have an appointment, to 约好了 yüe-hao le 161

have to, to (must) 必须 bee-shü 79

hayfever 花粉病 hwaa-fen-bing 141

head 头 tou 166

head waiter 领班 ling-ban 41

headache 头痛 tou-tong 163

heading, to be (in a direction) 去 chü 83

health food store 保健食品店 bao-jian sh-pin-dian 130

health insurance 健康保险 jian-karng bao-shian 168

hear, to 听到 ting-dao

hearing aid 助听器 joo-ting-chee

heart 心脏 shin 166; **~ attack** 心脏病发作 shin-dsarng-bing fa-dsuo 163; **~ condition** 心脏不好 shin-dsarng boo-hao 163

hearts (cards) 红桃 hong-tao

heat [heating] 暖气 nwan-chee 25

heater 暖气 nwan-chee

heavy 重 jong 14

height 身高 shen-gao 152

hello 你好 nee-hao 10, 118

help, to 帮助 barng-joo 18; **~: can you help me?** 请帮帮我。 ching barng-barng wo 71, 92

hemorrhoids 痔疮 j-chwarng 165

her(s) 她的 ta-de 16; **~: it's hers** 这是她的 jer-sh ta-de

here 这儿 jer-r 12, 17

hernia 疝 shan 165

hi! 你好 nee-hao 10

high 高 gao 122

high street 主商业街 joo sharng-ye-jie 96

highlight, to 用浅色染一染 yong chian-ser ran-yee-ran 147

highway 高速公路 gao-soo-gong-loo 94

hike (walk) 徒步旅行 too-boo lü-shing 106

hiking 徒步旅行 too-boo lü-shing; **~ boots** 长途行走靴 charng-too shing-dso-shüe 145; **~ gear** 远足用具 yüan-dsoo yong-jü

hill 小山 shiao-shan 107

hire, to 租 dsoo 83, 86

his 他的 ta-de 16; **~: it's his** 这是他的 jer-sh ta-de

hitchhiking 搭便车 da-bian-cher 83

HIV-positive 染有艾滋病毒 ran-yo ai-ds bing-doo

hobby 业余爱好 ye-yü ai-hao 121

hold on, to 稍等 shao-dung 128

hole (in clothes) 破洞 po-dong

holiday resort 度假胜地 doo-jia shung-dee

holiday, on 度假 doo-jia 66, 123

homosexual (adj) 同性恋 tong-shing-lian

honeymoon: be on honeymoon 渡蜜月 doo mee-yüe

A-Z

horse 马 ma; **~-racing**
赛马 sai-ma 114

hospital 医院 yee-yüan
131, 164, 167

hot 热 rer 14, 122; **~ dog**
"热狗" rer-go 110; **~ spring**
温泉 wen-chüan; **~ water** 热水
rer-shwee 25

hotel 旅馆 lü-gwan
21, 123

hour 小时 shiao-sh 97; **in an ~**
一小时后 yee-shiao-sh ho 84

house 房屋 farng-woo

housewife 家庭主妇
jia-ting joo-foo 121

hovercraft 气垫船
chee-dian-chwan 81

how 怎么 dsen-me 17

how are you? 你怎么样?
nee dsen-me-yarng? 19, 118

how far ... 有多远
... yo-duo-yüan 94, 106

how long ... 多久 ...
duo-jio 23, 75,
76, 78, 88, 94, 98,135

how many 多少 ... duo-shao 15, 80

how much ... (money) ... 多少钱
... duo-shao chian 15, 21, 65, 69, 84,
100, 109

how much (quantity) 多少
duo-shao 140

how often 多频繁 duo pin-fan 140

how old 多大了 ... duo-da le 120

hundred 百 bai 216

hungry: I am hungry 我饿了 wo e le

hurry: I in a hurry 我要赶时间
wo yao gan sh-jian

hurt, to 疼 tung 164

hurt, to be 受伤 sho-sharng 92, 162

hurt: my ... hurts 我的 ... 受伤了
wo-de ... sho-sharng le 162

husband 丈夫 jarng-foo 120, 162

I

ice 冰 bing 38; **~ cream** 冰淇
淋 bing-chee-lin 40, 160;
~-cream parlor 冷饮店
lung-yin-dian 35

icy, to be 结冰 jie-bing 122

identification 身分证明
shen-fen jung-ming

ill: I am ill 我病了 wo bing le

illegal: is it illegal 这不合法吗
jer boo her-fa ma

imitation 仿制的 farng-j de 134

immediately 立刻 lee-ker 13

in (place) 在 ... 里 dsai ... lee 12;
(time) 在 ... 之内 dsai ... j-nay 13

included: is ... included 包括在内吗
... bao-kuo dsai nay ma 86, 98

indigestion 消化不良
shiao-hwaa boo-liarng

indoor pool 室内游泳池
sh-nay yo-yong-ch 116

inexpensive 不贵 boo gway 35

infected, to be 感染 gan-ran 165

infection 炎症 yan-jung 167

inflammation of ... ... 炎 ... yan 165

informal (dress) 随便的 swee-bian de

information 资料 ds-liao 97

Information (telephone service) 查询台
cha-shün-tai 127

information desk 问讯处
wen-shün-choo 73

information office 旅游信息服务处
lü-yo shin-shee foo-woo-choo 96

injection 打针 da-jen 168

injured, to be 受伤
sho-sharng 92, 162

innocent 天真 tian-jen

insect 虫子 chong-ds 25

insect bite 虫咬/蚊叮虫咬 chong-
yao/wen-ding chong-yao 141, 162; **~
repellent** 驱蚊剂 chü-wen-jee 141

inside 在 ... 里面 dsai ... lee-mian 12

insist: I insist 我坚决要求
wo jian-jüe yao-chio

insomnia 失眠 sh-mian

instant coffee 速溶咖啡
soo-rong-ka-fay 160

instead of 而不是 er boo-sh

instructions 使用说明
sh-yong shuo-ming 135

instructor 教练 jiao-lian

insulin 胰岛素 yee-dao-soo

insurance 保险 bao-shian 86, 89, 93,
168; **~ claim** 保险索赔 bao-shian suo-
pay 153; **~ company** 保险公司
bao-shian-gong-s 93

interest 爱好 ai-hao 121

interesting 有意思 yo-yee-s 101

International Student Card
国际通用学生证 guo-jee tong-yong
shüe-shung-jung 29

Internet 因特网 yin-ter-warng 155

intersection 交叉路口
jiao-cha-loo-ko 95

introduce oneself, to 自我介绍
ds-wo-jie-shao 118

invitation 邀请 yao-ching 124

invite, to 邀请 yao-ching 124

iodine 碘 dian

Ireland 爱尔兰 ai-er-lan 119

Irish (person) 爱尔兰人 ai-er-lan-ren

is it ...? 是不是 ... ? sh-boo-sh ... 17

is there ...? 有没有 ... ?
yo-may-yo ... 17

is this ...? 这是不是 ... ?
jer sh-boo-sh ... 145

it is ... 这是 ... jer sh ... 17

Italian (cuisine) 意大利式
yee-da-lee-sh 35

itch: It itches 这儿痒 jer-r yarng

itemized bill 分项帐单 fen-shiarng
jarng-dan 32

J **jacket** 夹克衫
jia-ker-shan 144

jam 果酱 guo-jiarng

jammed, to be 打不开
da-boo-kai 25

January 一月 yee-yüe 218

Japan 日本 r-ben 119

Japanese (person) 日本人
r-ben-ren

jar 瓶 ping 159

jaw 下巴 shia-ba 166

jazz 爵士乐 jüe-sh-yüe 111

jeans 牛仔裤 nio-dsai-koo 144

jellyfish 海蜇 hai-jer

jet lag: I'm jet lagged 我有时差反应
wo yo sh-cha fan-ying

jet-ski 滑水快艇 hwaa-shwee
kwai-ting 116

jeweler 珠宝店 joo-bao-dian 130, 149

job: what's your job? 你是做什么的?
nee-sh dsuo shen-me de

join: may we join you? 我们插进来行
吗? wo-men cha jin-lai shing-ma 124

joint (of body) 关节
gwan-jie 166

joint passport 合用护照
her-yong hoo-jao 66

joke 笑话 shiao-hwaa

journalist 记者 jee-jer

journey 全程/旅程 chüan-chung/
lü-chung 76, 78, 123

jug 罐 gwan

July 七月 chee-yüe 218

jump leads 跨接电缆
kwaa-jie dian-lan

jumper 毛衣 mao-yee

junction 交叉路口
jiao-cha-loo-ko 95

June 六月 lio-yüe 218

A-Z

K

karaoke 卡拉OK ka-la-o-kai 111
keep, to 留着 lio-je 84
kerosene stove 便携式煤油炉 bian-shie-sh may-yo-loo 31
ketchup 番茄汁 fan-chie-j
kettle 水壶 shwee-hoo 29
key 钥匙 yao-sh 27, 28, 88
key ring 钥匙圈 yao-sh-chüan 156
kiddie pool 儿童戏水池 er-tong shee-shwee-ch 113
kidney 肾 shen 166
kilo 公斤 gong-jin 69
kilo(gram) 公斤 gong-jin 159
kilometer 公里 gong-lee
kind (pleasant) 友好的 yo-hao de
kind: what kind of ... 哪种 … na-jong ...
kiss, to 吻 wen
kitchen 厨房 choo-farng 29
knapsack 背包 bay-bao 31, 145
knee 膝盖 shee-gai 166
knickers 女内裤 nü nay-koo
knife 刀 dao 39, 41, 148
know: I don't know 我不知道 wo boo j-dao 14
Korea 韩国 han-guo 119
Korean (person) 韩国人 han-guo-ren

L

label 标签 biao-chian
lace 花边 hwaa-bian 145
ladder 梯子 tee-ds
lake 湖 hoo 107
lamp 电灯/灯 dian-dung/dung 25, 29
land, to 降落 jiarng-luo 70
language course 语言课程 yü-yan ker-chung
large 大 da 40, 110
larger 大点的 da-dian de 134
last 最后/上个 dswee-ho/sharng-ger 68, 75, 80, 218

last, to 持续 ch-shü
late (delayed) 晚点了 wan-dian le 70, 222
later 迟点 ch-dian 125, 147
laugh, to 笑 shiao 126
laundromat 自助洗衣店 ds-joo shee-yee-dian 131
laundry facilities 洗衣设备 shee-yee sher-bay 30; ~ service 洗衣服务 shee-yee foo-woo 22
lavatory 厕所 tser-suo
lawyer 律师 lü-sh 152
laxative 轻泻剂 ching-shie-jee
lead, to (road) 通到 tong-dao 94
lead-free (gas/petrol) 无铅 (汽油) woo-chian (chee-yo) 87
leader (of group) 领导 ling-dao
leak, to (roof, pipe) 漏 lo
learn, to (language) 学习 shüe-shee
leather 皮革 pee-ger 145
leave from, to (transport) 从 ... 发车 tsong ... fa-cher 78
leave me alone! 你走开! nee dso-kai 126
leave, to 离开/出发 lee-kai/choo-fa 32, 68, 70, 76, 81, 98, 126
leave, to (car) 停放 ting-farng 73
left, on the 左边 dsuo-bian 76, 95
left-luggage office 行李存放处 shing-lee tswun-farng-choo 71, 73
leg 腿 twee 166
legal: is it legal? 这合法吗? jer her-fa ma
leggings 绑腿 barng-twee 144
lemon 柠檬 ning-mung 38
lemonade 柠檬汽水 ning-mung chee-shwee
lend: could you lend me ...? 你能把 ...借给我吗? nee nung ba ... jie-gay wo ma
lens (camera) 镜头 jing-tou 151; ~ **cap** 镜头盖 jing-tou-gai 151

lens (glasses) 镜片 jing-pian 167

lesbian club 女同性恋俱乐部 nü-tong-shing-lian jü-ler-boo

less 更少 gung-shao 15

lesson 课 ker

letter 信 shin 154

letterbox 信箱 shin-shiarng

level (ground) 平坦 ping-tan 31

library 图书馆 too-shoo-gwan

lie down, to 躺下来 tarng-shia-lai 164

lifeboat 救生艇 jio-shung-ting 81

lifeguard 救生员 jio-shung-yüan 116

lifejacket 救生衣 jio-shung-yee

life preserver [belt] 救生带 jio-shung-dai 81

lift 电梯 dian-tee 26, 132

lift pass (ski) 缆车票 lan-cher-piao 117

light (of color) 浅 chian 14, 134, 143

light (of weight) 轻 ching 14, 134

light (bicycle) 车灯 cher-dung 83

light (electric) 电灯 dian-dung 25

light bulb 灯泡 dung-pao 148

lighter (vs dark) 光线好点的 gwarng-shian hao dian de 24

lighter (color) 更浅 gung-chian 143

lighter (cigarette) 打火机 da-huo-jee 150

like this (similar to) 象这个 shiarng jer-ge

like, to 喜欢 shee hwan 101, 111, 119, 121; **I don't ~ it** 我不喜欢 wo boo shee-hwan; **I ~ it** 我挺喜欢 wo ting shee-hwan; **I'd ~ ...** 我想 ... wo shiarng ... 18, 36, 37, 40, 133

limousine 豪华轿车 hao-hwaa jiao-cher

line (subway) 地铁路线 dee-tie loo-shian 80

linen 亚麻布 ya-ma-boo 145

lip 唇 chwun 168

lipstick 唇膏 chwun-gao

liqueur 烈性酒 lie-shing-jio

liquor store 酒类专卖店 jio-lay jwan-mai-dian 131

liter 公升 gong-shung 87, 159

little (small) 小 shiao

live together, to 生活在一起 shung-huo dsai yee-chee 120

live, to 住 joo 119

liver 肝 gan 166

living room 客厅 ker-ting 29

loaf of bread 大面包 da mian-bao 160

lobby (theater, hotel) 大厅 da-ting

local 当地的 darng-dee de 37

local anesthetic 局部麻醉 jü-boo ma-dswee 168

lock 锁 suo 25

lock oneself out, to 把钥匙锁在房间里了 ba yao-sh suo dsai farng-jian lee le 27

lock, to 锁 suo 88

locked, to be 上锁 sharng-suo 26

long 长 charng 144, 146

long-distance bus 长途汽车 charng-too-chee-cher 78

long-sighted 远视 yüan-sh 167

long: how long? 多久？ duo-jio 164

longer: how much longer? 再等多久？ dsai dung duo-jio 41

look for, to 找 jao 18;
I'm looking for ... 我想找 ... wo shiarng jao ... 143

looking for, to be 找 jao 133

loose 宽松 kwan-song 146

lorry (U.K.) 卡车 ka-cher

lose, to 丢失 dio sh 28, 138, 153

lose: I've lost ... 我丢失了 ... wo dio-shee le ... 71, 153

lost-and-found [lost property office] 失物招领处 sh-woo jao-ling-choo 73

louder 大点声 da-dian-shung 128

love: I love you 我爱你 wo ai nee

lovely 真好 jen-hao 122

low 低 dee 122

low-fat 低脂肪 dee-j-farng

lower *(berth)* 下铺 shia-poo 74

luck: good luck 祝你好运 joo-nee hao-yün 220

luggage 行李 shing-lee 32, 69, 71

luggage carts [trolleys] 手推车 sho-twee-cher 71

lump 疙瘩 ger-da 162

lunch 中饭/午餐 jong-fan/woo-tsan 98, 154

lung 肺 fay

M **machine washable** 可以用洗衣机洗 ker-yee yong shee-yee-jee shee 145

madam 女士 nü-sh

magazine 杂志 dsa-j 150

magnificent 宏伟 hong-way 101

maid 清洁工 ching-jie-gong 28

mail (n) 信件 shin-jian; **by ~** 写信 shie-shin 22; **to ~** 寄信 jee-shin 27; **~box** 邮筒 yo-tong 154

main 主要的 joo-yao de 130

main street 主街 joo-jie 95, 96

make an appointment, to 预约时间 yü-yüe sh-jian 161

make-up 化妆品 hwaa-jwarng-pin

Malaysia 马来西亚 ma-lai-shee-ya

male 男的 nan-de 152

mallet 大锤子 da chwee-ds 31

man *(male)* 男人 nan-ren

manager 经理 jing-lee 25, 41, 137

manicure 修指甲 shio-j-jia 147

manual *(car)* 手动变速 sho-dong bian-soo

many 很多 hen-duo 15

map 地图 dee-too 94, 106, 150

March 三月 san-yüe 218

margarine 人造黄油 ren-dsao hwarng-yo 160

market 集市 jee-sh 99, 131

married, to be 结婚了 jie-hwun le 120

mascara 睫毛膏 jie-mao-gao

mask *(diving)* 面具 mian-jü

mass 弥撒 mee-sa 105

massage 按摩 an-muo 147

match 比赛 bee-sai 114

matches 火柴 huo-chai 31, 148, 150

matin 日场 r-charng 109

matter: it doesn't matter 不要紧 boo-yao-jin

matter: what's the matter? 怎么了? dsen-me le

mattress 床垫 chwarng-dian

May 五月 woo-yüe 218

may I ...? 可不可以/我能不能 ...? ker boo-ker-yee/wo nung-boo-nung ... 18, 37

maybe 也许 ye-shü

me 我 wo

meal 饭 fan 38, 42, 124, 125, 165

mean, to 意思是 yee-s-sh 11

measles 麻疹 ma-jen 165

measure, to 量 liarng 146

measurement 尺寸 ch-tswun

meat 肉 ro 41

medication [medicine] 药 yao 164, 165

medium 中/中等 jong/jong-dung 40, 122

meet, to 会面 hway-mian 125

meet: pleased to meet you 幸会 shing-hway 118

meeting place [point] 约会地点 yüe-hway dee-dian 12

member *(of club)* 成员/会员 chung-yüan/hway-yüan 112, 115

men (toilets) 男厕所 nan tser-suo

mention: don't mention it 没关系 may-gwan-shee 10

menu 菜单 tsai-dan

message 留言 lio-yan 27

metal 金属 jin-shoo

meter (taxi) 计费表 jee-fay-biao 84

metro 地铁 dee-tie 80

metro station 地铁站 dee-tie-jan 80, 96

microwave (oven) 微波炉 way-buo-loo

midday 正午 jung-woo

midnight 半夜 ban-ye 220

migraine 偏头痛 pian-tou-tong

mileage 里程 lee-chung 86

milk 牛奶 nio-nai 160

million 百万 bai-wan 216

mind: do you mind 你介意吗 nee jie-yee ma 77, 126; **~: I don't mind** 我不在乎 wo boo-dsai-hoo 19

mine 我的 wo-de 16

it's ~ 这是我的 jer-sh wo-de

mineral water 矿泉水 kwarng-chüan-shwee

mini-bar 小酒吧 shiao-jio-ba 32

minimart 小型集市 shiao-shing-jee-sh 158

minute 分钟 fen-jong 76

mirror 镜子 jing-ds

miss, to 误了 woo le 79

missing, to be 不见了/失踪了 boo-jian le/sh-dsong le 137, 152

mistake 错 tsuo 32, 41, 42

modern 时髦 sh-mao 14

moisturizer (cream) 润肤霜 rwun-foo-shwarng

monastery 寺院 s-yüan 99

Monday 星期一 shing-chee-yee 218

money 钱 chian 42, 136, 139, 153

Mongolia 蒙古 mung-goo

month 月 yüe 218

monthly (ticket) 月票 yüe-piao 79

moped 机动自行车 jee-dong ds-shing-cher 83

more 更多 gung-duo 15

morning, in the 早上/上午 dsao-sharng/sharng-woo 221

mosque 清真寺 ching-jen-s 105

mosquito bite 蚊咬 wen-yao

mother 母亲 moo-chin 120

motion sickness 晕车 yün-cher 141

motorbike 摩托车 mo-tuo-cher 83

motorboat 摩托艇 mo-tuo-ting 116

motorway 高速公路 gao-soo-gong-loo 94

mountain 山 shan 107; **~ bike** 山地车 shan-dee cher; **~ pass** 山路 shan-loo 107; **~ range** 山脉 shan-mai 107

moustache 小胡子 shiao-hoo-ds

mouth 嘴 dswee 164, 166

mouth ulcer 口腔溃疡 ko-chiarng kwee-yarng

move, to 换 hwan 25

movie 电影 dian-ying 108, 110

movie theater 电影院 dian-ying-yüan 96, 110

Mr. 先生 shian-shung

Mrs. 夫人 foo-ren

much 很 hen 15

mugged, to be 被抢劫 bay chiarng-jie 153

mugging 抢劫 chiarng-jie 152

mugs 茶杯 cha-bay 148

multiplex cinema 多银幕电影院 duo-yin-moo dian-ying-yüan 110

mumps 腮腺炎 sai-shian-yan

muscle 肌肉 jee-ro 166

museum 博物馆 bo-woo-gwan 99

music 音乐 yin-yüe 111, 121

musician 音乐家 yin-yüe-jia

must: I must 我必须 wo bee-shü

mustard 芥末 jie-mo 38

my 我的 wo-de 16

A-Z

N name 名字 ming-ds 22, 118, 120

name: my name is 我姓 … wo shing 118

name: what's your name? 您贵姓 nin gway-shing 118

napkin 餐巾 tsan-jin 39

nappies 尿片 niao-pian 142

narrow 窄 jai 14

national 全国的 chüan-guo de

nationality 国籍 guo-jee

nature reserve 自然保护区 ds-ran bao-hoo-chü 107

nausea 恶心 e-shin

near 靠近 kao-jin 12

near-sighted 近视 jin-sh 167

nearby 附近 foo-jin 21, 87

nearest 附近 foo-jin 80, 88, 92, 130, 140

neck 颈 jing 166

necklace 项链 shiarng-lian 149

need: I need to … 我需要 … wo shü-yao … 18

nephew 甥侄 shung-j

nerve 神经 shen-jing

nervous system 神经系统 shen-jing shee-tong

never 从来没有 tsong-lai may-yo 13

never mind 不要紧 boo-yao-jin 10

new 新 shin 14

New Year 新年 shin-nian 219

newspaper 报纸 bao-j 150

newsstand [newsagent] 报摊/报刊店 pao-tan/bao-kan-dian 131, 150

next 下一个 shia-yee-ge 68, 75, 78, 80; **~ stop** 下一站 shia-yee-jan 79; **~ to** 在 … 旁边/紧靠着 dsai … parng-bian/jin-kao-jer 12, 95

nice 好 hao

niece 甥女/侄女 shung-nü/j-nü

night, at 夜里 ye-lee 221

nightclub 夜总会 ye-dsong-hway 112

no 不对 boo-dwee 10

no way! 我才不干呢! wo tsai boo-gan ne 19

no one 没人 may-ren 16, 92

noisy 吵 chao 14, 24

non-alcoholic 不含酒精 boo-han jio-jing

non-smoking 不抽烟 boo-cho-yan 36

none 一个没有 yee-ger may-yo 15, 16

nonsense 胡说 hoo-shuo 19

noon 中午 jong-woo 220

normal 正常 jung-charng 67

north 北 bay 95

nose 鼻子 bee-ds 166

not bad 不错 boo-tsuo 19

not good 不好 boo-hao 19

not yet 还没有 hai-may-yo 13

note (money) 钞票 chao-piao 139

nothing else 什么都不要了 shen-me dou boo-yao le 15

notify, to 告诉 gao-soo 167

November 十一月 sh-yee-yüe 218

now 现在 shian-dsai 13, 84

number 号码 hao-ma 138; **~ plate** 车牌 cher-pai

nurse 护士 hoo-sh

nylon 尼龙 nee-long

O o'clock, it's … 现在 … 点 shian-dsai … dian 220

occasionally 偶尔 o-er

occupied 有人 yo-ren 14

October 十月 sh-yüe 218

odds (betting) 赔率 pay-lü 114

of course 当然 darng-ran 19

off-licence 酒类专卖店 jo-lay jwan-mai-dian 131

off-peak 非高峰期 fay gao-fung-chee

office 办公室 ban-gong-sh

often 经常 jing-charng 13

oil 油 yo

okay 行/可以 shing/ker-yee 10, 19

old (vs new) 旧 jio 14

old (vs young) 年老 nian-lao 14

old town 旧城区 jio chung-chü 96, 99

old-fashioned 过时 guo-sh 14

olive oil 橄榄油 gan-lan-yo

omelet 煎蛋 jian-dan

on foot 步行 boo-shing 17, 95

on my own 我自己 wo ds-jee 120

on the hour 每个小时整点 may-ger shiao-sh jung-dian 76

on the left 在左边 dsai dsuo-bian 12

on the right 在右边 dsai yo-bian 12

on, to be (be showing of film, etc.) 上映 sharng-ying 110

on/off switch 开关 kai-gwan

once 一次 yee-ts 217

once a week 每星期一次 may shing-chee yee-ts 13

one like that 象那个一样 shiarng na-ge yee-yarng 16

one-way 单程 dan-chung 65

one-way ticket 单程票 dan-chung piao 68, 74

open 开 kai 14

open, to 开门 kai-men 77, 100, 132, 140

open-air pool 室外游泳池 sh-wai yo-yong-ch 116

opening hours 开门时间 kai-men sh-jian 100

opera 歌剧 ger-jü 108, 111; ~ house 歌剧院 ger-jü-yüan 99, 111

operation 手术 sho-shoo

opposite 在 ... 对面 dsai ... dwee-mian 12

optician 眼镜店 yan-jing-dian 131, 167

or 或者 huo-jer

orange 橘黄色 jü-hwarng-ser 143

orchestra 乐团 yüe-twan 111

order, to (taxi) 叫 jiao 32

order, to (in restaurant) 点菜 dian-tsai 37, 41

organized hike 有组织的徒步旅行 yo-dsoo-j de too-boo lü-shing

others 其它的 chee-ta de 134

our(s) 我们(的) wo-men (de) 16

outdoor 户外 hoo-wai

outrageous 漫天要价 man-tian yao-jia 89

outside 在 ... 外面/外面 dsai ... wai-mian/wai-mian 12, 36

oval 椭圆的 tuo-yüan de 134

oven 烤炉 kao-loo

over there 那儿/在那儿 na-r/dsai na-r 36, 76

overdone (food) 煮得太老 joo de tai lao 41

overheat 过热 guo-rer

overnight 一晚 yee-wan 23

owe, to 欠款 chian-kwan 168

owe: how much do I owe? 收多少钱? sho duo-shao chian

own: on my own 我自己 wo-ds-jee 65

owner 主人 joo-ren

P

p.m. 下午 shia-woo

pacifier (dummy) 橡皮奶嘴 sharing-pee nai-dswee

pack, to 打点 da-dian

package 包裹 bao-guo 155

packed lunch 盒饭 her-fan

packet 包 bao 159

packet of cigarettes 一包香烟 yee-bao shiarng-yan 150

paddling pool 儿童戏水池 er-tong shee-shwee-ch 113

padlock 挂锁 gwaa-suo

pagoda 宝塔 bao-ta 99

pail 小桶 shiao-tong 157

pain, to be in 感到疼痛 gan-dao tung-tong 167

painkillers 止痛片 j-tong-pian 141, 165

paint, to 画 hwaa

painter 画家 hwaa-jia

painting 画 hwaa

pair of ... , a 一双... yee-shwarng ... 217

palace 宫殿 gong-dian 99

palpitations 心悸 shin-jee

panorama 全景 chüan-jing 107

pants (U.S.) 裤子 koo-ds 144

panty hose 裤袜 koo-waa 144

paper 报纸 bao-j 150

paper napkins 纸巾 j-jin 148

paracetamol 扑热息痛 poo-rer shee-tong

paraffin 煤油 may-yo 31

paralysis 瘫痪 tan-hwan

parcel 包裹 bao-guo 155

pardon? 您说什么? nin shuo shen-me 11

parents 父母 foo-moo 120

park 公园 gong-yüan 96, 99, 107

park, to 停车 ting-cher 30

parking 停车 ting-cher 87; ~ lot 停车场 ting-cher-charng 87, 96; ~ meter 停车计时表 ting-cher jee-sh-biao 87

partner (boyfriend/girlfriend) 情人 ching-ren

party (social) 晚会 wan-hway 124

pass through, to 过境 guo-jing 66

pass, to 通过 tong-guo 77

passport 护照 hoo-jao 66, 153

pastry store 点心店 dian-shin-dian 131

patch, to 补 boo 137

patient (n) 病人 bing-ren

pavement, on the 在人行道上 dsai ren-shing-dao sharng

pay phone Ji Phons

pay, to 支付/付款 j-foo/foo-kwan 42, 67, 136

payment 付款 foo-kwan

peak 山峰 shan-fung 107

pearl 珍珠 jen-joo 149

pebbly (beach) 鹅卵石海滩 er-lwan-sh hai-tan 116

pedestrian crossing 人行横道线 ren-shing-hung-dao-shian 96; ~ zone [precinct] 行人区 hing-ren chü 96

pen 笔 bee 150

penicillin 青霉素 ching-may-soo 165

penknife 小刀 shiao dao 31

people 人 ren 92, 119

pepper 胡椒 hoo-jiao 38

per day 每天 may-tian 30, 83, 86, 87, 115; ~ hour 每小时 may-shiao-sh 87, 115, 155; ~ night 每晚 may-wan 21; ~ week 每星期 may-shing-chee 83, 86

perhaps 也许 ye-shü 19

period (menstrual) 月经 yüe-jing 167; ~ pains 痛经 tong-jing 167

petrol 汽油 chee-yo 87, 88; ~ station 加油站 jia-yo jan 87

pewter 白蜡 bai-la 149

pharmacy 药店 yao-dian 130, 140, 158

phone, to 打电话 da dian-hwaa; ~ call 电话 dian-hwaa 152; ~card 电话卡/电话磁卡 dian-hwaa-ka/dian-hwaa-ts-ka 127, 155

photo, to take a 拍照 pai-jao

photo: passport-size photo 二寸照片 er-tswun jao-pian 115

photocopier 复印机 foo-yin-jee 155

photograph 照片 jao-pian

photographer 摄影师 sher-ying-sh

photography 照相 jao-shiarng 151

phrase 词汇 ts-hway 11; **~ book** 词汇册 ts-hway tser 11

pick up, to (collect) 取/接走 chü/jie-dso 28, 113

picnic 野餐 ye-tsan

picnic area 野餐区 ye-tsan-ch 107

piece (of baggage) 件 jian 69

Pill (contraceptive) 避孕药 bee-yün-yao 167

pillow 枕头 jen-tou 27; **~ case** 枕套 jen-tao

pilot light 引火火苗 yin-huo huo-miao

pink 粉红色 fen-hong-ser 143

pipe (smoking) 烟斗 yan-dou

pitch (for camping) 宿营地 soo-ying-dee

place a bet, to 压赌注 ya-doo-joo 114

plane 飞机 fay-jee 68

plans 打算 da-swan 124

plant (n) 植物 j-woo

plastic bags 塑料袋 soo-liao-dai; **~ wrap** 保鲜纸 bao-shian-j 148

plate 盘子 pan-ds 39, 148

platform 站台 jan-tai 73, 76, 77

platinum 白金 bai-jin 149

play, to 参加 … 活动 tsan-jia … huo-dong 121

play, to (music/drama) 上演/演奏 sharng-yan/yan-dso 110, 111

playground 操场 tsao-charng 113

playgroup 游玩组 yo-wan-dsoo 113

playing field 运动场 yün-dong-charng 96

playing, to be (at movie theater) 上映 sharng-ying 110

playwright 编剧 bian-jü 110

pleasant, nice 好 hao 14

please 请 ching 10

plug 插头 cha-tou 148

pneumonia 肺炎 fay-yan 165

point of interest 游览点 yo-lan-dian 97

point to, to 指出来 j-choo-lai 11

poison 毒 doo

poles (skiing) 雪杖 shüe-jarng 117

police 警察 jing-cha 92, 152

police report 警察证明 jing-cha jung-ming 153

police station 公安局/派出所 jing-cha jü/pai-choo-suo 96, 131, 152

pollen count 花粉含量 hwaa-fen han-liarng 122

polyester 聚脂纤维 jü-j shian-way

pond 池塘 ch-tarng 107

pop (music) 流行乐 lio-shing yüe 111

popcorn 爆米花 bao-mee-hwaa 110

popular 流行 lio-shing 157

popular, to be 流行 lio-shing 111

port (harbour) 港口 garng-ko

porter 搬运工 ban-yün--gong 71

portion 份 fen 39

possible: as soon as possible 尽早 jin-dsao

possibly 很可能 hen-ker-nung 19

post (n) 邮件 yo-jian

post office 邮局 yo-jü 96, 131, 154

post, to 寄信 jee-shin 27

postage 邮费 yo-fay 154

postbox 邮筒 yo-tong 154

postcard 明信片 ming-shin-pian 154, 156

potato chips 炸土豆片 ja too-dou-pian 160

potatoes 土豆 too-dou 38

pottery 陶器 tao-chee

pound (sterling) 英镑 ying-barng 67, 138

power cut 停电 ting-dian ; **~ points** 电源插座 dian-yüan cha-dsuo 30

pregnant, to be 怀孕 hwai-yün 163, 167

premium (gas/petrol) 优级 (汽油) yo-jee (chee-yo) 87

prescribe, to 开处方 kai-choo-farng 165

prescription 处方 choo-farng 140, 141

present (gift) 礼物 lee-woo 167

press, to 熨 yūn 137

pretty 漂亮 piao-liarng

priest 教士 jiao-sh

primus stove 便携式煤油炉 bian-shie-sh may-yo-loo 31

prison 监狱 jian-yü

produce store 副食品杂货店 foo-sh-pin-dian 130

program 节目单 jie-moo dan 109

program of events 文娱活动时间表 wen-yü huo-dong sh-jian-biao 108

pronounce, to 发音 fa-yin

Protestant 基督教新教 jee-doo-jiao shin-jiao 105

pub 酒馆 jio-gwan

public building 公共建筑 gong-gong jian-joo 96

public holiday 公众假期 gong-jong jia-chee 219

pump (at gas station) 加油泵 jia-yo-bung 87

puncture 瘪了/打炮 bie le/da-pao 83, 88

puppet show 木偶戏 moo-o-shee

pure cotton 纯棉 chwun-mian 145

purple 紫色 ds-ser 143

purse/wallet 钱包 chian-bao 153

push-chair 婴儿车 ying-er-cher

---

quarter past ... ... 一刻 ... yee-ker 220

quarter to ... ... 差一刻 ... cha yee-ker 220

quarter, a 四分之一 s-fen-j-yee 217

queue, to 排队 pai-dwee 112

quick 快 kwai 14

quickest: what's the quickest way?
哪条路最快? na-tiao loo dswee kwai

quickly 快点 kwai dian 17

quiet 安静 an-jing 14

quieter 安静点 an-jing dian 24, 126

---

rabbi 拉比 la-bee

racetrack [race course] 赛场 sai-charng 114

racket (tennis, squash) 球拍 chio-pai 115

railway 铁路 tie-loo

rain, to 下雨 shia-yü 122

raincoat 雨衣 yü-yee 144

rape 强奸 chiarng-jian 152

rapids 急流 jee-lio 107

rare (steak) 半熟 ban-sho

rare (unusual) 罕见 han-jian

rash 疹子 jen-ds 162

rather 宁愿 ning-yüan 17

razor 剃刀 tee-dao; ~ **blades** 刀片 dao-pian 142

reading 阅读 yüe-doo 121

ready 修好了 shio-hao le 89; **to be ~** 能取 nung-chü 137, 151

real (genuine) 真的 jen-de 149

really? 真的? jen-de 19

receipt 收据 sho-jü 32, 89, 136, 137, 151, 168

reception (desk) 接待处 jie-dai-choo

receptionist 接待员 jie-dai-yüan

recommend, to 推荐/建议 twee-jian/jian-yee 21, 35, 141

recommend: can you recommend ...?
你能不能推荐 ...? nee nung-boo-nung twee-jian ... 97, 108

recommend: what do you recommend?
您能推荐一下吗? nin nung twee-jian yee-shia ma 37

record (LP) 唱片 charng-pian 157

---

record [music] store 音像店
yin-shiarng-dian 131

red 红色 hong-ser 143

red wine 红葡萄酒
hong poo-tao-jio 40

reduction [discount] 折扣 jer-ko
24, 68, 74, 100

refrigerator 冰箱 bing-shiarng 29

refund 退款 twee-kwan 137

refuse bags 垃圾袋 la-jee-dai 148

region 地区 dee-chü 106

registered mail 挂号信 gwaa-hao-shin

registration number 车牌号码
cher-pai hao-ma 88, 93

regular (gas/petrol) 普通 (汽油)
poo-tong (chee-yo) 87;
(of size) 中 jong 110

religion 宗教 dsong-jiao

remember: I don't remember
我不记得 wo bao jee-de

rent out, to 出租 choo-dsoo 29

rent, to 租 dsoo 86, 115, 116, 117

rental car 租来的汽车
joo-lai de chee-cher 153

repair, to 修 shio 89, 137, 168

repairs 修理 shio-lee 89

repeat, to 再说一遍
dsai shuo yee-bian 94, 128

repeat: please repeat that 请再说一遍
ching dsai shuo yee-bian 11

replacement (n) 替换品
tee-hwan-pin 167

replacement part 备用零件
bay-yong ling-jian 137

report, to 报告 bao-gao 152

required, to be 需要
shü-yao 112

reservation 预订 yü-ding
22, 36, 68, 77, 112

reserve, to 预订 yü-ding 21, 36, 74,
81, 109; **~: I'd like to reserve ...** 我想
预订 ... wo-shiarng yü-ding ... 74

rest, to 休息 shio-shee

restaurant 餐馆
tsan-gwan 35, 112

retail 零售 ling-sho 121

retired, to be 退休了
twee-shio le 121

return 往返 warng-fan 65

return ticket 往返票
warng-fan piao 68, 74

return, to (surrender) 归还
gway-hwan 86

return, to (come back) 返航/返回
fan-harng/fan-hway 75, 81

reverse the charges, to 对方付款
dwee-farng foo-kwan 127

revolting 难吃 nan-ch 14

rheumatism 风湿病 fung-sh-bing

rib 肋骨 lay-goo 166

right (correct) 对 dwee 14, 77, 94, 106

right: on the ~ 右边 yo-bian 76, 95

right of way 优先通行权
yo-shian tong-shing-chüan 93

right: that's right 对了 dwee-le

ring 戒指 jie-j 149

rip-off (n) 敲竹杠 chiao joo-garng 101

river 河 her 107; **~ cruise** 江上航游
jiarng-sharng harng-yo 81

road 路 loo 94, 95; **~ map** 公路图
gong-loo too 150

robbed, to be 被抢劫
bay chiarng-jie 153

robbery 抢劫 chiarng-jie

rock music 摇滚乐 yao-gwun-yüe 111

rolls 小面包 shiao-man-bao 160

romantic 很浪漫 hen larng-man 101

roof (house) 屋顶 woo-ding

roof-rack 车顶架 cher-ding-jia

room 房间 farng-jian 21; **~ service**
客房用餐服务 ker-farng yong-tsan
foo-woo 26

rope 绳子 shung-ds

round 圆的 yüan de 134

round (of golf) 一轮 yee-lwun 115

round neck 圆领 yüan-ling 144

A-Z

round-trip 往返 warng-fan 65; **~ ticket** 往返票 warng-fan piao 68, 74

route 道路 dao-loo 106

rubbish 垃圾 la-jee 28

rucksack 背包 bay-bao

rude, to be 粗鲁 tsoo-loo

ruins 遗址 yee-j 99

run into, to (crash) 撞车 jwarng-cher 93

run out, to (fuel) (汽油) 用完了 (chee-yo) yong wan le 88

running [training] shoes 运动鞋 yun-dong-shie 145

rush hour 高峰时刻 gao-fung sh-ker

Russia 俄国 e-guo

S **safe** (not dangerous) 安全 an-chüan 116

safe (lock-up) 保险柜 bao-shian-gway 27

safe, to feel 感到安全 gan-dao an-chüan 65

safety 安全 an-chüan

safety pins 别针 bie-jen

salad 凉拌菜 liarng-ban-tsai

sales 销售 shiao-sho 121

sales tax [VAT] 增值税 dsung-j-shwee 24

salt 盐 yan 38, 39

salty 咸 shian

same 同一 tong-yee 75

sand 沙 sha

sandals 凉鞋 liarng-shie 145

sandwich 三明治 san-ming-j 40

sandy (beach) 沙滩 sha-tan 116

sanitary napkins [towels] 卫生巾 way-shung-jin 142

satellite TV 卫星电视 way-shing dian-sh

satin 缎子 dwan-ds

satisfied: I'm not satisfied with this 我对这有意见 wo dwee jer yo yee-jian

Saturday 星期六 shing-chee-lio 218

sauce 佐料 dsuo-liao 38

saucepan 炖锅 dwun-guo 29

sauna 桑拿浴 sarng-na-yü 26

sausages 香肠 shiarng-charng 160

say: how do you say ...? ... 怎么说? ... dsen-me shuo

scarf 围巾 way-jin 144

scenic route 风景优美的道路 feng-jing yo-may de dao-loo 106

scheduled flight 定期航班 ding-chee harng-ban

school 学校 shüe-shiao 96

sciatica 坐骨神经痛 dsuo-goo-shen-jing-tong 165

scissors 剪刀 jian-dao 148

scooter 小摩托车 shiao muo-tuo-cher

Scotland 苏格兰 soo-ger-lan 119

Scottish (person) 苏格兰人 soo-ger-lan-ren

screwdriver 螺丝刀 luo-s-dao 148

sea 海 hai 107; **~front** 海滨 hai-bin; **~sick: I feel seasick** 我晕海 wo yün-hai

seasoning 调料 tiao-liao 38

seat 座位 dsuo-way 77, 109

seats (theater, cinema) 座位 dsuo-way 108

second 第二 dee-er 217

~ class 二等车厢 er-dung cher-shiarng 74; **~-hand** 二手 er-sho

secretary 秘书 mee-shoo

sedative 镇静剂 jen-jing-jee

see you soon! 回见! hway-jian 126

see, to 看 kan 18; (inspect) 看看 kan-kan 24, 37; (witness) 看见 kan-jian 93

self-employed, to be 个体户 ger-tee-hoo 121

self-service 自助式 ds-joo-sh 87

send, to 寄 jee 155

senior citizens 退休人员
twee-shio ren-yüan 100

separated, to be 分居了
fen-jü le 120

separately (adv) 分开 fen-kai 42

September 九月 jio-yüe 218

serious 严重的 yan-jong de

served, to be (meal) 供应 (饭菜)
gong-ying (fan-tsai) 26

service (religious) 做礼拜
dsuo-lee-bai 105

service 服务费
foo-woo-fay 42

serviette 餐巾 tsan-jin 39

set menu 套餐菜单
tao-tsan tsai-dan 37

sex (act) 性交 shing-jiao

shade 色度 ser-doo 143

shady 荫凉 yin-liarng 31

shallow 浅 chian

shampoo 洗发膏 shee-fa-gao 142;
~ and set 洗头加定型
shee-tou jia ding-shing 147

shape 形状 shing-jwarng 134

share, to (room) 合住 her-joo

shaving brush 剃须刷 tee-shü-shwaa;
~ cream 剃须膏 tee-shü-gao

she 她 ta

sheath (contraceptive) 避孕套
bee-yün-tao

sheet (bedding) 床单
chwarng-dan 28

ship 轮船 lwun-chwan 81

shirt 衬衫 chen-shan 144

shock (electric) 触电 c
hoo-dian

shoe repair 修鞋 shio-shie

shoe store 鞋店 shie-dian 131

shoes 鞋 shie 145

shop 店 dian 130

shop assistant 店员 dian-yüan

shopping area
商业区 sharng-yer-chü
99; **~ basket** 购物篮
go-woo-lan; **~ mall**
[centre] 购物中心 go-
woo-jong-shin 130; **~ trolley**
手推车 sho-twee-cher;
to go ~ 逛商店 gwarng sharng-dian

short 短 dwan 144, 146, 147

short-sighted 近视
jin-sh 167

shorts 短裤 dwan-koo 144

shoulder 肩 jian 166

shovel 铲子 chan-ds 157

show, to 指一下 j-yee-shia 133

show: can you show me?
能不能指一下?
nung-boo-nung j-yee-shia 94, 106

shower 淋浴间 lin-yü jian
21, 26, 30

shut 关 gwan 14

shut, to 关门 gwan-men 132

shut: when do you shut?
你们什么时间关门?
nee-men shen-me sh-jian gwan-men

sick: I'm going to be sick 我要吐了
wo yao too le

side order 配菜 pay-tsai 38

side street 后街 ho-jie 95

sides 两边 liarng-bian 147

sights 名胜 ming-shung

sightseeing tour 观光游
gwan-gwarng yo 97

sightseeing, to go 观光
gwan-gwarng

sign (road) 路标
loo-biao 93, 95

signpost 路牌 loo-pai

silk 丝绸 s-cho

silver 银 yin 149

silver-plate 镀银 doo-yin 149

similar, to be 类似 lay-s 11

singer 歌星 ger-shing 157

A-Z

single (for one person) 单人 dan-ren 81; (one-way) 单程 dan-chung 65; ~ **room** 单人房间 dan-ren farng-jian 21; ~ **ticket** 单程票 dan-chung piao 68, 74; **to be** ~ 单身 dan-shen 120

sink 水池 shwee-ch 25

sister 姐妹 jie-may 120

sit down, please 请坐下 ching dsuo-shia

sit, to 坐 dsuo 36, 77, 126

size 尺寸 ch-tswun 115, 146

skates 溜冰鞋 lio-bing-shie 117

ski boots 滑雪靴子 hwaa-shüe shüe-ds 117; ~**lift** 缆车 lan-cher 117; ~**school** 滑雪学校 hwaa-shüe shüe-shiao 117

skiing 滑雪 hwaa-shüe 117

skin 皮肤 pee-foo 166

skirt 裙子 chün-ds 144

skis 雪橇 shüe-chiao 117

sleep, to 睡觉 shwee-jiao 167

sleeping bag 睡袋 shwee-dai 31; ~ **car** 卧铺车厢 wo-poo cher-shiarng 74, 77; ~ **pill** 安眠药 an-mian-yao

sleeve 袖子 shio-ds 144

slice 片 pian 159

slippers 拖鞋 tuo-shie 145

slow 慢 man 14

slow down! 慢点! man-dian

slow, to be (clock) 慢 man 221

slowly 慢 man 11, 17, 94, 128

SLR camera 单镜反射式照相机 dan-jing fan-sher-sh jao-shiarng-jee 151

small 小 shiao 14, 24, 40, 110, 117, 134

small change 零钱 ling-chian 138, 139

smaller 小面值 shiao-mian-jee 136

smoke, to 吸烟 shee-yan 126

smoking (adj) 吸烟 shee-yan 36

snack bar 小吃部 shiao-ch-boo 73

snacks 小吃 shiao-ch

sneakers 运动鞋 yün-dong-shie

snorkel 潜水通气管 chian-shwee tong-chee-gwan

snow 雪 shüe 117

snow, to 下雪 shia-shüe 122

soap 肥皂 fay-dsao 142

soap powder 肥皂粉 fay-dsao-fen

soccer 足球 dsoo-chio 114

socket 插座 cha-dsuo

socks 袜子 wa-ds 144

soft drink 软饮料 rwan-yin-liao 110, 160

solarium 日光浴 r-gwarng-yü 22

sole (shoes) 鞋底 shie-dee

soluble aspirin 水溶阿司匹林 shwee-rong a-s-pee-lin

some 一些 yee-shie

someone 有人 yo-ren 16

something 某个东西 mo-ge dong-shee 16

sometimes 有时 yo-shee 13

son 儿子 er-ds 120, 162

soon 不久 boo-jio 13

soon: as soon as possible 尽可能早 jin ker-nung dsao 161

sore: it's sore 很疼 hen-tung; ~ **throat** 嗓子疼 sarng-ds tung 141, 163

sorry! 对不起 dwee-boo-chee 10

sort 类型 lay-shing 134

soul music 爵士灵歌 jüe-sh lin-ger 111

sour 酸 swan 41

south 南 nan 95

South Africa 南非 nan-fay

South African (n) 南非人 nan-fay-ren

souvenir 纪念品 jee-nian-pin 98, 156

souvenir guide 纪念品说明册 jee-nian-pin shuo-ming tser 156

souvenir store 纪念品商店 jee-nian-pin sharng-dian 131

spade 铲子 chan-ds 157

spare (extra) 备用 bay-yong

speak to somebody, to 跟某人说话
gen mo-ren shuo-hwaa 128

speak, to 说/说话 shuo/shuo-hwaa
11, 18, 41, 67, 128

speak: do you speak English?
你会说英语吗? nee hway shuo
ying-yü ma 11

special delivery 特快专递
ter-kwai jwan-dee 155

special rate 优惠价 yo-hway jia 86

specialist 专科 jwan-ker 164

specimen 标本 biao-ben 164

spectacles 眼镜 yan-jing

spell, to 拼写 pin-shie 11

spend, to 花费 hwaa-fay

spicy 辛辣的 shin-la de

sponge 海绵 hai-mian 148

spoon 调羹 tiao-gung 39, 41, 148

sport 体育 tee-yü 114, 121

sporting goods store 体育用品店
tee-yü yong-pin dian 131

sports club 体育俱乐部 tee-yü jü-ler-
boo 115; ~ ground 运动场 yün-
dong-charng 96

sprained, to be 扭伤了
nio-sharng le 164

spring 春天 chwun-tian 219

square 方的 farng de 134

stadium 体育馆 tee-yü-gwan 96

staff 职员 j-yüan 113

stain 污斑 woo-ban

stainless steel 不锈钢
boo-shio-garng 149

stamp 邮票 yo-piao 154

stand in line, to 排队 pai-dwee 112

standby ticket 剩余机票
shung-yü jee-piao

start, to 开始 kai-shu 98, 108

start, to (car) 发动 fa-dong 88

station 车站 cher-jan 96

stationer 文具店 wen-jü-dian

statue 塑像 soo-shiarng 99

stay (n) 住 joo 32

stay, to (at hotel) 住 joo
23, 123

stay, to (remain) 逗留
dou-lio 65

sterilizing solution 消毒液
shiao-doo-ye 142

stiff neck 脖子僵直
buo-ds jiarng-j 163

still: I'm still waiting 我还在等
wo hai dsai dung

sting 叮 ding 162

stockings 长统袜
charng-tong-waa 144

stolen, to be 失窃 sh-chie 71, 153

stomach 胃 way 166; ~ache 胃疼
way-tung 163

stools (faeces) 大便 da-bian 164

stop (bus, etc.) 站 jan 79, 80

stop (at), to 停 (站) ting (jan)
76, 77, 98

stopcock 总开关 dsong-kai-gwan 28

store 店 dian 130;
~ guide 商店示意图 sharng-dian
sh-yee-too 132

stormy, to be 雷雨 lay-yü 122

stove 炉子 loo-ds 28, 29

straight ahead 照直走 jao-j dso 95

strained muscle 肌肉拉伤
jee-ro la-sharng 162

strange 奇怪 chee-gwai 101

straw (drinking) 吸管 shee-gwan

strawberry (flavor) 草莓(味)
tsao-may (way) 40

stream 溪流 shee-lio 107

strong (potent) 强 chiarng

student 学生 shüe-shung
74, 100, 121

study, to 学习 shüe-shee 121

stunning 惊人 jing-ren 101

style 风格 fung-ger 104

subtitled, to be 配字幕
pay-ds-moo 110

subway 地铁 dee-tie 80

subway station 地铁站 dee-tie jan 80

sugar 糖 tarng 38, 39

suggest, to 推荐 twee-jian 123

suit 西服 shee-foo 144

suitable for 适合 sh-her

summer 夏天 shia-tian 219

sun block 防晒膏 farng-shai-gao 142

sunbathe, to 晒太阳 shai-tai-yarng

sunburn 晒伤 shai-sharng 141

Sunday 星期天 shing-chee-tian 218

sunglasses 太阳镜 tai-yarng-jing

sunshade 阳伞 yarng-san 116

sunstroke 中暑 jong-shoo 163

suntan cream 防晒油 farng-shai-yo 142

super (gas/petrol) 超级 (汽油) chao-jee (chee-yo) 87

superb 好极了 hao-jee le 101

supermarket 超级市场 chao-jee sh-charng 131, 158

supervision 照看 jao-kan 113

supplement 附加费 foo-jia-fay 68

suppositories 栓剂 shwan-jee 165

sure: are you sure? 你肯定吗? nee ken-ding ma

surfboard 冲浪板 chong-larng-ban 116

surname 姓氏 shing-sh

sweater 套衫 tao-shan 144

sweatshirt 针织套衫 jen-j tao-shan 144

sweet (taste) 甜 tian

sweets (candy) 糖果 tarng-guo 150

swelling 肿块 jong-kwai 162

swim, to 游泳 yo-yong 116

swimming 游泳 yo-yong 114; ~ **pool** 游泳池 yo-yong-ch 22, 26, 116; ~ **trunks** 游泳裤 yo-yong-koo 144

swimsuit 游泳衣 yo-yong-yee 144

switch 开关 kai-gwan 25

swollen, to be 肿大 jong-da

symptoms 症状 jung-jwarng 163

synagogue 犹太教堂 yo-tai jiao-tarng 105

synthetic 人造的 ren-dsao de 145

T T-shirt T恤衫 tee-shü-shan 144, 156

table 桌子 juo-ds 36, 112

tablet 药片 yao-pian 140

take away, to 不在店里吃 boo dsai dian-lee ch 40

take out, to (extract tooth) 拔掉 ba-diao 168

take photographs, to 拍照 paī-jao 98

take, to 要了 yao le 24; (buy) I'll ~ it 我买了 wo mai le 135

take, to (carry) 运 yün 71

take, to (medication) 服 foo 140, 165

take, to (time) 需要 (多久) shü-yao duo-jio 78

taken (occupied) 有人坐了 yo ren dsuo le 77

talk, to 说话 shuo-hwaa

tall 高大 gao-da 14

tampons 月经棉塞 yüe-jing mian-sai 142

tan 晒黑 shai-hay

tap 水龙头 shwee-long-tou 25

taxi 出租汽车 choo-dsoo-chee-cher 70, 71, 84

taxi stand [rank] 出租汽车站 choo-dsoo-chee-cher jan 96

tea 茶 cha 40; ~ **bags** 茶包 cha-bao 160; ~ **towel** 茶巾 cha-jin 156

teacher 教师 jiao-sh

team 球队 chio-dwee 114

teaspoon (measurement) 茶匙 cha-ch 140

teddy bear 玩具熊 wan-jü-shiong 157

telephone 电话 dian-hwaa 22, 92;
to ~ 打电话 da dian-hwaa 127, 128
~ bill 电话单 dian-hwaa-dan 32;
~ booth 电话亭 dian-hwaa-ting 127;
~ call 电话 dian-hwaa 32; **~**
directory 电话薄 dian-hwaa bo 127
~ number 电话号码 dian-hwaa
hao-ma 127

tell, to 告诉 gao-soo 18, 79; **~ me**
告诉我 gao-soo wo 79

temperature (*body*) 体温 tee-wen 164

temporarily 临时 lin-sh 89, 168

ten thousand 万 wan 216

tendon 腱 jian 166

tennis 网球 warng-chio 114; **~ court**
网球场 warng-chio-charng 115

tent 帐篷 jarng-pung 30, 31; **~ pegs**
帐篷桩 jarng-pung jwarng 31; **~ pole**
帐篷支柱 jarng-pung j-joo 31

terrible 很糟糕 hen dsao-gao 19, 101

terrific 太棒了 tai-barng le 19

tetanus 破伤风 puo-sharng-fung 164

Thailand 泰国 tai-guo

thank you 谢谢 shie-shie 10

that one 那个 na ger 16, 134

that's all 没别的了 may bie de le 133

that's enough 别再说了
bie dsai shuo le 19

that's true 是真的 sh jen de 19

theater 剧场 jü-charng 96, 99, 110

theft 盗窃 dao-chie 153

their(s) 他们的 ta-men-de 16

then (*time*) 那时 na-sh 13

there 在那儿 dsai na-r 12, 17

there is…/are … 有 … yo … 17

thermometer 温度计 wen-doo-jee

thermos flask 热水瓶
rer-shwee-ping

these 这些 jer-shie 134

they 他们 ta-men

thief 小偷 shiao-tou

thigh 大腿 da-twee 166

thin 瘦 sho

think: I think 我觉得 …
wo jüe-de … 42

third 第三 dee-san 217

third, a 三分之一
san-fen-j-yee 217

thirsty: I am thirsty 我渴了
wo ker le

this 这个 jer-ge 218

this one 这个 jer-ge 16, 134

those 那些 na-shie 134

thousand 千 chian 216

throat 嗓子 sarng-ds 165

thrombosis 血栓 shüe-shwan

through 通过 tong-guo

thumb 拇指 moo-j 166

Thursday 星期四 shing-chee-s 218

ticket 票 piao 65, 68, 75, 114, 153

ticket office 售票处 sho-piao-choo 73

tie 领带 ling-dai 144

tight 紧 jin 146

tights 裤袜 koo-waa 144

till receipt 收据 sho-jü

time 时间 sh-jian 76

time, on 正点 jung-dian 76

time: free time 自由活动时间
ds-yo huo-dong sh-jian 98

timetable 时刻表 sh-ker-biao 75

tin 罐 gwan 159

tire (*car*) 车胎 cher-tai 83

tired: I'm tired 我累了 wo lay le

tissues 卫生纸 way-shung-j 142

to (*a place*) 去 chü 12

tobacco 烟丝 yan-s 150

tobacconist 香烟店
shiarng-yan dian 131

today 今天 jin-tian 124, 161, 218

toe 脚趾 jiao-j 166

together (*paying*) 算在一起
swan dsai yee-chee 42

toilet 厕所 tser-suo 25, 26, 29; **~ paper**
卫生纸 way-shung-j 29, 142

tomorrow 明天 ming-tian 84, 124,
161, 218

tongue 舌 sher 166

tonight 今晚 jin-wan 108, 110, 124

tonsilitis 扁桃体炎 bian-tao-tee-yan 165

tonsils 扁桃体 bian-tao-tee 166

too (of extremes) 太 tai 17, 93, 146; **~ expensive** 太贵了 tai-gway le 135; **~ much** 太多 tai duo 15

tooth 牙 ya 168; **~ache** 牙痛 ya-tong; **~brush** 牙刷 ya-shwaa 142; **~paste** 牙膏 ya-gao 142

top 头顶 tou-ding 147

torch 手电筒 sho-dian-tong 31

torn, to be (muscle) 拉伤 la-sharng 164

tough (food) 嚼不动 jiao-boo-dong 41

tour guide 旅行团导游 lü-shing-twan dao-yo 27

tour operator 旅行社 lü-shing-sher 26

tourist 旅游者 lü-yo-jer; **~ office** 旅游服务处 lü-yo foo-woo-choo 97

tow truck 牵引车 chian-yin-cher 88

towards 往 … 方向 warng … farng-shiarng 12

towel 毛巾 mao-jin 27

town 市区/城市 sh-chü/chung-sh 70, 94

town hall 市政府大楼 sh-jung-foo da-lo 96

toy 玩具 wan-jü 157; **~ store** 玩具店 wan-jü-dian 131

traditional restaurant 传统风味的餐馆 chwan-tong-fung-way de tsan-gwan 35

traffic 交通 jiao-tong; **~ jam** 交通阻塞 jiao-tong dsoo-ser; **~ violation [offence]** 违反交通规则 way-fan jiao-tong gwee-dser

trail (path) 小路 shiao-loo 106

trailer 活动住房 huo-dong-joo-farng 30

train 火车/列车 huo-cher/lie-cher 76, 77; **~ station** 火车站 huo-cher-jan 73

tram 有轨电车 yo-gwee dian-cher

transfer 转移 jwan-yee

transit, in 过境 guo-jing

translate, to 翻译 fan-yee 11

translation 翻译 fan-yee

translator 翻译 fan-yee

trash 垃圾 la-jee 28

trashcans 垃圾箱 la-jee-shiarng 30

travel agency 旅行社 lü-shing-sher 131

travel sickness 晕车 yün-cher 141

traveler's checks [cheques] 旅行支票 lü-shing j-piao 136, 138

tray 托盘 tuo-pan

tree 树 shoo 106

trim (hair) 修一修 shio-yee-shio 147

trip 旅程 lü-chung 76, 78, 97, 123

trolley (shopping) 手推车 sho-twee-cher 158

trousers 裤子 koo-ds 144

truck (U.S.) 卡车 ka-cher

true: that's not true 那不对 na boo-dwee

try on, to (clothes) 试穿 sh-chwan 146

Tuesday 星期二 shing-chee-er 218

tumor 肿瘤 jong-lio 165

tunnel 隧道 swee-dao

turn, to (change direction) 转 jwan 95; **~ down, to** (volume, heat) 关小一点 gwan shiao yee-dian; **~ off, to** (appliance) 关掉 gwan-diao 25; **~ on, to** (appliance) 打开 da-kai 25; **~ up, to** (volume, heat) 开大一点 kai da yee-dian

turning 转弯 jwan-wan 95

TV 电视 dian-sh 22

tweezers 镊子 nie-ds

twice 两次 liarng-ts 217

twin bed 两张单人床 liarng-jarng dan-ren-chwarng 21

twist: I've twisted my ankle 我把脚腕扭伤了 wo ba jiao-wan nio-sharng le

two-door car 两门车
lian-men cher 86

type: what type 什么样
shen-me yarng 112

typical 典型的 dian-shing de 37

tyre 车胎 cher-tai 83

U United Kingdom 英国
ying-guo 119

United States 美国 may-guo 119

ugly 丑陋 cho-lo 14, 101

ulcer 溃疡 kwee-yarng

umbrella *(for sun)* 阳伞 yarng-san 116

uncle 叔叔 shoo-shoo 120

unconscious, to be 昏迷了
hwun-mee le 92, 162

under 在 ... 下方 dsai ... shia-farng

underdone *(food)* 不熟 boo-sho 41

underpants 内裤 nay-koo 144

underpass 地下通道
dee-shia tong-dao 96

understand, to 懂 dong 11; **do you ~?**
您懂了吗? nin dong le ma 11;
I don't ~ 我 不懂 wo boo-dong 11, 67

undress, to 脱衣 tuo-yee 164

unemployed 失业人员
sh-ye-ren-yüan 121

uneven *(ground)* 不平坦
boo-ping-tan 31

unfortunately 可惜 ker-shee 19

uniform 制服 j-foo

unit *(for a phonecard)* 单位
dan-way 155

unleaded petrol 无铅汽油
woo-chian chee-yo

unlock, to 开锁 kai-suo

unpleasant 不好 boo-hao 14

unscrew, to 拧开 ning-kai

until ... 前 ... chian 221

up to 直到 j-dao 12

upper *(berth)* 上铺 sharng-poo 74

upset stomach 肠胃不适
charng-way boo-sh 141

upstairs **(在)** 楼上
(dsai) lo-sharng 12

urgent 急诊
jee-jen 161

urine 小便
shiao-bian 164

use, to 用 yong 139

use *(n)*: **for my personal use** 个人使用
的 ger-ren sh-yong de 67

V V-neck V型领
vee-shing-ling 144

vacant 无人 woo-ren 14

vacation, on 度假 doo-jia 66, 123

vaccinated against, to be 打过 ... 预防
针 da-guo ... yü-farng-jen 164

vaginal infection 阴道炎
yin-dao-yan 167

valet service 洗车服务
shee-cher foo-woo

valid 有效 yo-shiao 75

validate, to 批准 pee-jwun

valley 山谷 shan-goo 107

valuable 值钱的 j-chian de

value 值多少钱 j duo-shaochian 155

valve 总开关 dsong-kai-gwan 28

vanilla *(flavor)* 香草(味)
shiarng-tsao (way) 40

VAT receipt 增值税收据
dsung-j-shwee sho-jü

vegan, to be 纯素食者
chwun soo-sh jer

vegetables 蔬菜 shoo-tsai 38

vegetarian, to be 吃素食 ch-soo-sh 39

vegetarian restaurant 素菜馆
soo-tsai-gwan 35

vein 静脉 jing-mai 166

venereal disease 性病 shing-bing 165

ventilator 通风机 tong-fung-jee

very 非常 fay-charng 17

video game 电视游戏机 dian-sh yo-
shee-jee; **~ recorder** 录像机 loo-
shiarng-jee

Vietnam 越南 yüe-nan
view: with a view of … 带 … 风景的
dai … fung-jing de
viewpoint 观光点
gwan-gwarng-dian 99, 107
village 村庄 tswun-jwarng 107
vinaigrette 香醋沙司
shiarng-tsoo sha-s 38
vineyard (winery) 葡萄园
poo-tao-yüan 107
visa 签证 chian-jung
visit (n) 走访 dso farng 119
visit, to 走访 dso-farng 123
visit, to (hospital) 探望 tan-warng 167
visit: places to visit 旅游点
lü-yo-dian 123
visiting hours 探望时间
tan-warng sh-jian
vitamin tablets 维生素药片
way-shung-soo yao-pian 141
volleyball 排球 pai-chio 114
voltage 电压 dian-ya
vomit, to 呕吐 o-too 163

W **wait (for), to** 等 dung 41, 76, 89, 140; **wait!** (exclamation)
等一等! dung-yee-dung 98
waiter/waitress 服务员
foo-woo-yüan 37
waiting room 候车室 ho-cher-sh 73
wake someone, to 叫醒某人
jiao-shing mo-ren 27, 70
wake-up call 叫醒电话
jiao-shing dian-hwaa
Wales 威尔士 way-er-sh 119
walk home, to 步行回家
boo-shing hway-jia 65
walking route 徒步旅行道路
too-boo lü-shing dao-loo 106
wallet 钱包
chian-bao 42

want, to 要 yao 18
war memorial 英雄纪念碑
ying-shiong jee-nian-bay 99
ward (hospital) 病房 bing-farng 167
warm 暖 nwan 14, 122
washbasin 盥洗盆 gwan-shee-pen
washing machine 洗衣机 shee-yee-jee
29; **~ powder** 洗衣粉 shee-yee-fen
148; **~-up liquid** 洗涤剂
shee-dee-jee 148
wasp 黄蜂 hwarng-fung
watch (wrist) 表 biao 149, 153
water 水 shwee 87; **~ bottle** 水瓶
shwee-ping; **~ heater** 热水器 rer-
shwee-chee 28; **~ skis** 滑水橇 hwaa-
shwee-chiao 116; **~fall** 瀑布 poo-boo
107; **~proof** 防水 farng-shwee;
~proof jacket 防水夹克衫 farng-
shwee jia-ker-shan 145
wave 波浪 bo-larng
waxing 热蜡脱毛 rer-la-tuo-mao 147
way (direction) 路 loo 94;
I've lost my ~ 我迷路了 wo mee-loo
le 94; **on the ~** 路过 loo-guo 83
we 我们 wo-men
wear, to 穿 chwan 152
weather 天气 tian-chee 122;
~ forecast 天气预报
tian-chee yü-bao 122
wedding 婚礼 hwun-lee; **~ ring**
结婚戒指 jie-hwun jie-j
Wednesday 星期三
shing-chee-san 218
week 星期 shing-chee 23, 97, 218
weekend, at (on) the 在周末
dsai jo-muo 218
weekend rate 周末优惠价
jo-muo yo-hway jia 86
weekly ticket 周票 jo-piao 79
weight 重量 jong-liarng
well-done (steak) 熟透 sho-tou
Welsh (person) 威尔士人 way-er-sh-ren
west 西 shee 95
wetsuit 潜水服 chian-shwee-foo

what do you do? (job) 你做什么工作?
nee dsuo shen-me gong-dsuo 121

what kind of ... 哪种...?
na-jong ... 37, 106

what time? 什么时间?
shen-me sh-jian 13

what's the time? 几点了?
jee-dian-le 220

wheelchair 轮椅 lwun-yee

when? 什么时间? shen-me sh-jian 13

where are you from? 你是哪国人?
nee sh na-guo ren 119

where is ...? ... 在哪儿?
... dsai na-r 99

where were you born? 你出生在什么
地方? nee choo-shung dsai shen-me
dee-farng 119

where 哪儿 na-r 12

which 哪个 na-ge 16

white 白色 bai-ser 143

white wine 白葡萄酒
bai-poo-tao-jio 40

who 谁 shwee 16

whose 谁的 shwee-de 16

why 为什么 way-shen-me 15

wide 宽 kwan 14

wife 妻子 chee-ds 120, 162

wildlife 野生生物
ye-shung shung-woo

windbreaker 连帽防风衣
lian-mao farng-fung-yee 145

window 窗户 chwarng-hoo 25, 77

window (store) 橱窗 choo-chwarng
134, 149; **~ seat** (on train, etc.)
靠窗座位 kao-chwarng dsuo-way 74

windscreen 挡风玻璃窗
darng-fung buo-lee-chwarng

windy, to be 大风 da-fung 122

wine 葡萄酒 poo-tao-jio 40, 160

wine list 酒单 jio-dan 37

winter 冬天 dong-tian 219

wishes: best wishes 最良好的祝愿
dswee liarng-hao de joo-yüan 219

with 用 yong 17

with milk 加牛奶
jia-nio-nai 40

withdraw, to 取钱
chü chian 139

within (time) ... 之内
... j-nay 13

without 不用 boo-yong 17

wood 树林 shoo-lin 107

wool 毛 mao 145

work, to (function) 用 yong 28;
it doesn't ~ 这个失灵了 jer-ger
sh-ling le 137

work for, to 雇主是 goo-joo sh 121

worse 更不好 gung-boo-hao 14

worst 最糟 dswee-dsao

wound 伤 sharng 162

write down, to 写下来
shie-shia-lai 136

wrong 错 tsuo 14, 136; **~ number** 拨
错号码 boo tsuo hao-ma 128; **to be ~**
错了 tsuo le 137

X-ray X光
ai-ker-s-gwarng 164

yacht 游艇 yo-ting

year 年 nian 218

yellow 黄色 hwarng-ser 143

yes 对 dwee 10

yesterday 昨天 dsuo-tian 218

yoghurt 酸奶 swan-nai

you 你 nee 118

you (formal) 您 nin

you (informal) 你 nee

young 年轻 nian-ching 14

your(s) 你 (们) 的 nee(-men)-de 16

youth hostel 青年招待所 ching-nian
jao-dai-suo 29

zebra crossing 斑马线 ban-ma-shian

zero 零 ling

zip(per) 拉链 la-lian

Glossary
Chinese -English

The Mandarin Chinese-English glossary covers all the areas where you may need to decode written Chinese: hotels, public buildings, restaurants, stores, ticket offices, airports, and stations. The Chinese is written in large type to help you identify the character(s) from the signs you see around you.

General 一般标志

左	*dsuo*	LEFT
右	*yo*	RIGHT
入口	*roo-ko*	ENTRANCE
出口	*choo-ko*	EXIT
厕所	*tser-suo*	TOILETS
男	*nan*	MEN (TOILETS)
女	*n*	WOMEN (TOILETS)
有人	*yo-ren*	OCCUPIED
禁止吸烟	*jin-j shee-yan*	NO SMOKING
危险	*way-shian*	DANGER
禁止入内	*jin-j roo-nay*	NO ENTRY
小心	*shiao-shin*	CAUTION
拉/推	*la/twee*	PULL/PUSH

General 一般标志

失物招领	*sh-woo jiao-ling*	LOST PROPERTY
禁止游泳	*jin-j yo-yong*	NO SWIMMING
止步	*j-boo*	KEEP OUT
饮用水	*yin-yong-shwee*	DRINKING WATER
非请莫入	*fay-ching muo-roo*	PRIVATE
请勿乱扔纸屑杂物	*ching-woo lwan-reng j-shie dsa-woo*	NO LITTERING
请勿随地吐痰	*ching-woo swee-dee too-tan*	NO SPITTING
地下通道	*dee-shia tong-dao*	UNDERPASS [SUBWAY]
小心台阶	*shiao-shin tai-jie*	MIND THE STEP
油漆未干	*yo-chee way-gan*	WET PAINT
软席	*rwan-shee*	SOFT SEAT (first class)
硬席	*ying-shee*	HARD SEAT (economy class)

Road signs 路标

停	*ting*	STOP
靠右行驶	*kao-yo shing-sh*	KEEP RIGHT
靠左行驶	*kao-dsuo shing-sh*	KEEP LEFT
单向行驶	*dan-shiarng shing-sh*	ONE WAY
不准超车	*boo-jwun chao-cher*	NO PASSING [NO OVERTAKING]
不准停车	*boo-jwun ting-cher*	NO PARKING
高速公路	*gao-soo gong-loo*	HIGHWAY [MOTORWAY]
通行费	*tong-shing-fay*	TOLL
交通灯	*jiao-tong-dung*	TRAFFIC LIGHTS
警告	*jing-gao*	WARNING
交叉口	*jiao-cha-ko*	JUNCTION

问询处	*wen-sh -choo*	INFORMATION
一号站台	*yee-hao jan-tai*	PLATFORM 1
一号登机门	*yee-hao dung-jee-men*	GATE 1
海关	*hai-gwan*	CUSTOMS
免税店	*mian-shwee-dian*	DUTY FREE
边防检查	*bian-farng jian-cha*	IMMIGRATION
抵达/到达	*dee-da/dao-jan*	ARRIVALS
离境/发车	*lee-jing/fa-cher*	DEPARTURES
行李认领	*shing-lee ren-ling*	BAGGAGE RECLAIM
公共汽车	*gong-gong-chee-cher*	BUS
火车	*huo-cher*	TRAIN
晚点	*wan-dian*	DELAYED
地铁	*dee-tie*	SUBWAY [METRO]

问询处	*wen-sh choo*	INFORMATION
浴室	*y sh*	BATH
接待处	*jie-dai-choo*	RECEPTION
保留座位	*bao-lio dsuo-way*	RESERVED
紧急出口	*jin-jee choo-ko*	EMERGENCY / FIRE EXIT
热水	*rer-shwee*	HOT (WATER)
冷水	*lung-shwee*	COLD (WATER)
闲人莫入	*shian-ren muo-roo*	STAFF ONLY
衣帽室	*yee-mao-sh*	COATCHECK [CLOAKROOM]
阳台	*yarng-tai*	TERRACE
花园	*hwaa-y n*	GARDEN
禁止吸烟	*jin-j shee-yan*	NO SMOKING
酒吧	*jio-ba*	BAR

Stores 商店

开门	*kai-men*	OPEN
关门	*gwan-men*	CLOSED
午休	*woo-shio*	LUNCH
部	*boo*	DEPARTMENT
楼层	*lo-tsung*	FLOOR
地下室	*dee-shia-sh*	BASEMENT
电梯	*dian-tee*	ELEVATOR [LIFT]
自动扶梯	*ds-dong foo-tee*	ESCALATOR
收款处	*sho-kwan-choo*	CASHIER
减价出售	*jian-jia choo-sho*	SALE

Sightseeing 观光

免费入内	*mian-fay roo-nay*	FREE ADMISSION
成人票	*chung-ren piao*	ADULTS
儿童票	*er-tong piao*	CHILDREN
学生票	*sh -shung piao*	STUDENTS
纪念品商店	*jee-nian-pin sharng-dian*	SOUVENIRS
茶点	*cha-dian*	REFRESHMENTS
请勿触摸	*ching-woo choo-muo*	DO NOT TOUCH
禁止拍照	*jin-j pai-jao*	NO PHOTOGRAPHY
请保持安静	*ching bao-ch an-jing*	SILENCE
请勿入内	*ching-woo roo-nay*	NO ACCESS

Public buildings 公共建筑

医院	yee-y n	HOSPITAL
医生	yee-shung	DOCTOR
牙医	ya-yee	DENTIST
警察	jing-cha	POLICE
银行	yin-harng	BANK
邮局	jo-j	POST OFFICE
游泳池	yo-yong-ch	SWIMMING POOL
市政府大楼	sh-jung-foo da-lo	TOWN HALL
出租车停靠处	choo-dsoo-cher ting-kao-choo	TAXI STAND [RANK]
公共浴室	gong-gong y sh	PUBLIC BATH
博物馆	bo-woo-gwan	MUSEUM

Numbers	216	**Public holidays**	220
Days	218	**Time**	221
Months/Dates		**Map**	223
Seasons	219	**Quick reference**	224
Greetings	220	**Emergency**	224

GRAMMAR

In Chinese, there are general numbers (listed opposite) used for talking about sums of money, telephone numbers, etc., and there is a system for combining a number with an object-specific *counter*. This system groups objects into types according to shape and size. Thus there are specific ways of counting flat objects, machines, animals, people, etc. When you are not sure of the correct counter, you can always try using the general numbers (yee, er, san, etc.) or better, the "all-purpose" counters listed below.

"All-purpose" counters

When you don't know the specific counter use:

1	yee-ge	2	liarng-ge*
3	san-ge	4	s-ge
5	woo-ge	6	lio-ge
7	chee-ge	8	ba-ge
9	jio-ge	10	sh-ge

* When the number 2 is used with any counter the word **liarng** is used rather than **er**, which is only used for general, arthimetical numbers.

If you don't know the specific counter for a bottle, use the "all-purpose" system, for example:

I'd like two bottles of beer.	I'd like two bottles of beer.
Lai liarng-ge pee-jio.	**Lai liárng-ping pee-jio.**
("all-purpose" counter)	(counter for bottles)

Note that the counter usually precedes the word it qualifies.

Other counters

Thin, flat objects (stamps, paper, etc.)		Small objects (indeterminate shape)		Packets (any size)	
yee-jarng	1	yee-j	1	yee-bao	1
liarng-jarng	2	liarng-j	2	liarng-bao	2
san-jarng	3	san-j	3	san-bao	3
s-jarng	4	s-j	4	s-bao	4
woo-jarng	5	woo-j	5	woo-bao	5

Numbers 数词

Alongside the traditional system of numerals, the Chinese are also familiar with the written form of Western numerals and you will find these used for telephone numbers, room numbers, and some prices.

0	零 *ling*	26	二十六	*er-sh-lio*
1	一 *yee*	27	二十七	*er-sh-chee*
2	二 *er (liarng)*	28	二十八	*er-sh-ba*
3	三 *san*	29	二十九	*er-sh-jio*
4	四 *s*	30	三十	*san-sh*
5	五 *woo*	31	三十一	*san-sh-yee*
6	六 *lio*	32	三十二	*san-sh-er*
7	七 *chee*	40	四十	*s-sh*
8	八 *ba*	50	五十	*woo-sh*
9	九 *jio*	60	六十	*lio-sh*
10	十 *sh*	70	七十	*chee-sh*
11	十一 *sh-yee*	80	八十	*ba-sh*
12	十二 *sh-er*	90	九十	*jio-sh*
13	十三 *sh-san*	100	一百	*yee-bai*
14	十四 *sh-s*	101	一百零一	*yee-bai-ling-yee*
15	十五 *sh-woo*	102	一百零二	*yee-bai-ling-er*
16	十六 *sh-lio*	200	二百	*er-bai*
17	十七 *sh-chee*	500	五百	*woo-bai*
18	十八 *sh-ba*	1,000	一千	*yee-chian*
19	十九 *sh-jio*	10,000	一万	*yee-wan*
20	二十 *er-sh*	35,750	三万五千七百五十 *san-wan-woo-chian-chee-bai-woo-sh*	
21	二十一 *er-sh-yee*			
22	二十二 *er-sh-er*	1,000,000	一百万 *yee-bai-wan*	
23	二十三 *er-sh-san*			
24	二十四 *er-sh-s*			
25	二十五 *er-sh-woo*			

Numerical expressions 数字表达法

first	第一 *dee-yee*
second	第二 *dee-er*
third	第三 *dee-san*
fourth	第四 *dee-s*
fifth	第五 *dee-woo*
once	一次 *yee-ts*
twice	两次 *liarng-ts*
three times	三次 *san-ts*
a half	一半 *yee-ban*
half an hour	半小时 *ban-shiao-sh*
half a tank	半箱 *ban-shiarng*
half eaten	吃了一半 *ch-le yee-ban*
a quarter	四分之一 *s-fen-j-yee*
a third	三分之一 *san-fen-j-yee*
a pair of ...	一双 ... *yee-shwarng* ...
a dozen ...	一打 ... *yee-da* ...
1998	一九九八 *yee-jio-jio-ba*
2001	二零零一 *er-ling-ling-yee*
the 1990s	九十年代 *jio-sh-nian-dai*

Days

Monday	星期一 *shing-chee-yee*
Tuesday	星期二 *shing-chee-er*
Wednesday	星期三 *shing-chee-san*
Thursday	星期四 *shing-chee-s*
Friday	星期五 *shing-chee-woo*
Saturday	星期六 *shing-chee-lio*
Sunday	星期日／天 *shing-chee-r/tian*

Months 月

January	一月 *yee-yüe*
February	二月 *er-yüe*
March	三月 *san-yüe*
April	四月 *s-yüe*
May	五月 *woo-yüe*
June	六月 *lio-yüe*
July	七月 *chee-yüe*
August	八月 *ba-yüe*
September	九月 *jio-yüe*
October	十月 *sh-yüe*
November	十一月 *sh-yee-yüe*
December	十二月 *sh-er-yüe*

Dates 日期

It's ...	今天是 ... *jin-tian-sh*
July 10	七月十号 *chee-yüe sh-hao*
Tuesday, March 1	三月一号，星期二 *san-yüe yee-hao, shing-chee-er*
yesterday	昨天 *dsuo-tian*
today	今天 *jin-tian*
tomorrow	明天 *ming-tian*
this ... / last ...	这个 ... / 上个 ... *jer-ge ... / sharng-ge ...*
next week	下个星期 *shia-ge shing-chee*
every month / year	每个月 / 每年 *may-ge yüe / may nian*
on [at] the weekend	在周末 *dsai jo-muo*

Seasons 季节

spring	春天 *chwun-tian*
summer	夏天 *shia-tian*
fall [autumn]	秋天 *chio-tian*
winter	冬天 *dong-tian*
in spring	在春天 *dsai chwun-tian*
during the summer	在夏天 *dsai shia-tian*

Greetings 问候

Happy birthday!	生日快乐!	*shung-r kwai-ler*
Merry Christmas!	圣诞快乐!	*shung-dan-kwai-ler*
Happy New Year!	新年好!	*shin-nian-hao*
Best wishes!	祝一切好!	*joo yee-chie hao*
Congratulations!	恭喜你!	*gong-shee-nee*
Good luck! / All the best!	祝你好运! / 祝你一切顺利!	*joo-nee hao-yün / joo-nee yee-chie shwun-lee*
Have a good trip!	旅途愉快!	*lü-too yü-kwai*
Give my regards to ...	代我问候 ...	*dai wo wen-ho ...*

Public holidays 节假日

There are seven days of official holidays for all Chinese people:

January 1	*yüan-dan*	New Year's Day
Spring Festival*	*chwun-jie*	Chinese New Year
May 1	*guo-jee-lao-dong-jie*	International Labor Day
October 1 – 2	*guo-ching-jie*	National Day

* 3 days in January or February, according to the lunar calendar

The remaining holidays are celebrated by particular groups and have little effect on daily life:

March 8	*foo-nü-jie*	Women's Day
May 4	*ching-nian-jie*	National Youth Day
June 1	*guo-jee-er-tong-jie*	Children's Day
August 1	*jian-jün-jie*	Army Day

Most Chinese stores are open on national holidays.

The Spring Festival (Chinese New Year) officially lasts three days, but many people take a week off from work. If you plan on visiting China during Chinese New Year, make your reservations well in advance as hotels will be full and public transportation more packed than ever.

Time 时间

...-dian woo-
sh-woo-
...-dian
...-dian ling-
woo-fen
sh ...-dian woo-
...-dian sh-fen
...-dian san-ker
...-dian yee-ker
...-dian s-sh
...-dian er-sh
...-dian san-sh-
woo-
...-dian
ban
...-dian
woo-
er-sh-

In ordinary conversation time is expressed as shown above. For airline and train timetables, however, the 24-hour clock is used.

Despite the size of China, there is only one time zone. China is eight hours ahead of GMT all year round: it does not change its clocks to reflect winter and summer time.

Excuse me, can you tell me the time?	请问，现在几点了？ *ching-wen, shian-dsai jee-dian le*
It's ...	现在 ... *shian-dsai ...*
five past one	一点零五分 *yee-dian-ling-woo-fen*
ten past two	两点十分 *liarng-dian-sh-fen*
a quarter past three	三点一刻 *san-dian-yee-ker*
twenty past four	四点二十分 *s-dian-er-sh-fen*
twenty-five past five	五点二十五分 *woo-dian-er-sh-woo-fen*
half past six	六点半 *lio-dian-ban*
twenty-five to seven	七点三十五分 *chee-dian-san-sh-woo-fen*
twenty to eight	八点四十分 *ba-dian-s-sh-fen*
a quarter to nine	九点三刻 *jio-dian-san-ker*
ten to ten	十点五十分 *sh-dian-woo-sh-fen*
five to eleven	十一点五十五分 *sh-yee-dian-woo-sh-woo-fen*
twelve o'clock (noon/midnight)	十二点 (正午/半夜) *sh-er-dian (jung-woo/ban-ye)*

at dawn	清晨，早晨	*ching-chen, dsao-chen*
in the morning	早上，上午	*dsao-sharng, sharng-woo*
during the day	白天	*bai-tian*
before lunch	中饭前	*jong-fan-chian*
after lunch	中饭后	*jong-fan-ho*
in the afternoon	下午	*shia-woo*
in the evening	晚上	*wan-sharng*
at night	夜里	*ye-lee*

I'll be ready in five minutes.
我五分钟后就好。
wo woo-fen-jong ho jio hao

He'll be back in a quarter of
an hour.
他十五分钟后回来。
ta sh-woo-fen-jong ho hway-lai

She arrived half an hour ago.
她半小时前到了。
ta ban-shiao-sh chian dao le

The train leaves at ...
火车 ... 离站。 *huo-cher ... lee-jan*

13:04
十三点零四分 *sh-san-dian-ling-s-fen*

0:40
零点四十分 *ling-dian-s-sh-fen*

The train is 10 minutes
late/early.
这趟火车晚点/提前十分钟。
*jer-tarng huo-cher wan-dian/tee-chian
sh-fen-jong*

It's 5 minutes fast/slow.
快/慢五分钟。 *kwai/man woo-fen-jong*

from 9:00 to 5:00
从九点到五点
tsong jio-dian dao woo-dian

between 8:00 and 2:00
八点到两点之间
ba-dian dao liarng-dian j-jian

I'll be leaving by ...
我 ... 之前离开。 *wo ... j-chian lee-kai*

Will you be back before ...?
你会在 ... 前回来吗?
nee hway dsai ... chian hway-lai ma

We'll be here until ...
... 前我们都在这儿。
... chian wo-men dou dsai jer-r

YELLOW
SEA

Taipei
Taiwan

Harbin

Changchun
Fushun
Shenyang
Dalian
Qingdao
Shanghai
Ningbo
Hangzhou
Wenzhou
Kaohsiung

**BEIJING
(Peking)**
Tianjin
Zhengzhou
Nanjing
Nanchang
Fuzhou
Xiamen
Victoria
Macau

Taiyuan
Luoyang
Wuhan
Changsha
Liuzhou
Guangzhou
Zhanjiang
Haikou

Xi'an
Chongqing
Guiyang

Xining
Lanzhou
Chengou
Kunming

C h i n a

Golmud

Lhasa

Karamay
Urumqi
Ruoqiang

Yining

Kashi
Shache
Yecheng

Quick reference 快速查找

Good morning.	早上好/你早。 *dsao-sharng hao/nee dsao*
Good afternoon.	你好。 *nee hao*
Good evening.	晚上好。 *wan-sharng hao*
Hello.	你好。 *nee hao*
Good-bye.	再见。 *dsai-jian*
Excuse me. (getting attention)	请问。 *ching-wen*
Excuse me? [Pardon?]	请再说一遍 *ching dsai-shuo yee-bian*
Sorry!	对不起! *dwee-boo-chee*
Please.	请 *ching*
Thank you.	谢谢 *shie-shie*
Do you speak English?	你会说英语吗? *nee-hway shuo ying-yü ma*
I don't understand.	我不懂。 *wo-boo-dong*
Where is …?	… 在哪儿? … *dsai na-r*
Where are the bathrooms [toilets]?	厕所在哪儿? *tser-suo dsai na-r*

Emergency 紧急情况

Help!	来人哪! *lai-ren na*
Go away!	走开! *dso-kai*
Leave me alone!	不要缠我 *boo-yao chan wo*
Call the police!	快叫警察 *kwai jiao jing-cha*
Stop thief!	抓贼! *jwaa-dsay*
Get a doctor!	快找医生 *kwai jao yee-shung*
Fire!	失火啦! *sh-huo la*
I'm ill.	我生病了。 *wo shung-bing le*
I'm lost.	我迷路了。 *wo mee-loo le*
Can you help me?	你能帮帮我吗? *nee nung barng-barng wo ma*

Emergency ☎ China

Fire **119**   First Aid (Beijing): **120**   Police **110**

Embassies/Consulates (Beijing)

Australia: 532 2331/fax 532 4605	Eire: 532 2691/fax 532 2168
Canada: 532 3536/fax 532 4072	U.K.: 532 1961/fax 532 1939
New Zealand: 532 2731/fax 532 4317	U.S.: 532 3831/fax 532 6057

There are also consulates for Australia, Canada, the U.K., and the U.S. in Shanghai; for Australia and the U.S. in Guangzhou; and for the U.S. in Shenyang.